This book is sent to you

through the courtesy of

the

OPINION EDITORIAL COMMITTEE

19 West 44th Street

New York, 18, N.Y.

AS I SEE IT

By STEPHEN S. WISE, *amuel, 1872-*

JEWISH OPINION PUBLISHING CORPORATION

1944

PRINTED IN THE UNITED STATES OF AMERICA
BY MARSTIN PRESS, INC., NEW YORK CITY
438

CONTENTS

AS I SEE IT

Foreword

I REMEMBER many years ago to have been asked to name the most hopelessly stupid person I had ever come upon. My answer referred to an outwardly successful New Yorker who, being asked whether there was not much in his life that he would fain change, replied, "There isn't a thing in my life that I would change!" I wonder whether it is in any degree less enlightened to reprint and thus give permanent form to fugitive pieces published over a period of more than a decade. These might have rested in undisturbed oblivion had not the editors of OPINION, for which they were written, decided to resurrect them and to make a more or less enduring volume of these editorial notes. Many were hastily penned, some have no permanent significance, and all were uniformly written under such pressure as to make impossible needed concern for form in addition to substance. I can have no pride in what I have written over the years, nor even in the accuracy of an occasional prediction. A reader may note that as early as 1932 I foresaw the Second World War and offered my humble, withal stern, warning against such conduct on the part of the Democracies as would make world war inevitable.

Jewishly it has fallen to me all my days to take the unpopular side, beginning with my support of the Zionist Movement, under the leadership of my old teachers, Dr. Gustav and Professor Richard Gottheil, as early as 1897. As for Zionism, I was a "natural," my paternal Grandmother having gone to Palestine to pray and to die, and there to be buried. She chose loneliness in Palestine and a grave facing the site of the Holy of Holies, rather than join her only surviving son, my father, in this country.

Throughout my life I have been actively associated with such movements as seek to bring about better relations between Jews and Christians. For many years, particularly in Portland, Oregon, which was the scene of my second congregational ministry, I began to feel that Rabbis must take a full part in bringing to Christian congregations an understanding of the truth with respect to Jewish life and faith, and to welcome Christians of every church to their own Synagogue pulpits. I venture to believe that I did this without such compromise and surrender as now often characterize efforts at inter-religious and inter-racial good will. Self-minimization is the poorest of passports to the altars of mutual understanding and reverence.

Much of the following pages deals with Hitler and Hitlerism, the terrible blight that has fallen upon the entire world and the earliest shadows of which have darkened the light of my people's life. I have written often and sternly, not merely with regard to the unmeasured evil of Nazism, but in the years from '32 to '39, of the sin of acquiescence, for the most part, of peoples and nations and even churches with respect to the limitless and indescribable wrong wrought against my people. Today the Democracies of earth must war for survival and, happily, too, for the rebirth of human freedom, because they failed to enlist in the cause of defending the earliest and least guilty of the hapless victims of the Nazi criminals. Some day I plan to write fully the story of what I know in relation to the long-continued failure of the Democracies, and the causes of the tragedy which is now upon us — soon to end in glorious triumph for freedom, for justice, for faith.

I purpose to continue as the editor of OPINION, and through its pages and with the cooperation of its board of distinguished editors to submit my own view of things to its subscribers. May the readers of this volume be as friendly and patient with the following pages as through the years they have been with the sometimes irritating, ofttimes impatient, but never timid writer, who has set down the truth as he saw it, and will continue to deal with men and things, within and without Israel, "As I See It."

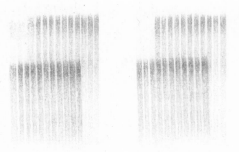

I

The Jewish Fate and Faith

The Jewish Heritage

THE UNIQUENESS of the spiritual heritage which is Israel's lies in the truth that no people or brotherhood was disinherited in order that Israel might become a people of inheritors. Truly Israel might say in the words of the poet, "Anybody might have heard it, but God's whisper came to me." Israel might more truly have said, "I followed after the whisper; I pursued the gleam; I claimed the heritage, when it promised, even as it became little more than a burden."

And the second peculiarity of the heritage is that, while material things which are inherited are often safeguarded from others, a spiritual heritage must be shared or else its ownership is made null and void. Israel is more truly the bestower of spiritual bounty than an inheritor. In many ways the world has sought to belittle the priceless heritage of Israel. Sometimes this has been done through denying the validity and the value of the heritage. Again the inheritors have been assailed, even while the assailants coveted and, in truth, lived upon the bounty of the heritage whose possessors they condemned. And there was another way of doing hurt to the heritage and its trustees, namely, to claim and withal deny it at one and the same time, in some wise to alter it and then to reclaim it as something unknown and unique.

And what has been the effect of the heritage upon its possessors, upon the world? In other words, what is the testimony to the value of the heritage on the part of its inheritors, on the part of them that would not share it and what has been its effect upon the moral and spiritual destinies of the human family? That this legacy of Israel enriched them to whom it came cannot be gainsaid. If the prophets and the seers and the psalmists made Israel, it is not less true that Israel made it possible for its sons to become among the prophetic and visioning teachers of the world. The Old Testament is only the first of the chapters of an endless story of moral and spiritual courage to which they were ever equal who claimed and prized the heritage. And the world at its justest has not failed by a thousand voices, among the noblest voices of history, to bear witness to what this heritage wrought for a God-intoxicated people who held it high.

But an awful problem faces Israel in our own time. In the world of material possessions, a legal title is the equivalent of an imprescriptible charter, but in the world of spiritual things a legal title, if such a thing can be, does no more than prove the spiritual poverty of them that hold no other title than the title of possession or tradition.

The business of Israel is not to vaunt itself as the historical possessor of a priceless heritage but to live and serve and teach in the sight of all the world as becomes the bearers of a great name and of a glorious tradition. One of the great English teachers of the eighteenth century declared "Happy, that while they lay down the rule, we can also produce the example." What shall it profit Israel, if its fathers have laid down the rule and we can no longer produce the example? And this is not a matter of verbal testimony or of spirited self-defense or of generous bounty to the needy or of boastful affirmation touching the past. This is to live again as did our fathers, as seekers after God, doers of justice, ever fanatical for social righteousness, possessed of childlike purity of heart. Whether the heritage is to be carried on depends upon the life of the Jew today, here and everywhere; upon the capacity of the individual Jew to give himself to those noble and consecrated ends of life which were the goal and the guerdon of the bequeathing Jew. And near be the day when it shall be said of us and of our children:

"And nobleness walks in our ways again
And we have come into our heritage."

— 1932

Jews Under Disapproval

"JEWS on Approval" is not another book by Maurice Samuel, though it come from his pen. It is really misnamed. It should be styled "Jews Under Disapproval." If published anonymously, it might almost be viewed as a Gentile's reply to Samuel's "You Gentiles." It is as frank and pitiless as "You Gentiles" and written from the inside. Like much of Maurice Samuel's work, it is done with a scalpel. One sees Jewish flesh bleed and Jewish nerves quiver at the scalpel's point.

The book raises two major questions, in addition to the many minor issues to be urged by sundry victims of Mr. Samuel's exposé. Query one: is a policy of silence and evasion possible or desirable with respect to the great shortcomings of American Jewish life? Shall the fear of Ford yesterday and of Hitler today move us to every manner of concealment touching evils in the Jewish household, the exposure of which lends comfort to Israel's traducers? Does not anti-Semitism hurt us most by inhibiting us from dealing courageously and radically with the sore places in the body politic of Jewry? If we seek a classic precedent for guidance, we have it in the utterance of the Hebrew prophets, whose every superbly self-critical word has been twisted and distorted throughout the centuries to Jewish hurt. And, yet, who would sacrifice one priceless syllable of prophetic denunciation at the behest of the "alrightnicks"—to use that delicious Anglo-Yiddish term?

When, some years ago, "Jews Are Like That," a collection of portraits of the great and near-great in American
Israel, was published, I called attention for the benefit
of some horrified readers of a critical analysis of certain
figures to the fact that an English writer had said of the
English king what no American Jewish writer would dare
say of a noted American Jewish banker or lawyer, namely:
that he is the "average man with an average mind."

In a community in which every giver is called a philanthropist, every lawyer a jurist, every politician a statesman, every preacher a prophet, it comes with a shock to
note the frankness and ruthlessness with which Mr. Samuel touches upon some of the dominant evils of American
Jewry. Insofar as there are vulgarity and self-seeking and
cowardice in the leadership of American Israel, whether
lay or clerical, it is well that some one, dissenting from
the chorus of bought and press-agented flattery, should
speak the truth and the whole truth.

And the second of the major queries is: granted that
there must be exposure—I had almost said explosure—
were it not well to have done the thing with some delicacy
and restraint? As a volunteer, Maurice Samuel "dis-
praises" with all the enthusiasm and energy, which ordinarily can be found in the professional output of Public
Service Counsels, to call personal lobbyists by their own
name. Query, again! Were not the Greeks right? It not the
half better than the whole? If adulation in Jewish life is
become sickeningly sweet, must unafraid appraisal read
like a page of Brann's erstwhile *Iconoclast?* "Economy of
Truth," to use a phrase which sounds more like Milne
than Mills, is indeed intolerable. But prodigality in the
mendacities of sycophantic dealing are not to be balanced
and corrected by fanaticism of denunciation. Intemper-
ance in dispraise does not become an aristocratic virtue,

because overmuch praise is the commonest of vices in a democracy. Yet despite the bitterness of its invective and the prodigality of its dispraise, it is an honest man's searching and above all a challenging analysis of some of the dominant problems in the American Jewish scene.

In an epistle of revealing frankness, Huxley said of himself: "I am full of faults but I am true." This book is marred by faults not a few, the error of hyper-criticism, the blunder of dealing with the first Jew of his age, Justice Brandeis, as if he were nothing more than the leader of American Zionist groups under the ban of Lipsky and Margulies. But it is the work of a man who will not lie for his people's sake, who, in his abhorrence of unsaving lies has taken into his hand the weapon of damning truth. The answer to "Jews on Approval" is not to be "You're another," or any succession of theatrical libel suits. For these are the children of the arrogance which Mr. Samuel justly pillories. An indictment is not quashed by *tu quoque*, or annulled by a libel suit. With charity to few, extenuating little and setting down much in malice, "Jews on Approval" brings with it an atmosphere of unpurchasable and unterrified truth-speaking after the vulgarity and indeed profanity of American Jewish "lick spittleism."

— 1932

Shema Yisraelism

IT WAS once said of Theodore Roosevelt that he was not so much the contributing as the distributing editor of the *Outlook*. I sometimes wonder whether, saving the difference, my function as a member of the editorial board of *Opinion* is to become its complaint-box. *Opinion* readers somehow may come to feel that a plaintiff of the pulpit may in the spirit of reprisal fittingly be made the object or recipient of complaints, objections, criticisms, and worse.

The first of such complaints or indictments is at hand from the pen of one who modestly styles himself "an ordinary reader." In straightforward fashion he asks the question: "Don't you realize that the ordinary reader would find it refreshing occasionally to hear that the authors of your articles have a well-defined, wholehearted belief in the *Shema Yisrael?*" There are two possible ways of interpreting this question. The writer may wish to be sure that the *Opinion* editors are theologically sound, or he confuses *Shema Yisrael* with Israel.

Let it be said flatly and bluntly that *Shema Yisrael* is no more equivalent to Israel than last year's proceedings of the Union of American Hebrew Congregations are equivalent to the whole of the chronicles of the people of Israel. *Shema Yisrael* is a terse way of expressing the central doctrine of the monotheistic faith of the Jewish people. It is inexpressibly precious and hallowed because it is bound up with the deathless memories of Jews in all generations, who chose to accept torture and even death rather than to forswear fealty to this basic affirmation of the religious faith of the Jew.

I repeat, for the benefit of the earnest writer of the epistle with which I am dealing, that the occasional or, after the manner of the Roman paternoster, even continuous recital of the *Shema Yisrael* is not co-terminous with the breadth and depth of a people's life. If "ordinary reader" believes that *Shema Yisrael* is all there is of Israel and that there is nothing else, then there is nothing for me to add except that I most earnestly and vigorously dissent. If Israel be a people, if Israel be a civilization, if Israel be a life—and Israel is all of these—then the *Shema Yisrael* has reference to no more than a phase, historical and evolutional though it be, of the credal division of that totality of life known as Israel.

Israel had and has a creed. But a creed, however valid, is not interchangeable with Israel. I frankly confess that I believe Israel without the *Shema Yisrael* would be infinitely poorer, but *Shema Yisrael* without Jews would be a cry into the void.

As I study Jewish life about me, I come to dread the peril of *Shema Yisraelism* becoming a substitute not only for Judaism, but even for Jewishness and Israel, instead of remaining its doctrinal parole. *Shema Yisrael* is fast becoming the all of Judaism for certain groups of Jewish assimilationists and semi-assimilationists who, lacking the courage of their cowardice, are not quite ready to take the final plunge into the seas of baptismal oblivion. To such, void of every shred of decent Jewish feeling and purged of every redeeming Jewish loyalty, the *Shema Yisrael* is no more than the last tolerable and the least intolerable of the links with a Jewish past. The easy recital with one's lips of a Jewish slogan serves as a self-palliating substitute for the loyalties of Jewish life. Even when uttered with mystic fervor, *Shema Yisrael* is no more than an affirmation of the soul's quest. Alas, that it can be and is uttered by Jews brutally callous to Jewish brothers faring upon the same pilgrimage of the soul!

I have no doubt that when in 1897 the *Protest-Rabbiner* succeeded in keeping Herzl and his Zionist Congress out of Munich and Germany, they recited the *Shema Yisrael* with the gusto of spirits that had faced and fulfilled without fear a soul-trying duty. One hopes the members of Congress were not unduly disturbed upon a recent occasion in Washington by the passionate cry of *Shema Yisrael* as it rang from throats weary with the effort of averting the introduction of an anti-Hitler resolution by Jews of doubtful *Shema Yisraelism* who realized the menace of Hitlerism to the life of German Jewry and the security of Israel. We are told that the very heavens of Philadelphia were recently rent by the perfervid cry of *Shema Yisrael* as it winged its upward way in the velvety accents of one who looked upon his godly work and was raptly grateful, for the work of "sneaking" what is known as the pogrom-hymn of Tzarist Russia into a place by the side of and parate with *Hatikvah,* long-challenged, bitterly-fought, ere it found its way into the new book of psalms compiled by the Central Conference of American Rabbis.

— 1932

Tragi-Comic History

SOME day a chronicler will write a comic history of the Jewish people. He will not fail to include mention of the Jewish home in California wherein a fortnight ago the Jewishly bemedaled Archbishop of the diocese performed a marriage ceremony before an improvised nuptial altar for the daughter of this Jewish home to the Catholic-reared scion of a Jewish line. He may narrate an incident of still more recent happening in New York, at the most expensive and long-exclusive of the Jewish clubs of New York. Not long ago invitations were issued for a bridge tournament and dinner. One member of the club is so hopelessly unmodern as to know how to consult a Jewish calendar, which of course is not to be found in this "most expensive and exclusive of Jewish Clubs." He noted that the bridge tournament and dinner were arranged for the Passover or Seder eve. He so informed the heads of the club, taking it for granted that a hint would suffice. The answer was that, although the tournament had been arranged without knowledge that the date coincided or conflicted with the Passover eve, the members of the club would have no objection to its adherence to the dinner and bridge tournament arrangements already made. And the dinner-tournament took place, attended by hundreds.

And we rail against those who make no provision in school and college and elsewhere for observance of the holidays and festivals! The Yom Kippur diners and revelers of a generation ago were less vulgar than these creatures. For the Atonement Day violators, however crude and blatant, embodied an attitude of protest against conformity. "Mistaken but in earnest" might have been spoken in condemnation of this blasphemy. But these new blasphemers represent no principle and embody no protest. This is unmitigated and brazen vulgarity. Granted the claim that the club diners would not celebrate Seder in their own homes! This is a Jewish club. So, at least, it was alleged when its members in war days sought to exonerate themselves from the charge of being a German social organization which in pre-war days it had loudly purported to be. Granted that not a single bridge player at the club that night would have had part in the Seder! If the membership were not woefully and wilfully ignorant, from the Jewish viewpoint, it would have remembered that tragic memories are bound up with that historic night in Israel, in many ways making it the most memorable of the Jewish year.

Possibly some of the older tournament dinner-guests remember the four types of sons mentioned in the classic Seder story. The Rashang asked: "What mean Ye by this service?"—"Ye" the narrative quaintly stresses, and not "we"!—It may be that in Berlin and Munich a generation ago the cousins of the members of the club in question held a Skat or Klabrias tournament on the Seder eve,

smiling at the superstitious practices of their East-European *Glaubensgenossen* and flattering themselves that
there was no more occasion to recall the days of bondage.
For are we not *Preussen* or *Bayern* or *Würtemburger*?
One fancies that in many a home in Berlin or Munich
this Passover eve family heads recited with a new solem-
nity "this year we dwell in bondage, next year may we
prove to be the children of freedom." So may it be! But
the old and empty boastings have died away. So nigh is
bondage to our freedom, no near is Hitlerism to overtak-
ing our manlike hope and trust.

Comic history of the Jews! Perhaps it should be serio-
comic or tragi-comic! For high comedy is never without
elements of tragedy. And there is tragedy, though not
without comic relief, in these ever-recurring tales whose
uniform theme is self-derision, whose never-failing motif
is self-contempt. The president of the local Communist
society in Russia, vainly hunted in order that he might
serve as chairman of a pre-Passover demonstration of the
Atheistic Society and at last discovered baking Matzoth
in a village cellar, is of the essence of the comic: but beneath the comic there is the tragic element of spiritual
self-recovery. There lies the austerity of a will to loyalty
that neither gods nor men can bend. Another and greater
Zangwill will yet arise to write this comic history. His
must be the homeliness of Sholem Aleichem, the penetration of Maurice Samuel, the wisdom of Ludwig Lewisohn,
the wit of Heinrich Heine—and the compassion of the
Jew!

— 1932

World Jewish Conference

THE American Jewish Congress was called into being for two purposes: To bring about the establishment of the Jewish National Home in fulfillment of the ancient and unrenounced ideal of our fathers. This means a Jewish majority on both sides of the Jordan, and is in conformity with the vision and the program of Theodor Herzl. The second purpose was and is to safeguard rights of Jews in all lands in which they dwell. The founders of the Congress and their tens of thousands of comrades throughout our land believed and continue to believe that a people honorable and proud cannot live on benefactions from without or from within, that it must subsist upon its own strength.

As a result of the moral and political retrogression since the war, there are nations great and small which have repudiated the democratic ideal and renounced its principles and policies. In Jewish life, too, there are those who have lost faith in democracy, and are eager to revert to the autocratic process of management which was ever nearer to their heart's desire. This unhappy day may witness wide and grave defections in one way or another from the ideal of democracy. This, after all, is nothing more than a people's faith in its capacity to be self-governing, in its ultimate right of self-determination. Surely, we, the Jewish people, earliest among self-governing national groups, whose charter of democracy harks back to earliest beginnings and antedates the complex of Christian life and civilization, ought to be the last among peoples to renounce and betray the democratic hope. Herzlism means that people cannot be saved by favor or bounty, means self-salvation without external mediation. What kings and czars could not do for us yesterday, Jewish oligarchs and autocrats, however unlimited their self-approval and however genuine their good will, cannot do for us today.

If we of the Congress had as little faith in the power of the Jewish people understandingly to consider and courageously to face our problems, we, too, would lament that nothing is to be gained by conference and consultation. But it must be noted that unfaith is the attitude of the outspoken opponents of a World Jewish Conference, however limited and informal, not only with respect to the Jewish people, but just as truly with respect to the judgment and conscience of mankind. Despite all that has been visited upon our people in various lands, we declare that we have not lost our faith in the Jewish people or in the will of mankind to be just to the Jewish people. We put it in this way—and we assume that the world will understand—Professor Cuza and Rumania are not interchangeable terms. The mind of Cuza is not the mind and spirit of Rumania. Nor do we believe that Hitlerism is the last word of the German people. We believe that Schiller and Lessing more truly express the soul of Germany than do Hitler and Goebbels. And, above all, whatever political and partisan changes may for a time threaten the peace of Germany, the more than half million Jews, descendants of Jewish dwellers in and builders of Germany for a thousand years will not be physically exiled from the Germany of Heine and Boerne, Wasserman and Ehrlich, Lasker, Bamberger, and Albert Einstein, nor be doomed to the spiritual fate of eviction from fullest sharing in the life and status of German citizenship.

The objections that are urged against a Conference we cannot hope at this time adequately to consider. But this may briefly be said. The claim that money alone can help our fellow Jews, if it were true, were a sign of something graver than financial need or distress, namely of moral bankruptcy. To maintain that unless we can bring great financial resources to the succor of our fellow-Jews is to malign our brothers, however desperate their economic status.

As for the allegation that a World Conference would in some degree and a World Congress in still greater measure arouse against us the suspicion that we are banded together internationally in self-defense, it is too contemptible and cowardly to be taken seriously by a self-respecting company of Jews. If we are not strong and brave and wise enough to meet together in the sight of men to consider what can be done to lighten the burdens unjustly laid upon our people, then, in truth, we do not deserve a better fate. Slaves sullenly acquiesce in, even as free men earnestly and publicly protest against wrong.

If, too, our status as citizens of the nations in which we dwell is as precarious as some Jews imagine it to be, then, indeed, we have nothing to lose. The truth is that the world understands that in addition to the fullest discharge of our duties as citizens and nationals of the lands of which we are a part, we have an inevasible obligation to our fellow-Jews, to one another, to our brothers. The world will understand and honor our decision to consult *with* brother Jews, representative of the Jewries of many lands, and our irrepealable decision not to act, not to legislate, not to decide *for* other Jewries, howsoever afflicted or wronged. Masters may speak to their subjects, brothers meet and consult with one another.

— 1932

A Tragic Blunder

REFORM Judaism has borrowed too much from the alien church ideal of Western lands. The Church was for Christendom an easy and inexigent substitute for the more rigorously exigent moral and spiritual demands of Christianity. The State magnified the Church in extenuation and exoneration of itself. Again the Church, whether Roman or Protestant, was sturdily and shrewdly upheld by the State as the one symbol of unity in a world rent by every manner of conflict and division. Church and State indeed offered a dichotomy which had no parallel and could achieve no parallel in Jewish life. The unconscious assimilation of Jewish life to such utterly alien and un-Jewish dichotomy was a tragic blunder insofar as it was violative of an immemorial Jewish tradition. This tradition regarded people and synagogue or people and religion as one and inseparable.

Jewish Reformism—for there was no movement needed or possible, which ranked in point of importance with the Reformation—unconsciously or subconsciously followed the non-Jewish model. At first purposing and later purporting to magnify the Synagogue, it began to move in the direction of holding the synagogue, its worship, its practices, and its mores, as distinct or distinguishable from the Jewish people. Some unhappy results followed. There ceased to be an understanding of the truth that people and faith were reciprocally pervasive, and again, almost equally lamentable, it came to be believed that people and faith moved in unconcentric spheres. Coupled with this a process of alienation began, in the end almost avowed and purposive, of Jews from what was an alien and borrowed concept of Jewishness.

The synagogue and "religion," using that debatable

term, were given a false emphasis, not a larger but a mis-
leading emphasis. Ignoring Jewish precedent, it somehow
set up a credal test with even more lively zest than had
been done by Orthodoxy, and this test, un-Jewish and
untraditional, proved to be repulsive and expulsive to
great numbers of Jews, our best in truth, not void of some
measure of the Jewish consciousness, but still justifiably
unready to submit themselves to credal test or dogmatic
authority. Unversed in Jewish learning, these yet dimly
or clearly sensed that they were members of a fellowship,
not communicants of a sect or church. And the un-Jewish
superimposition of credal test or dogma either impelled
them into an attitude of negation or else afforded a not
undesired method of escape from rigors which, stern in
themselves, proved intolerable to unheroic souls.

The perhaps inevitable mistake has been that the
credal test, though implicit and informal, has external-
ized the synagogue to the Jew, rather than made him a
part thereof so that he had to be re-absorbed within it or
else come to think of himself as a faithless Jew. However
winsome this utterly un-Jewish point of view may have
been to Lutheranized, Anglicanized, Romanized Jews in
Germany, England, France, and America, grave and as
yet cureless evils have followed thereupon.

The un-Jewish stress upon Credo, which is only another name for the Temple fixation of Reform Judaism,
was bound to eventuate in an underemphasis of the Jewish people concept; and in what might be called a major
emphasis upon the Jewish church, a minor emphasis upon the Jewish people. The major emphasis became
paramount and all but solitary, the minor emphasis ultimately became an insistent negation, virtually the primary article of the Credo of Jewish Reform. Within the
Temple the Jew proclaimed the Lord as One. Outside of

the Temple and in the midst of life, the Reform Jew continuously echoed: "We are not a living and eternal people; we are not a people at all."

Thus American Israel developed too deep a passion to be like unto the majority people in the midst of which it lived. Too much that was Jewish was forsworn; and under the aegis of liberation or emancipation, too much that was un-Jewish was assimilated. The most grievous effect of this was that we as a people made minimal effort to affect and to influence, to pervade and to transform the people among whom we had come to find home and freedom and asylum. We Jews in America had something, yea much, to give, not merely something to get. Out of political bondage we came, but not even American freedom could make us freemen as long as we strove wholly to adjust ourselves to circumstance and environment instead of with the genius of the Jew achieving mastery over environmental circumstance.

The time is come for us to behold the truth that we are not to suffer ourselves to be consumed and devoured, overborne and assimilated. Rather are we to be a constitutive and creative factor, a transforming force in American life. We must cease to think of finding shelter in America and begin to think of our people as enrichers and not beneficiaries of America. As a people, we too have been docile and acquiescent instead of being inflexibly self-insistent as Jews.

Today we Jews must no longer be ready to be "liberalized" into a Semitic version of Unitarianism, nor yet to be Jewish Humanists with a Jewish accent whether that Jewish accent be imported from Pinsk or Posen, whether from Bambach or Altkunstadt. Never was there less valid figure or illustration than the figure of "the

melting pot" applied to America. To accept it were trea-
son to our capacity for contribution to the treasures of
American life. We would be more than Jewish clay in the
hands of alien potters. We would be potters shaping the
vessel of our fate as men and Jews.

— 1933

A Century of Jewish Progress

IN DEALING with the century of Jewish progress, one ought
seek to single out the more hopeful and joyous items of
that century. And yet it is most painfully difficult to make
any draft upon the spirit of cheerfulness in one of the
blackest hours of Jewish history. And before dealing with
the latest phase of one hundred Jewish years, one must
needs attempt to summarize the major happenings of that
period. Happenings have reference not chiefly to events
and episodes however striking and dramatic, but to the
currents and movements that underlie historic development.

Outwardly the dominant factor and movement of the
century, 1833-1933, has been the emancipation movement, that movement making for political emancipation
which was well under way in 1832 in France and America, about to dawn in the England of that day, after little
more than a decade to come to light in the German-
speaking countries, somewhat later in Italy, and last of
all in cataclysmal ways and days in East European lands.

Within the century just ended, the world has looked
upon the joyous beginnings and, it may be the tragic ending, of the processes of political emancipation for the
Jews. In the life of the Jew, enghettoed for a millenium,
the opening of the ghetto gates meant for too many re-
pressed and suppressed Jews not merely political libera-

tion, but liberation from things that were not chains, from status that was not binding nor repressive. One of the nothing less than tragic by-products of the Jewish century of progress has been the fanatical quest of the Jew for withdrawal and separation from all that was Jewish, because the world bade him be free from chains and bonds.

From and after 1832, holding fateful and historic thirty-two to be the beginning of the current Jewish century, and ever since, emancipation has been the major disintegrative force of Jewish life. Imagined to spell release from the bonds of Rabbinism, it builded up a new prison house the dwellers within which conceived themselves to be unfettered mortals, when in truth they had been forging new and self-enslaving chains.

To waive and repudiate the right to be unchallengeably oneself is a species of intellectual and spiritual self-enslavement. And this forfeiture of the right to be frankly and fearlessly oneself became the sin of the Jew in the name of and under the guise of emancipation. This must always signify outer and inner freedom, and Jewish emancipation in many lands became nothing more than the substitution of new self-enslavement for the lack of outward freedom.

Against the myriad disintegrating influences of so-called emancipation, which for a time opened only the outermost doors of Jewish isolation, there arose as the century under consideration was two-thirds spent, the only completely integrating force and factor of Jewish being, namely Zionism. Zionism is not to be imagined to be a Jewish species of land-hunger, nor a yearning for shelter and refuge, nor even to be solely a nostalgia of the landless for the people's only refuge worthy of the name, a National Homeland. Nay, Zionism, as conceived and in

part executed by Theodor Herzl was the half conscious
instinct of a people integrating past and future together
into the totality of the will to live and to be itself and
only itself.

1933 then finds World Jewry impacted upon by two
dominant influences, the integration of political Zionism
and the disintegration of quasi-emancipation. Such prog-
nosis as might have been attempted three months ago
appears strongly in favor of reintegrative Zionism since
the fifth day of March, the day of Hitler's rise and civilization's fall. Hitler may yet cost world Israel the 600,000
Jews of Germany for whom there remain according to
the best informed students of Germany, three courses:
(1) economic extermination from without, (2) self-de-
struction, another tragic form of external coercion, and
(3) emigration, which may be said to be a union of outer
compulsion, and inner resolve.

Today, as perhaps never before in the early nineteenth
century of the Diaspora, the Jew faces the problem in
some such terms as Moses Hess set up—Rome or Jerusalem. Backward to any one of a hundred Romes of assimilation, whether it be through the political gateway of
emancipation or the quasi-religious vestibule of that substitute for the totality of Jewishness which calls itself Reform Judaism. Would that the answer to the query addressed to the Jew by the passing of the century and the
beginning of a new era had been offered by the Jew without the compulsion of Hitler or the barbaric coerciveness
of the German Reich. Hitler may yet prove like many
another Baalam, Haman, Pharaoh and Titus and Torquemada before him, to have been a great preserver of
all truest Jewish interests, a unifier of the severed and
sundered fragments of Jewish life as these have come under the disintegrative impact of Jewish "otherism," to use

Emerson's term for contemptuous self-alienation from one's own innermost life. In that case German Jewry's sacrifice will not have been made wholly in vain.

Today as never before for a thousand years and more, the Jew must answer not only before the forum of world opinion, but before the tribunal of his own soul: Shall I lose myself in the sea of commonplaceness and security into which I may fling myself in the quest for surcease from Jewish wound and woe or shall I once again and forevermore accept for myself a place in the advancing ranks of those fellow-Jews who are resolved to end the fiction of Jewish dissolution and to achieve again the miracle of Jewish rebirth? It may yet be that the century ended will prove to have been the century of the Jewish life of will-lessness and the century that is about to begin become the century of the Jewish will to live.

— 1933

Why Not Jewish Unity?

IT ALMOST seems at times as if "unity" had become the "Mesopotamia," with all of the weird and anesthetic quality of that term, in American Jewish life. One of the best known of American Jews followed up a plea for unity at a Jewish meeting some years ago by stating with regard to a man whom he imagined to be averse to unity, "if that fellow is not for unity, I will break his neck."

Unity is an admirable thing but they who strive for it, they who ceaselessly prate about it ought to reach some understanding with respect to its content. The term unity is often used by those who, if they but knew, were reaching out for uniformity or for unanimity, whether these take the form of explicit agreement or the assent of unchallenging silence. Most important of all and most often forgotten is the truth that unity is not a thing to be sought, is not to be pursued as a goal, but is nothing more than a method of quest, an item of technique.

Such is become the fetish and superstition of unity in Jewish life that effectiveness of action is less earnestly sought after than unity. One is tempted to suspect that Jews almost believe and more than half hope that somehow the magic that resides in unity may become a substitute for vigorous effort and unremitting devotion and the reality of sacrifice.

If American Jewry did not think in terms of shibboleths, it would begin to ask whether much of the ceaseless and raucous cry for unity does not grow out of the things which are more evil than the absence of unity— namely intolerance, self-distrust when not self-contempt, over-much concern for manner and even manners and too little concern for matter and substance. The insistence upon unity comes oftenest from them for whom unity is a paraphrase for dominance which were grave enough, for minimum rather than maximum Jewishness. Unity is not seldom the watchword of those who seem prepared to surrender to the forces of assimilation and to yield to the pressure which would obliterate everything that is Jewish.

IN RECENT years Jewry has looked upon several illustrations of the way in which unity works out. The Jewish Agency was to be a union of Zionism and non-Zionism in the upbuilding of the Jewish national home. The truth is that the Jewish Agency has paralyzed Zionism, has made the Zionist Organization far less effective and vigorous than it was in pre-Agency days, whilst it has failed to galvanize non-Zionists. To Zionists the Agency has afforded an alibi and to non-Zionists it has offered the benefit of

self-exoneration, ending that sense of guilt and of desertion from Jewish life which touched the souls of them
who became the non-Zionist authors of the Agency. The
Agency, instead of bringing unity, has given non-Zionists
control minus responsibility and continues to burden
Zionists with responsibility minus control.

The so-called Synagogue Council, one of the many de-
vices of them that cry for unity, has within a few months
reached an agreement on the lowest common denominator of all the Jewish groups which it purports to represent.
That lowest denominator is virtually a zero or a politely
paraphrastic substitute for zero. Those of us who are
deeply in earnest about things Jewish may not forget
that, whilst unity is a good eagerly to be striven for, there
are certain things which stand definitely and uncancel-
ably in the way of it and that there can be no unity without fatal surrender on one side or the other. If the surrender were on the other side, the fatality might be viewed
with some measure of resignation. Behold the conflict between Jewish self-affirmation and Jewish assimilation,
between them limiting Jewishness to the recital of a
statement of creed and an intellectual dogma and they
who hold that Judaism is the way of life of a people. Need
one do more than hint at the infinite hurt which has been
wrought by the creed or dogma theory of Jewishness, supremely effective only in shutting out the intelligentsia
from Jewry. One may speak of unity everlastingly, but
what unity save of action, it may be in self-defense, can
there be between those whose Jewishness consists only in
the recital of *Shema Yisrael*, whose Jewishness consists
chiefly in the denial of the reality of the peoplehood or
racehood of Israel, and those to whom Judaism is co-terminous with life, to whom the Jew is the symbol of a
deathless people and an imperishable ideal of life.

What approximation, summing it up, can there be between these two irreconcilable viewpoints, the viewpoint
of such Jews as virtually say, "The past may not have been
bad, the present must be endured, but as for a future, we
are done" and of those who believe that Israel's past has
been great, that the present, despite every difficulty and
burden and challenge, is glorious and that the future of
Israel is to be greatest of all?

Jewish unity should be sought after, provided it be
clearly understood that no unity is worth the name that
rests on the basis of fears, of self-contempt and of pro-
scription, that unity in order to be worth-while must be
bound up with hope, with the mood of self-trust and with
a spirit of mutual reverence. And this means that there
must be complete respect for every group or faction in
Jewish life in our land, whatsoever be its European origin,
whatever be its viewpoint on Jewish problems. Unity to
be dreaded and fought against is such unity as means
dictation by the few to the many, dictatorship over the
many by the few, the dictation of such as reject the view
that Judaism is a people's way of life rather than a sense
of misfortune of the hour pending final dissolution. Unity
can and must be; provided they who are to be unified are
not to be submitted to the processes of Judean *Gleichschaltung*, that is to say as long as unity be not made an
instrument of coercion; provided the passion for unity
be bound up with the basic hunger of the Jewish people
—its will to live.

— 1934

Notable Anniversaries

IT IS early in the year to take account of the more important anniversaries which it is to include. But special men-

tion may fitly be made at this time of several which merit
and will have widest commemoration throughout World
Jewry. The over-shadowing anniversary event of 1935
promises to be the Octocentenary of Maimonides on the
Passover eve. The man and his age will have fullest celebration unless we unwisely suffer the drear shadow of
Central European Hitlerism to mar the holiday mood of
a people which may look back 800 years to the birth of the
son of Maimon. He, than whom there was only one
greater Moses in all the centuries, points not to the dark
and medieval century of his birth. His people, our fathers, were during his life in the midst of one of the gold-
en epochs of alternately glowing and drab Jewish history.
For the Maimonidean epoch witnessed the rise of poets,
scholars, philosophers, and scientists, whose names and
works still gleam in the annals of their people. It was an
age which Jewishly was as rich in many realms as was the
later Elizabethan of the North. From Saadya of the tenth
to Rambam of the twelfth century was one of the golden
ages of the long Jewish centuries. And Rambam, *primus
inter pares*, was greatest in two fields in which the Jew
has oft if not uniformly excelled, medicine and philosophy, that is to say, pure and applied science. But great as
was this neo-Aristotelean of the twelfth century, he was
greatest in the humanely applied science of medicine,
which through the ages has claimed or inspired some of
our best.

But one must not linger unduly on this commemoration of some months hence lest one overlook another and
even greater. This year's *Channukah* will mark the completion of twenty-one centuries since the re-dedication
of the sanctuary which marked the triumph of the Maccabeans—thirteen hundred years prior to the birth of
Maimonides. Such is the span of Jewish history, current

English speech having no term or name for a celebration which looks across the vista of two millenia with a century superadded.

Does this mean nothing to devouring foes or faltering friends and sons of Israel? Hitlerism is but another Aryan-accented resurrection of the Hellenic paganism, which vainly pitted its destructive wrath against indestructible Judea. Will not the faltering and the fearful among us learn that nothing less than Maccabean self-reverence, battling in the name of the Eternal and of eternal things, can offer effective resistence to hosts that would crush our ethical and spiritual values—the traditions which embody these and the obligations which derive from them? If the Jewish people fail proudly and grandly to observe the twenty-one hundredth anniversary of the Maccabean miracle of self-deliverance, it will be only because the self-obliterative passion which is assimilation in action dreads the remembrance of sustaining triumph ever more than the memory of unhappy defeat.

Let the celebration be in the key of high resolution and emulation which alone can justify commemoration. Maimonides was four hundred years before Columbus and Torquemada. The Maccabeans were nearly two hundred years before the beginning of that movement which gives its name to an era. The Maccabeans, in truth, antedate Christendom itself, for all else the starting point of the modern world. Dare Jews not feel that they belong to an enduring people in whose "sight a thousand years are as yesterday when it is past, and as a watch in the night"?

Maccabeans, unheroic and craven, would have been the heralds of Jewish destruction. They were not warriors by choice or training, but men who felt threatened by the extinction of country and faith and sanctuary and they fought like men and warred as greatly as men ever dared to war. They feared not to excite the ill-will of neighboring peoples nor did they improvise a theory of non-resistance, trusting through "ideas and ideals" to spare themselves laborious days and endangered nights. Let the great Maccabean celebration of the year's end, to be inaugurated December 20, be more than a proud and chauvinistic spectacle. If we never cruelly sang *vae victis*, let us not belatedly stoop merely to hail the victorious. Rather let us find sustaining and warning in one of the supreme triumphs of history for a people of undefeatable resolve and indeflectible purpose.

And when the year 1935 shall have ended, we shall move swiftly after four days to still another commemorative day. January 4, 1936, will mark the completion of one hundred and fifty years since the death of the third Moses, Mendelsohn. Strange as my word may seem, it is still too early to evaluate the ultimate place of Mendelsohn in Jewish history. The late scholar, Professor Max L. Margolis, some decades ago hinted in the pages of the *Jewish Quarterly Review* at the need of radical re-evaluation of Mendelsohn and his age. Are we not coming to see that Mendelsohn, despite personal piety and Jewish devoutness, prepared the way for an emancipation which was to be tragically less than auto-emancipation? Self-adjustment may be an amenity of the individual, but when it becomes the law and passion of a people is pleasantly but effectively suicidal.

The Mendelsohnian *Aufklaerung* or Enlightenment became too much the feeble and flickering lamp of assimilation. It began with light from the Gentiles, but it ended with reversion to the misunderstood *Missionstheorie* of "light to the Gentiles." An infinitude of self-betrayal and self-surrender of a people lay between the 1786 of Mendelsohn's death and the rebirth of a people which came with the 1896 of Theodore Herzl's *Judenstaat*. It may be, despite Herzl and all that he has come to mean to the Jewish people, that the self-inflicted hurt of the century from Mendelsohn to Herzl may prove to be irreparable. It will be if Jews meet the new day with less than Maccabean strength of self-insistence, if we fail to understand that the ceaseless negations of a hostile world can only be met by that self-affirmation which the past demands and the future shall yet justify. Rich and exhaustless, and abiding, the life of a people which within a twelvemonth commemorates Maimonides and Mendelsohn and the Maccabeans—nor yet chooses to forget.

— 1935

An Hour in Warsaw

I SHALL not seek to convey in these paragraphs even a summary of the impressions gathered over some days in Warsaw. These impressions were for the most part poignant and saddening though conveying a sense of indomitably mystic hope. I limit myself to one unforgettable hour and scene, which told me much touching the horror and the grandeur of the life of Polish Jewry.

To the Keren Hayesod Chambers came a group of men from Przytyk, a town become famous in recent days. A number of the group had been under arrest, some of whom had been discharged and some only released though not discharged, pending appeal to a higher court. These were not beggars, nor even complainants, though there was bitterness in their accusing speech. Only a few months ago there had been 600 Jewish families in Przytyk, living as Jewish families do for the most part, in the smaller Polish towns, that is to say, in half-decent poverty. A day came when these people felt that growing out of the general Jewish disorders in the land, an attack would be made upon them. A member of the group speaking with inward fire in his voice, said, in Yiddish of course: "They thought they could do anything to us Jews, and that we would die like lambs in the hands of a butcher without offering resistance. But we did resist, and one of them, who rushed forward to murder our wives and children, fell."

They told of the unbelievable injustice of a quasi-judicial trial, which freed the pogrom-makers and sentenced to prison the Jewish defenders of their community. One after another spoke with passionate tenseness, their chief plea being to secure mitigation somehow of grievously unjust sentences imposed upon some of their kinsmen, one pleading particularly on behalf of a very young brother under heavy sentence. The crime of self-defence they admitted, self-defence provoked by fierce and murderous attack.

They asked for something more. And the Zionist party leaders who sat with me were no less deeply moved than I. The substance of their petition was—we are not trying to make capital out of our misfortune; we are not like those Jews who begin to think of Palestine only after they are threatened with destruction or homelessness; we were and are, all of us, Zionists; we know that the still nearly five hundred Jewish families of our community cannot be transported to Palestine; we do not deserve it more than others, and we understand that if there were certificates enough for all of us, then all that the Poles would require to do in order to get rid of their Jews would be to begin pogroms in all the Polish cities and villages. We know that we must stay where we are, though we do not know how we shall be able to live through the winter. The police already get in the way of peasants who would, if left free, bring food to the hungry among us.

But—and here was the heart of their cry—we are not *Gezwungener Juden*, like some other Jews and they named these geographically. If we lived in Palestine we could defend ourselves. We are ready to die for the Jewish land, and to endure for Jewish honor. Let some of us go. A number was mentioned and at once another named a lesser figure. If ever so few—and a most modest figure was mentioned—we feel life is not so dear to us, and if we fall, it will be for Eretz Israel that we die. With tear-choked voice I asked: "How long have you lived in Przytyk?" Swiftly the answer came: "There are *Mazevot* in our cemetery which are 600 years old." Two things stood out, one, the tragic humility of the Jew, dating his history of centuries by gravestones, and, two, that moral grandeur which, with the patience of its eternal faith, "I shall not die but live," plans to tell the works of the Lord anew in his own land.

There came yet another moment; this band of heroes pleaded with united fervor for one of their number, Eleazer Feldberg, a man of noble visage, as the photograph in their hands revealed, sentenced to prison for ten months. Father of the community he must be, for they were at one in their story of the dignity and courage with which he had borne himself throughout a cruelly vindictive trial. The prosecutor, seeking to fasten upon him membership in a radical Zionist group, questioned him with respect to his party affiliations. Quietly his answer was given, "I belong to the party of Abraham, Isaac and Jacob." Hence the eternal people! I went to Poland to observe and to learn. What I beheld of Jewish misery and learned of Jewish nobility touched my heart with sorrow not unmingled with pride.

— 1936

The Ancient Vision

To many seated at the Seder table, the story of the Egyptian Passover deliverance will sound this year like a mocking myth. For the Jewish burden grows heavier every hour and the world's yoke ever more crushing to the Jew in land after land. Pre-Nazi Germany contained as many Jews as did Pharaoh's Egypt, but after four black and bitter years those who are left to make up German Jewry still number nearly 400,000—as many Jews as dwell in Palestine. And without reciting all the plagues that afflict and smite Israel in our day, alas, we know how terrible has been the lot of Israel throughout the year. Without as well as within Germany, for Polish Jewry has looked upon affliction and nearly one million Jews in Rumania are still troubled sore. The enemies of Israel have lifted up their hands against us even in Palestine though not without calling forth the strength of perfect self-discipline and inspiring that highest form of courage which is unshatterable self-restraint.

When the voices of Israel cry in the unison of the Seder petition to the end that Israel be delivered from the darkness and death of bondage to the light and life of freedom, shall we hear as without hope and scoff at the futility of re-echoing an ancient piety? Or shall we rather seek to recall that freedom is not only a Jewish aspiration but the Jew's achievement and gift to the world from earliest days? Wherever he has lived and been denied, he has nonetheless moved men's hearts to seek freedom and that larger life of opportunity which cannot be for those who are not free.

Thus the paradox—the Jew freed the world and the world enslaved the Jew. The Jew blessed the world with his own passion for that human liberty which for thousands of years the world denied the Jew. And still forever the chant of the Jew is, "Next year may we be in Jerusalem." Not that the Jews all together dream of returning to any earthly Jerusalem, but they have not given up their dream of bringing all mankind to the Jerusalem of human liberty for all the inhabitants of all the lands. That dream the Jew refuses to relinquish. A thousand Hitlers cannot rob Israel of a vision undimmed by his tears and his blood. The more cruelly the world seeks to shatter his dream, the more deeply the Jew remains under its spell. Whether the world shall yet choose to enter into the heritage of human freedom we do not know. But this Jewish history makes sure—that the Jew will never revise downward his eternal insistence upon every manner of freedom. Woe unto him who would exchange the safety of the Jew or the security of Jews for the freedom of mankind. Blessed they whose soul remains true to the ancient vision of their people ready to suffer and endure and strive that all men may be "in Jerusalem next year."

— 1937

"Dayenu"

DAYENU is not only one of the dominant key-notes of the approaching Passover holidays, but is through the ages become an expression of the Jewish faith. Beginning as a symbol of grateful piety, it has acquired a secondary significance as token of reluctance to yield up faith under any temptation or provocation. It would have been enough, thus runs the quaint refrain, if God had led us out of Egypt, though He had not brought us to Sinai. Not in generations, perhaps centuries, has there been another Passover season in which the lips of piety will not inevitably read a reverse meaning on the Passover or Seder eve

into the ancient saying, "It would have been enough"—
if the Nazi crime against Jewry had been continued without becoming more ruthlessly cruel day by day, it would
have been enough: if, as a result of Nazi gold and influence, the Jews of Poland would have continued to suffer
economic boycott without the indignity of the Ghetto
benches being forced upon them, it would have been
enough: if the Nazi and Polish wrongs to Israel had not
been paralleled by ferocious Goga-Cuza interlude in Rumania, it would have been enough. If the Nazi Reich
had tortured its Jewish subjects without crowning the
horror by annexing Austria to the Empire of shame and
thus bringing one of the finest Jewries of history, the
Viennese, within the orbit of evil, *Dayenu!*

Dayenu! Verily, anyone of these would have been
enough to try our souls and test our spirits. Comes the
Passover treasure-store of a myriad memories, chiefly
mournful! And the miracle of salvation which it unfolds
and the many miracles bound up with its observance
through the ages remind one that hard and bitter as is the
lot of millions of our brothers, our fathers too were enslaved and felt the lash. Pharaoh made them slaves. God
and Moses made them free-men. Hitler like Pharaoh will
pass. God and his people Israel will endure.

— 1938

Eternal Reminder

IF EVER a Passover message was needed by the Jewish
people to make almost insupportable burdens less crushing and to light up the darkness of a grievous time, such
message is needed now. And nothing can help that shall
be less than the faith that made the Egyptian Passover
possible, than the faith which evoked the unshattered
spirit of the Jewish people, as it was compelled to choose

between the ease of Egypt and the bitterness of exile to a strange land.

Things are happening in the world today as by-product and cause alike of the world disaster that is upon mankind, which bitterly afflict and most cruelly try the patience and strength of our people—incidents of a war by a mighty foe against the most defenceless of all peoples, children, women, men, Jewish all, in the Nazi-seared territory of Poland. One wonders whether the human spirit, however resilient, can longer endure. And yet to one's infinite satisfaction, one learns that whatever the sufferings of old and young, rich and poor, learned and unlettered, the spirit of Polish Jewry remains what it was, the crown and glory of world Jewry, unshatterable at its core, fortified into invulnerableness by a faith which all the rapacious Nazi soldiery cannot affect.

Even we, their brothers, children of a common heritage, heirs of a common hope, can hardly believe that the Jewish masses in Poland can survive the orgy of suffering and torture in which their Nazi masters revel. And yet those of us who know Polish Jewry, who have seen the poorest of the poor, the lowliest of the lowly, lift themselves up to levels of spiritual faith and ethical self-enrichment, of which Park Avenue denizens have never caught the faintest gleam—know that such faith will not falter, such strength will not break, such hope will not yield.

The light of the Passover still shines into the darkness of that new enslavement of which our fellow-Jews are for a time the victims. And when on the Passover eve we lift up the cup and give thanks that the day will come, that the day has come for emergence from bondage into freedom, from grief into joy, from darkness into light, we feel that that prayer represents an ancient fulfillment and an ever-present and inviolable promise. The day of the enslaving tyrants, from Pharaoh to Hitler, though it may know a momentary recrudescence, will yet be ended. The night of suffering will pass, the darkness will lift and, as the rule over the universe is divine, neither fiendish nor adventitious, so we Jews who have suffered most will be most glad in the morning of freedom and enlightenment which is soon to dawn.

The Passover is the eternal reminder to Israel—after Pharaoh comes Moses, after Egypt Sinai, after bondage deliverance, and God give it that our faith be triumphantly vindicated in an early day, that Israel and all mankind be free after having put away from before its eyes the evil forever to be ended.

— 1940

The Indestructible Jew

FOR THE tenth time it falls to me as Editor of OPINION to write a review of the Jewish happenings in the year about to end. Year after year it has seemed well to move from land to land, and give a resume of leading events and tendencies since 1931. These reviews have, we fear, tended to sound monotonous as land after land has stood out as yet another victim of Nazi diabolism — what Churchill called "a crime without a name." The pen of Edgar Allen Poe, at his most weird and sanguinary, would alone be equal to the successive horrors of these unutterable years. Last year OPINION dealt with that series of crimes which began with the devastation of Poland, continued in the subjugation by stealth of Denmark and Norway, the conquest, after more or less stout resistance, of the Lowlands, and culminated in the unimaginable tragedy of France's surrender, so that the year 5700, which ended with the epic glory of Dunkirk and the no less epic resistance of London and other English cities, was on the whole one of the most tragic years of a millenium.

And the following year, still current, to be brought to a close by the New Year's Festival, has hardly been more benign. For it has witnessed rather than given rise to mountainous wrongs and woes, which stamp the authors with blackest guilt, and mark the victims as bravest of the brave. Within the year the war has moved South and East. Some of the Balkan and near-Balkan lands have crumbled under the mere threat of Nazi force—lands such as Hungary, Roumania, Bulgaria: others of the Baltic lands, notably Jugoslavia and Greece, have yielded neither to threat nor force, and have heroically fought, though vainly, to defend themselves.

As if the infamies of betrayal had not been enough, the Nazi Reich turned in mid-July, 1941, against the Soviet Union, to which two years earlier it had pledged enduring friendship. And the result—the fiercest, bitterest bloodiest battle in history, not fewer than three millions of the two mighty opposing armies having been lost within the first three months of the war. The battle scene, the most murderous in history, has been the densely populated Jewish belt, stretching from the Baltic to the Black Sea, including some of the classic communities of East European Jewish history. As if this were not terrible enough, the Nazis have not merely overrun the Jewish regions of Poland and Russia but have concentrated their fiendish destructiveness against such Jewish towns and cities, singling out Jews as responsible for Communist leadership.

And that leads immediately to the consideration of one, probably fatal, strategic blunder of Hitler. Lightly and inadvisedly he took it for granted that the mere cry of "Down with Bolshevism" would win and unite the world against Russia, and, therefore, in his own support. Never was graver miscalculation. Even the Catholic Church has refrained from supporting Hitlerism against the Bolshevist regime. Some of the finer voices of American Catholicism—like those of Bishop Hurley of Florida, and Dr. Agar of Louisville, and Professor Sheehy—have spoken out against the Nazi attempt to capture such Christian support as it has long repelled by program and acts alike.

As a result of the Nazi-Soviet war, the issue is clearer than ever before. The foes of Hitler are united not only outwardly by the dread of him but inwardly by common aims, even though the Soviet Union does not purport to be a democracy in the Western sense of the term. Britain and our own country are evidently resolved to give maximum aid and reinforcements to the Soviet, the resistance of which to the Nazis is beyond belief.

Roughly estimated, two-thirds of world Jewry dwell within the nations resisting Hitlerism—one-third in the English-speaking lands, and one-third in the Soviet Union. What the fate of the latter is to be, no one can foresee. But surely the part taken by Jews in unexampled defense ought to bring to Jews in the Soviet not a status of favor, but a position to which they are become entitled by reason of their contributions to Russia both in peace and war, a position such as is their own in democratic lands.

THE NOW famous Eight Points Proclamation of Roosevelt and Churchill clearly foreshadows what in a new dehitlerized world is to ensue upon the victory of the democracies. And yet the reading of the Proclamation and the hearing of the Prime Minister's speech left one wondering whether it would not have been possible for Churchill to add a word of apostrophe to that people, first and last of Hitler's victims, the Jews, and speak solace to them made homeless in a score of countries. For these home can be found if England, mindful of its pledged word, remember the passionate yearning of homeless Jewry to rebuild the land of their fathers.

And world Jewry is deeply disturbed over constant rumors and more of Arab Federations and other readjustments of problems in the Near East. These are propounded—it may be more than propounded—as if Jews had nothing at stake and were peripheral or irrelevant to any solution of the Palestine problem. This is false, for a number of reasons: one, Jews in Palestine alone have done a great and creative work; two, England is under solemn and inevasible obligation to safeguard in every sense the contributions of Palestine to the well-being of Britain and the Arab world; three, the service of Palestine Jewry to Britain, which could not have been more significant unless the Palestine Government had distinctly and wisely cooperated. For all these reasons it should be clearly stated by Jews everywhere, and not solely by the Jewish Agency, that we have the right to assume that there is to be no discussion of the fate of the peoples of the Near East, including more than a half a million Jews in Palestine, without Jewish participation in such discussion and in all decisions arising therefrom.

If Chamberlain and Simon, Hoare and MacDonald were still the leaders in the Cabinet, we would have reason to be apprehensive. These happily are gone—all of them. And he is in command who first said that "Jews are in Palestine of right and not on sufferance." But Palestine Jewry and world Jewry ought not to be dependent upon the Prime Minister's good will or the President's favor. "Of right and not on sufferance" and it was the Prime Minister in the House of Commons little more than two years ago who spoke most vigorously against the inequity of the White Paper, which must be abrogated, that the uncancelable Balfour Declaration stand again. Our own country, by every administration since Wilson's has uttered itself unmistakably in support thereto, none more so than the Government under Roosevelt, Hull and Welles.

IF THE contemplation of the year has taken the form of forecast of the future rather than review of the past, it is because the review of the year's suffering would be almost as unendurable as the fate of them whom it has been sought to crush. One year ago, it was clearly seen, indeed ever since the beginning of the war, that a factor of the first importance had entered into the Jewish position. For six years and more, from January 1933 to September 1939, and except for the seizure of Austria and the violation of Czechoslovakia, Jews had stood alone in their sorrow. Not only had they had to live with little help, save from their own, but they had had to bear the burden of an unequaled misery without more than conventional sympathy and understanding from the world without.

What the brutally broken promises of the Nazis up to September 1939 had failed to do, the violation and subjugation of Poland at last succeeded in making clear. Namely, the war of Hitlerism upon the Jew, though primary in point of time, was merely an incidental preliminary to a world revolution or world war against the things which together comprise Western civilization. At one fell blow, which brought Poland to the dust, Hitler made clear that his was a war of lawlessness against law, of maniacally exaggerated nationalism against an international order of law, of racial mastery against a world to be enslaved, of the doctrine of might glorified against the ideals of negotiation, adjustment and understanding between peoples and races and faiths. Everything that has happened since 1939, the infinite wrongs which Hitlerism has perpetrated, has served to confirm the truer understanding of what it means and what it would effect.

Today, it might be said that the Jew no longer fights alone, nor stands alone. It is he who stands with the Democracies, with the peoples who, though temporarily subjugated, constitute a world of free men. It is not the Jew so much who has united with the forces of freedom, it is the forces of freedom that recognize that the Jew is the symbol of the will of men to remain free and unconquered. The Totalitarian states have done what they could to destroy the life of the Jew. The Jew knows his life to be indestructible and today, as never before, is in the midst of a world which understands that the fate of one is bound up with the fate of all, that a world which permits the Jew to be wronged cannot be a world of justice. At last the Jew lifts himself to a higher stature, and takes his place among the unconquered and unconquerable peoples of the democratically governed world of brother peoples, races, faiths of tomorrow.

— 1941

Inter-American Jewish Unity

THE AMERICAN JEWISH CONGRESS, a democratic Jewish organization, basing itself upon the hopes and ideals of the Jewish masses, founded by the leadership of that moral genius, the late Justice Louis D. Brandeis, has long felt that there should be some consciousness of relationship between the Jewish groups of the Americas, and the very special duty of calling this Conference* naturally

---

* Excerpts from an address delivered at the Inter-American Jewish Conference in Baltimore, November 23, 1941.

rested with the largest of the American Jewish groups, that of the United States, which represents five-sixths of the Jewish population of the Western hemisphere.

The Jewries of all the American countries, other than our own, are still in process of becoming; in time they will come to face the problems and responsibilities which rest upon the Jewish people of the United States. The Jewries of the Central and South American countries stand where the Jewry of the United States stood in 1880. This Conference is summoned in order that we may share the fruit of our experience with you, that we may not only teach but learn, sitting together as brothers, dwelling together as brothers in the unity of inquiry and of search. Our one common purpose above all else is to integrate the Jews of every land in the Western hemisphere into the fullness of the American way of life. That American way of life may express itself differently in the Americas of the South and the North. America does not mean uniformity but unity. External uniformity is totalitarian. Inward unity is democratic and American. Our own country does not wish to impose any way of life or any program upon the other American countries, but it is the hope and purpose of our country to integrate the people of the Western world not only into the bond of hemispheric defense against the enemy who will at a not far distant day be destroyed, but into a common idealism, into a common way of life, into a common destiny.

The Jews of the American countries must be in the vanguard of those who accept the program of identification with the higher viewpoints and the nobler purposes of the American or Democratic way of life. We are not met in order to ask but to give, not to demand privilege but to render service. We have no mandate over the Jewries of any land. We know that after the current fanaticisms shall have passed from the horizon of political life, no special problems or burdens will be laid upon the Jewish population of any American country. Our own United States is the denial of the validity of anti-Semitism. The one commanding intolerance of my own country is its intolerance of racial and religious intolerance. If the Church or Churches be not supported by the State, the State leaves the Churches and faiths and their communicants as free as is the State, and the State in turn remains undominated by the control of Church or Churches, though it may be permeated by the spirit of religious faith at its highest.

WE ARE GATHERED in part in order to bethink ourselves touching the infinitely mournful fate of our fellow-Jews, who have dwelt in European lands. Addresses other than my own will deal with the oceanic tragedy which has befallen the peaceable and loyal populations of many European lands, who were the first and will be the last victims of Nazism until the day of liberation from the monstrous calamity of Nazism. And that day is not far off. For if our country remain, as it is resolved to be, the arsenal of Democracy, and if it give the fullest measure of its unshatterable strength to Britain and its Allied countries, the day of the final overthrow of Nazism will not, cannot, be far off.

But even though, not if, Hitlerism or Nazism is to be banished from the earth, as it will be, there will still remain a number of most difficult and taxing Jewish problems. The economic basis of Jewish living has been wilfully destroyed by Nazism. Jews who, like you and like us, are free must give to the succor of Jews who for nearly a decade have been enslaved and dispossessed. Even though after the war, inter-governmental programs must have special reference to a people in many lands deprived of the basic possibilities of self-support, the fate of our brother-Jews in European lands cries out to us for immediate succor. When peace shall have come, as it will, demands will be made for ultimate and permanent redress from the nations which will have it in their power to bring about the organization of a new world.

Woe betide us, if amidst the comparative plenty and prosperity of American life, we forget our brother-Jews, whose agonies of suffering have come about largely, if not solely, because they are Jews. The self-styled "master-race" has undertaken to enslave. The Democracies will liberate and then as their brother-Jews, we must come to the help of such of our brothers as have been made homeless, as have been reduced to the lowest deeps of want and need, to whom we can bring some measure of solace that they may rise again and lift their eyes unto the hills whence by our hands under God shall come their help.

You and I need not be reminded that when the war shall have ended and even before, we are never, never to lose out of mind Eretz Israel, the land of Israel. More than half a million Jews have come to dwell within its walls, in part with England's help and the help of the League of Nations. Within Palestine the miracle has been wrought by the pioneers of transforming a barren wasteland into one of the most fertile fields of earth, and Palestine breeds not only superior citrus fruits but superior men and women, who are learning to ignore their personal needs and uniting in devotion to the ideal of making a home for the largest number of their fellow-Jews. Loyalty to the Palestine ideal does not divide any Jew from the country in which he dwells and of which he is a citizen. It unites him more profoundly with the ideals of the country. It enriches his loyalty to his country by bringing to the altar of its patriotism the inspiring remembrance of Palestine, its ancient ideals, its present hopes, its dreams for the future.

I call attention, as I close, to a question which Lord Bryce asks in his volume on South America: "Is there, in fact, such a thing as that which the word 'Pan-Americanism' is intended to describe, or does the expression denote an aspiration rather than a fact?" We assume today that Inter-Americanism is both an aspiration and a fact: a fact of world-wide significance; an aspiration which represents the common idealism of the American Republics.

I remember that Lord Bryce speaks rather sadly in one passage of his great book on the imperfections and blunders of Democracy, and most especially of that phase of Democracy known as Municipal Government about which he would have thought better could he have foreseen the achievements of a Latin-American, whose name is La Guardia. Still he maintains that every other form of government has been tried and found wanting. Under Democracy he believes men are still free to choose. Under Democracy we have chosen, who are Jew of many lands in South, in Central America and in North America, from Canada to Argentina, to unite in a new appraisal of our larger duty as Americans. As dwellers in the hemisphere of unassailable and inevasible freedom, this Conference represents a gathering of Jews, American Jews who are at one in their loyal adherence to the American program of the "Good Neighbor," to the American policy of indivisible and impregnable defense and at the same time of unforgetting loyalty to Jewish ideals, to Jewish memories, to Jewish hopes, to the right of the Jew to live as Jew, unashamed and unafraid, proud and eager and enrichingly contributing sharer in the life of every country of which he has become a citizen.   — 1941

The Jew — and Tomorrow's World

IN his chiefly melancholy Last Testament to his people, shortly before his tragic suicide, Stefan Zweig said to a Jewish group in Rio de Janeiro, "We are living through the darkest hour that our people or any people have ever had to face. Only a miracle can help us to live through it, but miracles do not happen as they did in Biblical days. We must create one." Has the miracle come to pass and if so, how? Have we in any sense helped to create it?

Readers of OPINION may recall that from year to year the Editor has prepared the story of the year's happenings. Only one such tale since 1931, the year of OPINION's founding, has failed to be a saddening chronicle, and the review of 1932—5692, was full of drear forebodings because Hitler seemed to the writer to be on the eve of emergence as dictator of the German Reich. As the years passed, it became more and more difficult to picture the blackness of the fate visited upon the victims of Nazism— first among whom were the Jews of Germany, last among whom were the Jews of Hitler-conquered territories.

The term "tragic" loses its power of characterization of what the world has perforce endured at the hands of Hitlerism, and Jews to an even larger degree than any other people or group. Lands have been overrun. Peoples have been pillaged and enslaved. Every manner of barbarism has been inflicted upon the subjugated. But it is only against Jews that the unashamed threat or edict of extermination has been pronounced. Jews have suffered a thousandfold from wrong and evil and injustice devised by the savage Fascists. But against Jews something unique in its enormity of humiliation and torture has been perpetrated, namely, the reestablishment of the Ghetto, with all that it means of enslavement and torture and exile. No wrong, not even slave labor, equals the horror of the Ghetto, itself a symbol of reversion to an era before men knew pity or even practiced the rudiments of Justice.

These facts of cruelty in all their stark and grim horror have etched themselves ineradicably upon the memory of the Jew. So unendurable had the mere recital of these oceanic wrongs against European Jews become from day to day to their fellow-Jews in our own land that the American Jewish Congress, together with the B'nai B'rith and the Jewish Labor Committee, found it imperative to summon the people to a mighty demonstration of their souls' protest and sorrow over the ever deepeningly bitter lot of their Jewish brothers in all Fascist lands.

That demonstration of grief and horror evoked two messages of the highest importance—not only because of the distinction of their authors but because of the context, President Roosevelt forecasting the day of justice to be meted out to the offenders who have violated the moral laws of the Hebraic-Christian civilization, and Prime Minister Churchill making acknowledgment of the very significant contribution of Jewish Palestine to the war effort.

While there is no measuring the hurt and suffering wrought against the Jew wherever men are not free, two things stand out amidst the grimness of the story: One, the heroism of the invincible Jew and the little less heroic acts of many in high and low place who have been moved to compassion with ineffably wronged and tortured Jews. The human shame of Nazi maltreatment of the Jew was in truth mitigated if not redeemed by the unyielding heroism of its victims and the oftimes heroic conduct of non-Jews. These in a thousand ways large and small ministered to the afflicted Jew, always at heavy cost, oftimes at dire peril, sometimes even unto death.

No VOLUME could encompass the story of the horrors of the Jewish year, 5702, coming after "nine iron years of terror and of evil led by the screaming voice that is war and hate." Almost the direst of tragedies is to be found in the spread of most terrible persecution to lands of considerable Jewish populations, which for centuries had deemed themselves completely bound up with the wellbeing, the fortunes good or evil, of their beloved lands. I name only Hungary and Bulgaria—one can hardly include the old anti-Semitic center of Roumania — into which anti-Semitic theory and practice were successfully imported by Nazi occupation and dominance. So that now these lands have come to be, for a time in any event, within the area of anti-Semitic exploitation, though it must in fairness be added, without the approval of the populations. This is almost uniformly true in the countries of France, Holland, Belgium, Czechoslovakia, Poland, Denmark, and of course, Jugoslavia and Greece, in the guerilla warfare of which last named lands Jews have taken their rightful and honorable place.

Individuals and communities alike have felt the shame of the Nazi torture of the Jew and have paid the penalty of their courage as they revolted in the presence of day-by-day atrocities—to look upon which had become intolerable for beings of humaneness and decency. Church groups and Councils, Catholic and Protestant alike, have in many lands taken their unafraid stand, within and without the Fascist countries, against the policy of humiliation and degradation, when not actually extermination, adopted against the Jew. Thus Protestantism in the Canton of Geneva uttered its solemn protest in the words, "Our duty of justice and charity extends to all men, our brethren. The race from which have come the prophets and the apostles deserves our respect. We invite the members of our Church to resist all attempts to introduce among us anti-Semitic concepts condemned by the spirit of our Master and by all our traditions nurtured on Holy Writ."

Even more significant is the truth that the Nazis in a number of their terrorized lands have found it necessary to bring pressure upon Clergy and people, in lands such as Czechoslovakia, Belgium and Holland, in order to compel them to change their pro-Jewish attitude. Thus the Dutch Prime Minister, speaking for his brave and unbowed Netherlands people, recently expressed horror in the name of his countrymen and his Queen against the crime of deporting Jews from the Netherlands—"a crime which breaks the centuries-old Netherland tradition, and violates the Netherlands constitution according to which all citizens are equal before the law." In Holland, moreover, Protestant and Catholic Churches, aroused by these mass deportations of Dutch Jews, petitioned the Occupation Commander, requesting better treatment for the Jews, so that the Nazi authorities found it needful to have Jewish deportations take place at night, in order to avoid pro-Jewish demonstrations by the Dutch.

The Gauleiter of Holland frankly disclosed that Dutch Jews converted to Catholicism had been transported to occupied Poland in retaliation for the protest of Catholic and Protestant Church leaders against deportation of Jews—"We consider the Jews our worst enemy and all those who intervene for them will be punished by sharing the Jewish fate." Still more foul and brutal deeds have been wrought, chiefly by the Gestapo, against men and women whenever found guilty of the crime of mercy to Jews. Thus was a Polish woman executed for providing Jews with bread; thus was a German baker executed as an accomplice of the deed, in addition to the two Jews ac-

cused of purchasing the bread. Reading the story of these
unmentionable deeds, one must even give credence to the
deed of the Nazis in driving hundreds of Jews to a barge
in Yelsk without food and shelter. And when a peasant,
hearing their maddened cries, swam at night to the barge
to feed them, was discovered, twelve peasants from the collective farm were executed, after which the barge was
exploded and all the Jews drowned. It is safe to say that
such diabolisms as these moved the League of Nations
Union of Great Britain by its Executive to urge "the
Statesmen of all Nations whose moral conscience is not
dead to express their sorrow at this relapse into barbarism," thus unmeasuredly condemning the cold-blooded
extermination of the civilian populations of occupied
countries by the German military commanders and the
Nazi officials.

Better than any official declaration of abhorrence were
such acts as those of the Czechs, who after the introduction of the Yellow Badge, themselves wore the Star of
David to express their sympathy with Jews even after
being warned that they must bear "all the merciless consequences of their attitude and be treated as Jews." Five
German peasant women of villages in the Koenigsberg
District brought up eight small Jewish children as their
own, whose parents had been deported to Poland for
forced labor. After eighteen months the "crime" was discovered and the women sentenced to long prison terms.
This deed of tender charity will not be forgotten on the
Day of Deliverance.

It was inevitable that some of the great Church leaders
of Christianity should speak out and they have done so
without reservation. The newly named Archbishop of
Canterbury, Dr. Temple, in his Preface to his Report of
the Commission of Churches for International Friend-

ship and Social Responsibility, declaring: "Doing justice to the Jews will be one text of a juster world order." And the Catholic Primate of England, in a memorable message to the Federation of Czechoslovakian Jews, put the case of Christian decencies versus Nazi savageries in the following unforgettable statement: "The cruel persecution of Jews simply because they are Jews is an outrage to all principles of justice and humanity. We condemn in strongest terms the massacre of innocent people, the appalling horror of deportations of whole populations, the hideous concentration camps and the savage methods of the Gestapo as well as the pillage and robberies."

But even above and beyond Archbishop and Cardinal, the Holy Father of the Catholic Church, the writer has reason to believe, sought to intervene on behalf of the Jews of Slovakia. If intervention, it was in vain, for the Nazi rulers of Slovakia, Tiso and Mach, unmoved even by the benign plea of the Head of the Church to which they purport to yield obeisance, continued their unutterable treatment of Slovakian Jews, who like hunted beasts were forced to flee into the deepest recesses of the woods.

It appears to be more than rumor that His Holiness, Pope Pius XII, urgently appealed through the Papal Nuncio to the Vichy Government to put an end to deportations from France and the appeal of the Pope is said to have been reinforced by petition and protest from the Cardinal Archbishops of Paris and Lyons. But, alas, Marshal Petain is not the ruler or leader of France and power, alas, is vested in the agent of Hitler—Laval—who will hardly take risks for the sake of refugees, however lawless and shameless their return to the Nazi territories of their origin. If such Papal intervention be factual, then Pius XII follows the high example set by his saintly predecessor, whose word in reprobation of anti-Semitism, "Spiritually we are all Semites," will never fade out of the memory of a people which does not forget but forgives. Irrespective of the outcome of Papal intervention, it is certain that the French people as a whole deeply disapprove of Vichy's attitude to the Jews, which will prove to be not the least of the causes of Vichy's downfall.

JEWISH fortitude and Christian neighborliness are not the only brighter aspects of the gloomy picture of the year. In Palestine and its relation to the Mandatory Government, there have been too many unhappy incidents, apart from the tragedy of the Struma. But outstanding are two major items. One is that Palestine has not fallen into the omnivorous Nazi maw; second, that Jews have not only borne themselves most creditably in the British Army but after infinite effort a beginning has been made in organizing a Jewish military force in Palestine. Though limited for the present to a Jewish battalion, there can be little doubt that despite the incredible shortsightedness and worse of the Palestine Government, the Jewish Battalion is bound to be the forerunner of a Jewish fighting force that shall worthily represent the numbers and will of the Jewish people in Palestine, one-third of whom have fled from the Nazi terror. Knowing the Maccabean mood of Palestine's young Jews, one is certain that given the opportunity these will battle in defense of Palestine even as Britons have defended England. Dr. Weizmann put it best when, in his now famous letter to Winston Churchill of June 25th, he said: "If we go down in Palestine we are entitled to go down fighting. The Mandatory Power is in duty bound to grant us this elementary human right." In the meantime and pending the necessity of defending Palestine, its Jewish population chiefly continues to make a most important contribution in many respects to the war program of the United Nations.

In Russia, the bitter and magnificent struggle of the Soviet army has had its marked Jewish repercussions. The anniversary of the Nazi invasion of Russia heard a second appeal to the Jews of the world to help Russia. The appeal urged that planes and tanks be sent to Russia in her hour of desperate resistance. But under the operation of the Lend-Lease Act it would be impossible for any non-official group to dispatch munitions or any war items. Moreover, our business as Americans is not to favor one rather than another of the United Nations but to give maximum war aid to all, without partiality or favor. Many American Jews, led by the American Jewish Congress, have come to see that it is Russia that has borne the heaviest blows, fought most bravely and endured the largest losses of life and land and substance. For the sake then of the United Nations of which Russia with China at her side has most endured, we as a people are bound to do all that may be done for Russia. The veil that hid Russo-Jewry for two decades has in part been lifted and as American Jews we rejoice in the freedom Russia has held for its sons and daughters. We rejoice, too, in the part which Jews have played in building a mighty nation, free today and, it may be, to achieve Democracy on the morrow.

In our own country, we have seen the beginning of the end of the anti-Semitism that seemed and was wholly alien to the American spirit. If not an end, like every alien and anti-Democratic trend, it has been driven underground. The mood of our country, forging its way toward national unity, is utterly intolerant of the gross and Fascist-derived anti-Semitism which for some years has tainted the very atmosphere of our Democracy. It is of more than passing interest that a large batch of men and women arraigned at the bar of Justice for one or another of the crimes of disloyalty to our country should include virtually all the anti-Semitic leaders of the last decade—all save Messrs. Coughlin and Curran, who seem destined to go unwhipped of justice. If the present mood of purposive national unity persist, our country may never again witness a recurrence of that dread and divisive anti-Semitism which cannot co-exist with Democracy.

The people of the United States begin to recognize a profound truth, that Hitler's attack upon the Jews was token of a threefold determination: (1) To allure the strong by attempted destruction of the weak; (2) To exterminate the most ancient protagonists of human freedom and thus weaken men's faith in its self-guarding efficacy; (3) To wipe out the people who had stood throughout the ages as the guardian of religious faith. The plan almost succeeded, aided and abetted in a thousand unholy ways by a thousand unholy forces. For a time Hitler threatened to succeed—even in our own country. There arose a movement, if possible more malign than the Ku Klux Klan, which, utilizing America's natural abhorrence of war, dealt with Hitler's Jewish victims as if these had brought about and were responsible for the war designed to destroy them. Alas, that even some teachers of religion, such their outward calling, had part in a nefarious attempt to fasten blame for the war of irreligion against all religion upon the people of the Mother faith, Hebraic-Christian, of the Western World, for such is the basic faith of the Jew.

The spirit of fairness and decency, fundamental to the American Democracy, crushed this conspiracy which imitated and feebly paralleled the foul plotting of the

Nazis. Best of all the Nation was supremely fitted to avert the evil, because of the leadership of that friend of man, himself of deepest faith, apostle of tolerance, who first among Americans urged a quarantine against the aggressor nations, who stands valiantly and undefeatably in the vanguard of those bent upon overwhelming freedom's foes so that men everywhere may be free. It is the President of the United States whom fate, as well as the American people, has chosen to make and keep human freedom and faith forever inviolable.

In his best known peom, Bialik, dealing with the tragic lot of his people, gives expression to the fear that the world may yet come to accept the ethical and spiritual teaching of the Jew, but that the Jew may be gone before the hour of his spiritual triumph be at hand. Today witnesses to the truth that the mournful prophecy of Bialik is not destined to come true. In the world of tomorrow the Jew will not only live in its acceptance of the gospel of freedom and justice and faith for which he has lived and fought, but the Jew will live within the brotherhood of earth's faiths and peoples, continuing to take his full and heroic and, when necessary, sacrificial part in shaping, maintaining and further ennobling the newer, truer, juster world on behalf of which earth's freemen are bound to be victorious.

— 1942

A Passover Message

No people has known the bitterness of enslavement as often and as fully as the Jewish people. Alas, within the year 5703, the bitterest of bondage has seared the soul of Israel as never before. Awful though it sound, even Egyptian bondage was less bitter than the fate of our enslaved people since July of last year. Hundreds and hundreds of thousands have been slain, and, worse than slain, our brother Jews from nearly all the lands of Europe have endured torment and torture foully devised and fiendishly executed.

Today it is not Moses who demands of Pharoah, "Let my people go that they may serve me," but Jews who are free, particularly in the English-speaking lands, beseech the leaders of the United Nations, as men have never pleaded before, to help our people go out of Hitler-Europe. The madman who rules Hitler-Europe may choose to deny the request of them whose military overthrow he seeks. A terrible guilt is and a still greater guilt would be upon his head. But our country and England dare not share that guilt. They must, in language used at the Madison Square Garden protest demonstration, storm heaven by prayer and move Hitler-Germany by every earthly means in order that the unspeakable horror of Jewish mass-slaughter may end and end at once.

The above is the saddest of preludes to the Haggadah of this year's Passover. Tears will be in millions of Jewish eyes when, at the Seder table in conformity to the custom of our fathers, we recite "this year in bondage, next year in freedom." For we shall be thinking of a bondage that has led to death and while it has lasted has been worse than death. And still we dare not forget—next year freedom and the year to come the land of Israel! Such will be the two deepfelt supplications of all Jewish hearts which are still free to pray—freedom for all our people within the year to come and freedom for all peoples through the triumphant defeat of the Axis nations and the glorious victory of the Nations united in and for freedom.

Next year in the land of Israel! That will be the most fervent prayer of Jews everywhere. For Palestine has

meant deliverance for more than half a million of our
people who but for it would have shared the fate of the
unhappy millions in Hitler-Europe. The restoration of
Palestine to the Jewish people with exact and undeviat-
ing justice to the Arab, the establishment of a Jewish
Commonwealth of Palestine as the world's reparation to
the Jew—this must come to pass. Jews have not only been
the most tragic victims of Hitlerism but the earliest and
most vigorous of resistants thereto. May it come to be that
the Passover mark the beginning of the end of the worst
regime of enslavement, and the dawn of a new day of liberation for the Jew and for all peoples who would be free.

— 1943

Russo-American Jewish Rapprochement

THE question, "What are to be the after effects of the
visit of the two representatives of the Jewish anti-Fascist
Committee of the Soviet Union?" is bound to occur to
Jewish persons and organs which, unlike the *Vorwaerts*,
are concerned with Jewish problems larger than the
demolition of Sholem Asch. The remarkable demonstration at the Polo Grounds in honor of Professor Mikhoels
and Colonel Feffer embodied a number of trends. Above
all, the gratitude of Jews to the Soviet Union, whatever
its attitude to organized religious life, which has led the
world in actually outlawing anti-Semitism. Herein, it may
be said parenthetically, the United Nations will follow
the Soviet Union, or England and America will come to
see anti-Semitism utilized as an instrument of anti-Democratic divisiveness, even within their own borders.

Coupled with the instinctive gratitude of the Jewish
masses to the nation which has pioneered in dealing with
anti-Semitism as a crime against the unity and integrity

of the State, remains the moving appreciation of the Soviet armies and people which have done most to limit Nazi barbarities. But there was something more and profounder in the Polo Grounds welcome. Too long have the Jews of our country, many of East European origin, deplored the severance of every link between Russo-Jewry and the Jews of America, lamented the parting of the two largest groups within world Jewry. After the floods of misunderstanding which have raged for twenty years and more, these two Jewish anti-Fascists have flown here and alighted upon the Ark of our own country's life. Hence the genuine Jewish enthusiasm which welcomed these ambassadors from a lost member of Jewish life, apart from common devotion to the anti-Fascist cause.

As was aptly hinted by a Yiddish journalist, the path between Russo-Jewry and our own must be a two-way street. As long as the Comintern divided our countries, American Jews desired not to break down and through the wall of separation. Now that our governments and armies stand embattled together within the framework of the United Nations, we are eager to join hands with the Jews of the Soviet. But not only in the destruction of Fascism, which is the task of all free peoples, but in the reconstruction of Jewish life where Fascist brutality and Nazi savagery have struck at the very heart of the life of world Jewry. To the task of immediate healing and of permanent rebuilding of that shattered and tortured but still indestructible life, Jews, whether in Moscow or in New York, singly or united, cannot decently remain indifferent.

— 1943

The American Jewish Conference

THIS is an American Conference. We are Americans, first last, and all the time. Nothing else that we are, whether by faith or race or fate, qualifies our Americanism. Everything else we are and have deepens, enriches and strengthens, if that can be, our Americanism. We and our fathers chose to be, and now choose to abide as Americans. One hundred generations have chosen that we be Jews, and for another hundred and more generations our children and children's children will choose to be heirs of the Jewish past, builders of the Jewish future. Our first and sternest task, in common with all other citizens of our beloved country and with the citizens of the United Nations, is to win the anti-Fascist war. Unless that war be won, all else is lost.

The question before this American Jewish Conference is: Shall Hitler's attempted extermination of the Jewish people be accepted as the solution of the Jewish problem, or have we American Jews another solution to offer? To ask the question is to answer it—with a deep, solemn, unanimous negative. And we have a solution to offer!

We were recently reminded in a collection of the noble prose of the late Mr. Justice Holmes: "Not the least Godlike of man's activities is the large survey of causes, that to know is not less than to feel." This Conference is to be such a large survey of a cause, that we may know as well as feel.

Five thousand seven hundred and three soon to end has not only been the saddest and mournfullest year in Jewish history, but its sorrow equals, alas, the combined sorrows of the last thousand years. The entire Jewish year has been one prolonged, continued, never ending day of mournful commemoration. The first Tishah b'Ab marked the wanton and vandalistic destruction of the holy of holies 1873 years ago. This year of our calendar will forever be commemorated because of the attempted extermination of the whole Jewish people. Attempted and, alas, not in vain, for within the Axis world, excluding of course Great Britain and Palestine, Russia and our own country, two-thirds and more of the Axis world's Jewish population has been murdered, most foully and unnaturally murdered, by methods of open and devastating terror. The aim was, as was recently reported by a Christian who has just emerged from the Polish Underground, "to wipe out Jews as a people and individuals, to exterminate them systematically as a race by sheer mass murder without any exceptions."

The Polish Underground relates the unbelievably hideous details of the death camps at Tremblinka, for example, on the railway running from Warsaw to Bialystok, the death houses, the special extermination machinery, the liquidating gases piped into death cells, the victims dying daily by thousands. A huge poster greets the newcomers to Tremblinka: "You can be confident of your future!" An ironic invitation to death at its cruelest! For the victims, we say to these bestial executioners: Unlike death with honor you have brought to your victims, death and shame are swiftly becoming your portion. The United Nations have made us confident of your immediate future and there is and will hereafter be no future anywhere on earth for such as seek to set race against race and faith against faith. Yours have been ten years of horror and pillage and rapine. Oblivion were your more merciful fate! We have lived and served throughout millenia. Your thousand years have ended within a decade. We resume life with gladder hope, because civilization and freedom are about to extirpate their organized and united enemies—the Axis Powers.

We do not parade our suffering. The casualties we suffer in war we bear as do all Americans, proudly, even gladly. But we can bear neither proudly nor stoically "the horrifying barbarism" which has resulted in the slaughter of millions of our brothers and sisters, whether three or four, what Harold Laski calls "the foulest crime in history." The brave and noble Dutch Government-in-Exile put it: "Such abominable mass murder must be avenged." What solemn and inevasible obligation this lays upon us, who are become far and above the largest Jewry of history. Not only to bind up their wounds, but to take counsel with the surviving, that together we may plan their and our future and bethink ourselves as one with respect to the fate of that world Jewry, including Russo-Anglo-Palestine Jewry, which is no larger than our own.

We have learned lessons and the world has learned lessons. We learned slowly and late. The world learned still more slowly and even later. Learned what? That the only safe foundation of law is freedom; that the only certain guarantee of freedom is law. First to learn that Cherut and Charut, freedom and the written law, are interdependent; liberty based on law; law safeguarding freedom. We have through the centuries incurred and we still incur the implacable enmity of all those to whom human freedom is an abominable heresy, to whom human equality is the sin of sins, to whom political democracy is the unforgivable assault upon the sacred ark of privilege and power.

A good rule for this Conference would be that of a recent writer on the "Captains of Their Souls." "For this is the hour of decision; it is the most fateful moment of our lives, and only if we believe truly, can we hope to think clearly and then to act effectively." In what are we to believe truly? Is it necessary to say again that we believe in the speedy triumph of our country, the triumph of the great task it has set out to perform, the saving of itself, the safeguarding of human freedom everywhere, even ultimately for those violators and betrayers of the conquered and the enslaved, the creation of a new and better, because juster, world.

We believe truly in ourselves, in our people, in our faith and fate or destiny! Though our hearts are full of sorrow, we stand unshaken by the evil of the ten years drawing to a close, by the nameless horror of all the past year. We believe more truly than ever in Israel as in Israel's God. Millions of victims within the life of our people, more, if not all, of them, martyrs. Those conscious witnesses to the truth which was their life and death as it is our life and deathlessness, move us to believe more truly and surely than ever before in our people, its great past, its momentous though mournful present, its puzzling withal certain future.

THIS is an American Jewish Conference. American and Jewish! Jewish, because as a people, we have lived and battled, with uncountable victims and casualties through the most awful year in history. Not war but wars! One war in which all the nations, the free nations, fought, and Jews among the free nations fought as of them and with them and for them, in every country in which Jews dwell —goodly numbers throughout the British Empire, the Soviet Union, and these United States. And we have fought or been fought and outfought in another war. The war of the enemies of freedom against Jews in fulfillment of a thousand threats to exterminate the Jews. We have borne our full share of the war. In addition, there has been a Jewish war, a war in which Jews were singled out as the victims, not as casualties of war but as victims of extermination, the dread and, alas, almost completely successful threat of extermination. No people, though its population were five or ten times as large as the numbers of world Jewry, has suffered losses comparable to that of the Jewish people in the war of Jewish extinction. In that war of Jewish extinction one-fourth and more of our numbers have perished.

As every American gathering aims to preserve and safeguard America, so the American Jewish Conference aims to preserve and safeguard America, and beyond that, to preserve and defend the Jewish people. Hitler said, and Goebbels echoed: "The Jewish people must be exterminated." The American Jewish Conference accepts the challenge and answers: The Jewish people will not be exterminated and joins in the high resolve and resistless determination of the United Nations that nevermore shall leader or gangster, Chancellor or President, be permitted even to threaten unrebuked and unpunished the extermination of a people or race or faith. A free world will never again passively wait for the fulfillment of such a threat, as it, alas, waited from 1933 to 1939. Such a threat will indict and convict its authors, in the sight and with the sanction of all the world, of destructive intent and purpose not against the Jew alone, not against any people or faith, but against our common civilization and freedom.

We are bidden to think clearly and to act effectively. To think clearly is to think not with confusing prepossessions or prejudices but with open-mindedness and clarity, with mind single to the needs of the hour. The proposal that when the delegates enter the Conference they must forget their partisan labels is only partially valid counsel. The delegates are to act in the name and in the spirit of those who chose and delegated them for the good of all. Each of us represents a segment of Jewish life. All of us together serve the whole of Israel. We shall be truer to Jewry in its entirety only if we remember the best and highest in the group or faction that sent us here.

As for acting effectively, when Jews were threatened, beginning in 1933, Jews failed to unite save for those groups, too few and too limited, which dared to do so. Such a policy of extermination obtained as men have not aforetime known. Neither did the world unite when Hitler uttered most terrible of threats against freedom, nor until he attacked and devastated Poland. Even then men and nations did not unite, but waited and temporized until it became too late. Holland, Belgium, Norway, Denmark, Greece, Yugoslavia fell by the wayside, one by one. Hitler's war upon a free world began not on August 31, 1939, when he invaded Poland, but on January 30, 1933, when he was by appointment enabled to renew his pre-electoral threat to exterminate the Jewish people.

To act effectively is to act in unison. Action in unison does not mean identity of thinking. Effective action is born of the capacity for adjustment in situations which call for agreement without compromise. Never did a people come under deeper or more compelling motivation. We stand under the shadow of a great and oceanic sorrow, sorrow over the extinction of uncounted numbers of our people, a sorrow too deep for tears. And yet not without hope we suffer and we mourn. We have suffered. We have mourned. We hope. However measureless our grief, we cannot live without hope. "Our hope is not destroyed."

That American Jewry be united through this Conference is not enough. It must be united with Jews the world over, reforging the old bonds with the reenforced and un-lost Jewish population of the Soviet Union and eager to act with, not merely for, the reviving Jews of the Axis lands. For them that have survived and may survive, let the report of this Conference serve as tonic, stimulus, revival. Their hurt at the hand of Hitler does not unfit them for comradeship and counsel with us, their free and happier brothers, who, but for the Grace of God and our fathers' earlier migrations, would be they. Hitler's unpitied victims have not ceased to be our beloved and honored blood-brothers, to be heeded, to be revered, to be cherished.

Within this chamber I behold the spirits of the millions slain. These plead with us not for revenge—for sufferance hath too long been the badge of all our tribe—but for other and nobler acts, that we, like them, may choose death rather than the shame of desertion of the God of Israel. If the United Nations and we could not save them, these shall now save their and our brothers who may yet be saved. The only redress and reparation the martyrs seek are freedom and justice and peace at last for all mankind, a world wherein the great nations and the great faiths, led by Christianity, shall nevermore endure such a Jewish holocaust as the Hitler horror. This assurance may be granted by stamping out the evil forces out of which grew the shame of history's most terrible Jewish slaughter.

I behold the tear-stained survivors, few in number, who have lost all but life and honor, and these place their trust in us. For these are confident that our sorrowful guardianship invites and will avail itself of their mature wisdom and tragic experience. These shall not be set aside as merely pitiable victims, to be fed and clothed and sheltered as our wards, but, however terrible and exigent their needs, to be counselled with as brothers, for the metal of their Jewish loyalty has been tempered by passing through the fires of almost unpitied torture and wholly unredressed wrong.

Within this chamber are gathered, too, not only some hundreds of chosen representatives of American Jewry but millions by whom these have been directly or indirectly chosen. Out of a heart of deepest sorrow, these, our fellow-Americans, invisible but not inaudible to our spirits, plead with us to deal wisely as American Jews, soberly, courageously and nobly with the problems of the Jew in a new and free world. One of the wisest, noblest of American Jews has phrased it: "It is only by our own efforts and endeavor, by our confidence in the rightness of our purposes and in our own power, if fully organized, that we have the means of accomplishing our aims!" Unless we are resolved to face the task with such sustained wisdom as may God give us, with such a noble vision and purpose as the hour demands, let us relinquish the task to other hands. To that task, to that burden, we solemnly resolve that we shall not be unequal. Israel Zangwill once said: "We are a people of lost opportunities." This Conference is to proclaim that we are a people of unlost opportunities. Such be the meaning of this Conference.

I HAVE not chosen to anticipate the program which only this Conference can adopt after the fullest consideration and fairest discussion. But viewing the record of the speaker, he will not be expected to refrain from adverting upon that which may be arguable from some points of view, withal has come to contribute a glory to the whole Jewish people—not merely an unparalleled achievement of the Jewish population of Palestine.

Two years ago and less Palestine stood under the

shadow and terror of Nazi invasion. Whatever the virtually neutral Arab population might or might not have
done, our brother Jews, men and women alike, were
ready to do and dare all in defense of freedom and the
cause of the United Nations, including Palestine. The
brilliant feat of the Alexander-Montgomery armies, not
without Jewish participation, averted that Rommel peril.
In all the vast Arab complex of populations and territories and amid its kingdoms, great and small, that of Palestine, which is Jewish, stood out alone in passionate and
unreserved support of freedom's cause as safeguarded by
the United Nations.

In the meantime a policy has been continued in respect
to Palestine by the Mandatory Government upon which
Britain and the free world set their stamp of disapproval
when appeasement was finally rejected in September
1939. The White Paper of the Spring of that year is the
last vestige of that unhappy and unworthy policy. Despite
the repudiation of appeasement its spirit and its letter,
alas, still obtain in Palestine and this, too, although the
greatest of disasters has befallen the Jewish people, re-
sulting first in exile and later in horror throughout Hitler Europe.

The humane and generous thing for the Mandatory
Government would have been, in frank disregard of the
appeasement-dictated White Paper survival of the pre-
Churchillian regime, to open the gates of Palestine to
Jewish exiles, even though parallel action might have become necessary on the part of England and America within the law. No act of relief on the part of the United
Nations will seem sincere or be worthwhile as long as the
gates of Palestine threaten to close. Whatever we may
hope and plan is to be the future status of Palestine, and
there may be room for discussion, its gates must not be

closed. There must be Jewish migration under Mandatory and Jewish control, under the direction and super-
vision of that Jewish Agency which is instrument of and
by covenant confederate to the Mandatory Power.

Herzl beheld only the glorious ideal of Zionism; but he
truly forefelt the mournful necessity, to use his own term,
which is become the lot of continental Jewry, truly the
only hope of the surviving less than 3,000,000 Jews of the
Europe that is. Much has been made of a word uttered by
one of the responsible heads of the Jewish Agency for
Palestine.—"It would be wrong to consider the Jew in
Palestine incapable of deeds of despair, if driven to the
extreme of exasperation by a decision to persevere in
what is a cruelly unjust policy." Who would wish Jews
to be incapable of deeds of despair? Such deeds, for example, as were performed by the glorious heroes and hero-
ines of the last Jewish stand at Warsaw. Only cowardly,
self-hating, self-obliterating Jews! Even deeds of despair
are treasonable to such as will to die and not to live.
Whatever the decision of this Conference in relation to
Palestine, let us so bear ourselves within these walls that
deeds of despair shall not be needed in Palestine. But if
such deeds be done, they must be accepted by us as inexor-
able as is our centuried story. It must have been deeds of
despair that called forth from the Psalmist his immortal
word:—"For the sake of Zion I will not be silent." Today,
after the lapse of twenty-five centuries, "I will not be silent" means I will not be inert, I will not be passive, I will
not be non-resistant.

The tragedy of tragedies that has been and, alas, still is
changes the character and content of this Conference. It
was organized with a view to two major objectives: The
rights and status of Jews in the post-war world; the imple-
mentation of the rights of the Jewish people with respect

to Palestine; the choice of those who would pursue and prosecute these objectives to the end in connection with the after victory conference or conferences.

But a new and more, indeed most, immediate objective presses itself upon this body of American Jews—solemnly to demand of the United Nations that not another hour be lost in rescuing from the lands in the hands of Hitler the remaining Jews, the less than 3,000,000 survivors of the 8,000,000 Jews who lived in pre-Hitler Europe. Further delay in rescue would doubtless mean that there would be no Jews to save in what was Hitler Europe. Never was it truer that a way, the way, the ways of rescue will be found, provided the United Nations, led by our own, have the will to rescue our harassed, despoiled, tortured brothers. Such rescue of the surviving may in part redeem the world's shame of the years, 1933-1939. Throughout these years every manner of nameless crime was committed against our brothers with none save a handful of Christians such as Cardinals Faulhaber and Mundelein, the Archbishop of Canterbury and Dr. Cadman, to plead angel-tongued for the victims of the devils of extermination.

Bermuda was a poor and sorrowful beginning. The Inter-governmental Committee of Refugees, led by London and Washington, if summoned at once, may prove to be a second step. Is it necessary in the face of one of the nearly consummated crimes of history to insist that there be no further and fatal delay, that the United Nations avert Jewish destruction by every method of rescue? There are many such, as the Joint Emergency Committee for European Jewish Affairs has pointed out, by which the United Nations, with the help of the no longer undecided and hesitating Neutrals, can rescue the elsewise doomed civilian victims, including women, children, aged men.

Let not the unjust reproach be incurred that more could
and would have been done if the threatened and endangered had not been Jews! This were too terrible a reflection upon the professions and principles and practices of
the United Nations, and above all upon the moral quality
of our own nation and its leadership.

As a spokesman of the Conference at its opening hour,
I choose to register my unchanged faith in the deep humanity of the foremost leader of free men in the world
today, Franklin Delano Roosevelt. This body of delegated
and widely representative American Jews, dedicated to
the triumph of our Nation's cause, declares its deep and
unchangeable confidence in the integrity and goodwill
of its Commander-in-Chief. This Conference trusts that,
in response to the deepest promptings of humanity and in
compliance with the will of the American people, our
President, together with Prime Minister Churchill, will
insist upon the acceleration of the tempo of rescue and
take the lead in performing the supremely imperative
task of Jewish rescue with that unwithstandable resolve
which is become the habit of their great souls.

Yesterday, in the Synagogue, the words were read:—
"Behold, I set before you this day a blessing and a curse."
The evil and the curse have been throughout this bitter
and awful year. The good and the blessing may be if we
here resolve that what our dead, the innumerable army of
our dead, ask of us is only what a self-reverencing people
may be and do and achieve, the reparation of security for
the living in a free world.

This is the soul of goodness in things evil, would we
but knowingly distill it out. The soul of goodness to be
distilled out of the evil of the past year is not merely the
physical rescue of the surviving, but the unity of Jewish
life in our country, striving earnestly and devoutly for

the deliverance and the unchallenged freedom of the
Jewish people wherever they may dwell. "Behold, I set
before you this day a blessing and a curse." We choose the
blessing for our country and for Israel.

— 1943

The Final Liberation

ONCE again the Passover is at hand. It has ever been a
season of mingled joy and sorrow. Joy because it is a season of deliverance, the birthday of a nation and its freedom! Sorrow because often and again the festival of liberation has been observed by them that dwell in bondage.
Not Christian blood, as the wicked maligners allege, but
Jewish tears and Jewish blood have marked the largest
number of Passover celebrations throughout the centuries.

In all the millenia of Jewish history, no Passover will be
observed more tearfully and more hopefully than the
Passover which is now to be celebrated. For the tenth
time since the advent of Hitler, Jews will, at their Passover tables throughout the world, find that the bread of
affliction is again become their fare. We dwell in freedom
but even our land of freedom and light is threatened and
assailed by the forces of darkness and enslavement. Never
before have the Pharaohs been mightier than the three
miscreants who lead the armies that would enslave mankind, and in this no account is taken of the tens and even
hundreds of thousands who have not survived the year
but lie buried within the blood-soaked soil of their countries, helpless victims of a diabolical fury which slew multitudes the sooner to enslave the sons of men.

But the Passover festival is a reminder, too, that bondage, however long continued, ends when men are re-

solved that enslavement shall cease to be their portion and that life without freedom is a life which humans cannot accept as the portion of the children of the living God. Tears will flow at many Passover tables this year. But the Jew, communing with the spirit of his great history, will remember that there are alternations of joy and sorrow, darkness and light, enslavement and freedom. Today slavery seems in the ascendant, but freedom is bound to dawn on the morrow and with its dawn the recognition will come that no people in history have wrought more earnestly, have suffered more bravely, have battled more heroically for man's freedom than the Jews. That recognition on the part of mankind, save for an embittered Nazi-like remnant, will mark the final liberation of all humanity, will bring to the Jew the guerdon of a long, patient, glorious battle for life's highest good.

II

Hitlerism and Beyond

German Jewry at the Crossroads

THE conventional reflection at this time on the imminence of the threat of Hitlerism is that governmental responsibility always tends to sober and to restrain. Such is the sage and soothing counsel of the Stadtlanim—really, we must not be unduly alarmed about the menace of Hitlerism. For, it is added, Hitler the propagandist is one being and Hitler, the dictator, would prove to be quite another being. But is account taken of two elements in the case? That it may not be possible for Hitler to carry out his program? In those aspects which concern repudiation of unpopular international treaties this involves relations between Germany and its creditor nations. France, insatiable and unappeasable, will not refrain from the threatened violation of the Ruhr in order to enable Hitler to keep his pre-election promises.

What is more, Hitler has with calculated frenzy made promises which of necessity are irredeemable. However raucous these promises, he cannot cancel reparations nor will the magic of his *Bier Stube* eloquence avail to solve the economic problems of his people and free it from the burdens of crushing taxation.

One thing he can do. In truth, it is not merely the one thing he can do, but it is that which he can hardly avoid doing. Here let Albert Einstein speak: *"Hitler will be powerless to halt the forces of evil he has let loose, even though he has no present intention of carrying out his threats against the Jews."* This sums up the present prospects of the Jews of Germany. They face not so much the enactment of monstrously unjust laws, as the cumulative onslaught of the hatreds which Hitlerism has invoked and evoked from the German people after a decade of ruthless exploitation of the gospel of ill-will. How can a people be expected suddenly to stay the hand of hate, after it has for years been bidden to wreak itself on "an alien people dwelling in its midst"?

In the eighties and nineties there was a parallel situation in Germany. If there was no blood-letting then, despite the Treitschkes and Stoeckers, the Ahlwardts and the de Lagardes, it was because Russia across Germany's Eastern frontiers executed the deed which Germans merely devised in the terms of a new pseudo-ethnic philosophy of life. And, even more important, because the then unexhausted liberal tradition of German life and letters, which ran from Lessing and Schiller to Virchow and Mommsen, was still dominant in Germany. That liberal tradition seems to have waned, if not to have passed, and the forces of moral anarchy rather than spiritual culture have come to prevail.

The query then is, as the great physicist definitely envisages it, dare we hope that the powers of evil can be checked which Hitlerism has long and assiduously cultivated? It were almost unfair to the followers of Hitler to deny them in the hour of triumph the attainment of the awful goal which has been their goad and incentive through the years. Either Hitler will be true to the basest hopes which he has raised in his followers and Israel will be engulfed in disaster or else he will disappoint and betray these followers. But such betrayal offers no guarantee of Jewish security in Germany.

It is a ghastly outlook which, according to Dr. Einstein and all save the professional optimists, German Jewry faces. If Germany is not to witness a recrudescence of anti-Jewish medievalism, its Jewry must be wise and resolute, the true and finer spirit of Deutschtum must make itself felt. World Jewry must unite as it has never been united, even in the minor function of relief. And world opinion—shall we not say the opinion of Christendom—must be invoked lest a monstrous wrong be inflicted upon Israel and Germany suffer unspeakable and uncancellable shame.

— 1932

To the Conscience of the World

THE American Jewish Congress has called but not caused this protest meeting tonight. The American Jewish Congress has not aroused this protest against anti-Jewish wrongs in Germany but has brought within the bounds of law and order an oceanic tide of indignation against the outrages inflicted upon Jews in these days under the Nazi Government.

Not out of the bitterness of anger but out of the deeps of sorrow and the spirit of compassion do we speak tonight. For Germany we have asked and we continue to ask justice and even magnanimity from her erstwhile foes. We demand in the sight of humanity the right for Germany from the nations and the right from Germany for the Jewish people. No wrong under the heavens could be greater than to make German Jews scapegoats because Germany has grievances against the nations. We who would secure justice from the nations for Germany and justice to Jews from Germany affirm that Germany cannot hope to secure justice through injustice to its Jewish people.

This protest of tonight is not against the German people whom we honor and revere and cherish. How could we, of the household of Israel, fail to cherish and honor the German people, one of the great peoples of earth, a people that has made monumental, indeed eternal, contributions to human well-being in the domains of religion, literature, and the arts. How could we fail to cherish and to revere the people of Goethe and Schiller, Kant and Hegel, Beethoven and Wagner, Heine and Einstein?

This protest of tonight is not against the political program of Germany, for Germany is master within her own household, but it is against the present anti-Jewish policy of the Nazi Government. There is no need for our German-born neighbors in America nor for our fellow Jews in Germany to appeal to us to avoid an anti-German demonstration. We are not against Germany, and it is an unforgivable calumny to declare that we are *"Deutschfeindlich."* We are the friends of and believers in Germany. Germany at its highest, at its truest, the German nation at its noblest. Because we are the friends of Germany, because we have inextinguishable faith in the basic love for righteousness of the German people, we appeal to Germany in the name of America which has been stirred as rarely before against wrongs perpetrated upon Jews.

We know that it is not easy to cancel the Nazi program of thirteen years and still we know that it can be done. A dictatorship is omnipotent and above all the German people at its best will support the Government in every honest effort to avert the shame of the medievalization of German Jewry. If the Nazi Government will use for the suppression of the anti-Semitic campaign in Germany one hundredth part of the vigor and rigor with which it has suppressed differing or, as it believes, dangerous political parties, anti-Semitism will perish in Germany.

We understand the plea and the plaint of our brother Jews in Germany. There are German patriots who love their Fatherland and have had reason to love it. Some of their leaders are under the impact of panic and terror, others under some form of compulsion, in any event the compulsion of a great fear if not actual coercion. Do they appeal to the Nazi Government to bring about a cessation of its anti-Jewish campaign as they have appealed to us to end our protest? We have no quarrel with our Jewish brothers in Germany and their leaders, but their policy of uncomplaining assent and of super cautious silence has borne evil fruit. They who have virtually been silent through the years of anti-Jewish propaganda cannot be followed by us as the wisest of counsellors. And if things are to be worse because of our protest, if there are to be new penalties and new reprisals in Germany, which I cannot bring myself to believe, then humbly and sorrowfully we bow our heads in the presence of the tragic fate that threatens, and once again appeal to the public opinion of mankind and to the conscience of Christendom to save civilization from the shame that may be imminent.

To those leaders of German Jewry who declare that the present anti-Jewish situation in Germany is a local German question, we call attention to the word of Abraham Lincoln. Defenders of slavery urged and excused slavery on the ground that it was local. Lincoln's answer was "slavery is local but freedom is national." The conscience of humanity has made a world problem of the present situation of the Jews in Germany. We lay down no conditions, we make no stipulations, we do not even urge demands. But we do affirm certain elementary axioms of civilization. The Jews of the world, no more than the Jews of Germany, do not demand exceptional treatment or privileged position or favored status for themselves. We do not even ask for rights. We ask only for the right.

What are these elementary maxims of civilization as we call them? The immediate cessation of anti-Semitic activities and propaganda in Germany including an end to the policy of racial discrimination against and of economic exclusion of Jews from the life of Germany. That is, Jewish life and the human rights of Jews must be safeguarded. One other absolutely reasonable and just axiom rather than demand: The revocation of all special measures already taken against Jewish non-nationals and their equal treatment with all other non-nationals in Germany. Which of these demands shall we abate? Whatever be the threat of reprisal, none of these can be withdrawn or altered or moderated without insult to Germany and without tragic self-stultification on the part of Jews.

But it must be made clear in the hearing of men that even if life and human rights are to be safeguarded, there must not be a substitution of the status of helotry for violence. Such substitution will not satisfy us nor satisfy the aroused conscience of humankind even though Jews in Germany must sink into the horror of seeming acquiescence. Every economic discrimination is a form of violence. Every racial exclusion is violence. To say that there will be no pogroms is not enough. A dry and bloodless economic pogram remains violence and force.

Hear the word of a great English statesman, of one who did as much as any other Englishman of his day to make England mighty: "Providence would deal good or ill fortune to nations according as they dealt well or ill by the Jews." This is not a warning but a phophecy. May the German people merit the fulfillment of this prophecy of good fortune by dealing well and justly and as a Christian nation by the Jews.

I close as I began. We are not met in the spirit of bitterness, hatred, or revenge. We do not desire that the German people be punished because of the unwisdom of the measures and the injustice of some practices of its Government. Whatever nations may ask in the spirit of reparation and reprisal, we who are Jews know that our spirit must be in consonance with the high tradition of Jewish forbearance and Jewish forgiveness. But there must be no further reprisals against our fellow Jews, no penalizing them as German hostages because the conscience of the world utters its mighty protest.

— 1933

Civilization is at Stake

IT IS an admirable withal saddening practice of OPINION to prepare an annual symposium of what Hitlerism has meant and wrought from year to year. The symposium, contributed by representatives of the Protestant, Catholic and Jewish groups, sets out to tell the story of the Hitler influence within and beyond the Reich. I must be pardoned if I refer to the contribution to last year's survey by that preacher-prophet, Samuel Parkes Cadman, who all his life stood and fought the fight for freedom, whose majestically eloquent voice was the first in America to ring out against Hitler violation of religious freedom and Hitler destruction of every manner of human freedom.

One year ago, after three years of Nazi shame, OPINION dealt with the Nuremburg Laws, which in September, 1935, canonized racial oppression and erected anti-Jewish persecution into the law of the State. The Nuremburg *Gesetz* was the unblushing disclosure of the Nazi will to effect *Gleichschaltung*, racial and religious, in the terms of the most rigid laws. This added nothing to the horror endured by Jewish residents of the Reich. But it shattered a Jewish illusion that only some of Jewry's sons and daughters were intolerable to the Aryans, and that the oldest German-Jewish families might look for less humiliating treatment.

But Nuremburg, 1935, also had its lessons for the two chief religious groups in German life, Protestant and

Catholic. And this be said without abating one jot or tittle
of world-wide reverence for those teachers in religion in
both divisions of Christendom, who alone have stood
contra mundum Hitleri. Protestants have looked upon
ill-disguised attacks upon the inviolate integrity of their
church organizations and Roman Catholics have beheld
with consternation the narrowing range of their freedom
to teach, and the crescent strength of that movement,
which save in moments of political crisis is almost frankly
a substitution of neo-German paganism for the Christian
faiths.

Not for generations will it become possible to tell the
whole tale of Jewish humiliation under Hitlerism, which
may be bravely glossed over by its victims but none the
less remains the most diabolically organized assault upon
the honor, life and possessions of a people that the world
has known. Nothing less than the infinite capacity of the
Jew to suffer and endure, fortified by unbroken faith, has
made it possible for nearly four hundred thousand Jews
in the Reich to survive up to this hour. Survive is the exact term, for they hardly live whose daily portion is con-
tumely and every new device of persecution, deprivation,
humiliation.

The past twelvemonth has witnessed two developments
of Hitlerism both of which are clearly the concern of all
mankind. The 1936 Nuremburg celebration was little
more than a call to the world to arms against Bolshevism
coupled with the oft-repeated attempt to identify the
Jewish people with the authorship and upbuilding of the
Soviet Union.

But no mad repetition by Hitler and Goebbels of the
Jewish-Bolshevist accusation could blind the world to the
fact that the gravamen of the Nuremburg speeches lay in
the emphasis upon the Soviet resources and the Ukraine

granary, the Nazi possession of which would promptly change everything. What need for Western democracies to wait upon the fourth anniversary speech of Hitler with its undeceiving evasions and unmistakable ambiguities after the Nuremburg utterance and its dire threats!

And long before that, two things happened of deepest moment. Nazism had set out effectively to enmesh the Central and South Americas in the Nazi net. The political trends of countries such as Brazil and the Argentine lend themselves readily to the Nazi design. So that the South American World is becoming almost uniformly unsafe for democracy. And the Pan-American Peace Conference, despite the noble utterances of President Roosevelt and Secretary Hull, has availed chiefly to strengthen the status of the lesser Hitlers of the Latin Americas.

As for world-resistance to the ever-deepening menace of Nazism, Britain's recent proposal to expend millions in preparation for defense is a symptom of democratic awareness of the Hitler peril. Is that enough in the light of the political and economic conquest of the Latin Americas and the Nazi-Fascist assault upon Spain, which may soon prove to be tragically overwhelming? And any national arrangement in the West that leaves Hitler free to move to the East and South and crush Poland or Czechoslovakia will solve no problem but merely ensure the coming of the day of doom for all the West.

March 5, 1933, after ten years and more of brazen campaigning, should have been the day of understanding for England, France and other nations that choose to be free. Peoples and churches permitted themselves to be lulled into unawareness, because it was only or chiefly the Jew who at the outset was hurt. Men heeded not that the Jews were assailed as symbol of that civilization, the values of which Nazism was resolved to destroy. Today, after four years of ever increasingly arrogant Nazi conduct, the nations appear to begin to understand. And even so there is not full understanding, for there are still those in the democracies of the West, England, France, the United States, who are ready to be deceived by the promise of Hitler to defend and safeguard the world against the onrush of Sovietism. Only the crassest and blindest possessors—not all of the capitalists—can desire to utilize Hitlerism as bulwark against Communism. Communism may radically revise the values of life which Nazism is resolved not to revise but to destroy. Liberty may, however, unjustly be withheld for an hour; but the denial of the vital and sovereign qualities of freedom and justice is their destruction. The world that Hitlerism can save or defend is a world destroyed. Unless free peoples come to understand this truth, the menace is not to the Jew but to mankind. The Jew rises with humanity free of which he has been forerunner and apostle. The Jew falls with the precious and timeless values which Nazism is sworn to cancel and annul. The now imperiled world failed the Jew for the most part in the earliest days of the Hitler scourge. The world that would be free must forever find in the Jew a fearless defender and tireless ally.

— 1937

LaGuardia vs. Nazism

FIORELLO LAGUARDIA has in these days writ his name large in the story of such struggle as is being waged in resistance to Nazism. The story may briefly be rehearsed. At a luncheon of the Women's Division of The American Jewish Congress, Dr. Michael Williams, Editor of the Catholic *Commonweal*, speaking more or less in the name of the Committee on the Rights of Racial and Religious

Minorities, suggested that at the New York World's Fair of 1939, a shrine of religious and racial freedom be reared as example and inspiration to all peoples and lands. Mayor LaGuardia added the suggestion that an annex be added to the shrine of freedom, such annex to be a chamber of horrors containing the figure of "that brown-shirted fanatic who is the greatest menace to world peace." The Nazi press, which operates under orders more completely than any privately owned press agency in any other land, began to fulminate against the Mayor and his hostesses in the terms of foulest vituperation, descending to the use of such terms as "pimp and procurer entertained by 1200 women of the streets." The State Department politely suggested to the Nazi Government that this was not really nice, whereupon the Nazi press pointed to the extreme irritation it had suffered because of the Mayor's remarks. The President of the Women's Division of the American Jewish Congress asked that the State Department protest against the indecency of the Nazi allusion to the Women's Division. This was done with somewhat more vigor.

After that came the remarkable anti-Nazi boycott Demonstration held under the joint auspices of the American Jewish Congress and the Jewish Labor Committee. Despite the stormy night, twenty thousand people crowded the great hall and heard a series of addresses which will long be enshrined in the record of civilization's self-defense against its would-be destroyers. Most notable were the utterances of John L. Lewis, speaking in the name of the temporarily crushed Labor Front of Nazi Germany and insisting that the surest defense against Nazism is the organization of the workers. On the same high level were the words of General Hugh Johnson, picturesque, strident, massive, and Dr. Frank Bohn, an

Aryan of German parents, who electrified the audience
by his appeal to Americans to stand against Nazism even
to the point of defending the threatened victims of Nazism, the Soviet Union. Unforgettable was the impression
made by Erika Mann, whose intellectual charity and spiritual power were a surer reminder of her father even than
her name.

The unforgettable climax of the evening came when
the Mayor appeared in a box and after the audience had
shouted itself hoarse in its demand that he speak to it,
the Mayor again limited himself to one incisive and mor-
dant phrase, calling Hitler *nicht satisfaktionsfaehig* which
means: "I have no need to deal with one who is so base
that I must disregard his challenge." Whereupon Germany's Hans, but not Luther, made a further appearance
at the State Department and demanded another apology.
The State Department spoke in terms which will satisfy
no American, least of all those who feel that nothing can
be more infelicitous than to allude to meetings of the
brother-Jews of the victims of Nazism and brother humans of all the victims of Nazism as a "vituperative row."
For surely it cannot be meant that there is not to be even
spoken resistance to the most terrible of human tyran-
nies and even that, though our government must be
silent, there is to be no frank speaking such as that of the
Mayor concerning him who is, whether the Nazi Ambassador admit it or not, the "greatest menace to world
peace." The State Department knows quite as well as
Mayor LaGuardia that the gigantic war preparations and
war expenditures are chiefly the result of Hitler's dominance in the European situation.

Opinion rejoices that one man has seen fit to speak the
truth. And best of all on the Mayor's part it was not a belated improvization. Thus has he spoken since the be-

ginning of the Nazi regime. Standing ever under the banners of human freedom and human justice, the Mayor of New York has given only another example of a lifelong devotion to those ideals, which Hitlerism would destroy, about which the State Department imagines that Americans ought to remain politely acquiescent, and touching which men who are free as Americans happily still are, will speak with something of the courage and power of New York's great Mayor.

— 1937

Ambassador Dodd and World Nazism

JANUARY 1938 will long be remembered as one of the blackest months in the Jewish calendar. The sudden reinforcement of Nazism at its worst after the Rumanian elections by the royal designation of Goga and Cuza as the heads of the Rumanian Cabinet is a Jewish disaster of the first magnitude. And the disaster and menace are not merely to a million Rumanian Jews but to the League of Nations, the democratic ideal and to the sanctity of Treaty obligations. All these are bound up with the misfortune which threatens Rumanian Jews. For a Cabinet headed by Goga and Cuza means that King Carol of whom so much was alas vainly hoped, has gone over to the Berlin-Rome axis and has deserted the democratic nations including our own, which remade the Rumanian kingdom and which alas entrusted millions of men and vast areas to the reconstituted Rumania. England and France acted promptly, as did the World Jewish Congress, which promptly and bravely presented the case to the Council of the League of Nations. Alas, that American failure to ratify the Versailles Peace Treaty seems, according to legal authorities, to deny to our country the right of intervention in the unspeakable situation that has arisen—unspeakable because of the brutally frank declarations of the Rumanian Premier with regard to violation of Minority Rights.

Yugoslavia appears to be prepared to imitate the infamous example of Rumania. Verily, blackest of months, moving the *Times* in a flaming editorial to condemn the Rumanian government for its repudiation of the Minority Treaties and to refute the lying government claims of "a Jewish invasion."

If January 1938 will long be remembered as one of the dismalest periods in the dismal Jewish centuries, bound up as it is with the fifth anniversary of the advent of Hitler and the Nazi regime, the month was also marked by one of the finest and most heroic acts of a great American —Ambassador William E. Dodd. Returning from Germany after five years of service, he gave a statement to the American people which as a document will rank with refugee High Commissioner MacDonald's indictment of Germany in his letter of resignation. One is loath to believe that Ambassador Dodd's discontinuance in office at Berlin was bound up with his manly counsel to the State Department not to be represented at the annual Nuremburg carnival of murderous hatred. Our government, unhappily, did see fit to send a representative to Nuremberg, which decision at one and the same time gave immense help to the Hitler regime and implicitly repudiated the American Ambassador.

Professor Dodd, who is now a free man, for he is no longer technically in the service of his country, has not so much insulted Nazi Germany or its leader as he has effectively laid bare the danger of the Nazist-Fascist conspiracy against the well-being and security of the world's democracies. President Roosevelt's historic appeal to his countrymen, to use the non-violent weapon of "moral quarantine" against the oppressor and lawless nations, found its first significant reinforcement in the utterance of Ambassador Dodd upon his arrival.

If the American people will not awake after the thrilling summons of Ambassador Dodd, then the question arises whether we are not doomed impotently to face the overwhelming disaster that confronts the few surviving democratic peoples. It is not possible to know what Professor Dodd's plans as teacher and publicist may be. But certain it is that the leadership of liberalism and the democratic ideal in our country has been enormously enriched by the accession thereto of a sturdy liberal whose liberalism is challenging, penetrating, effective. Americans should be grateful for what Professor Dodd has been and done in Berlin. It may well be that the nearly five years in Berlin have been a period of preparation for still more notable service to Virginia, the State whence he hails and to our country which needs such informed and enlightened, wise and heroic leadership as he has shown himself qualified to give his country.

— 1938

Five Mournful Years for Jewry

FIVE years have passed since that mournful 5th of March, which witnessed the so-called election of Hitler as Chancellor of the German Reich. It might long have been foreseen and perhaps even averted, had they been prepared, whose minds were under the moral obligation to be ready. Save for Labor and handsful of radicals who paid a terrible price, few resisted or even challenged the advent of the deadliest regime in a millenium. Least prepared were the Jews of Germany, about half a million, who had with

most explicit insults been warned. At first some of the
older and better circumstanced Jewish groups assented
with incredible baseness to the diverting of anti-Jewish
Nazi wrath to the newer East European emigrants who
since war days had made their home in Germany. This
was exactly as the Jews of Southern France more than a
century earlier had attempted to burden their hapless
Alsatian brother-Jews with the weight of putative Jewish
iniquity.

Despite every escape mechanism, including cabled sup-
plication to the leaders of the American Jewish Congress
in our country, to desist from attack upon the new Nazi
regime, what was threatened in pre-Nazi years has come
to pass and German Jewry, which may no longer so style
itself, lies prostrate and helpless beneath the iron heel of
Nazi law and practice. In a review of five years of Nazism
from the Jewish point of view, certain things stand out
that justify special consideration. For years before Hitler's
accession and for a time thereafter and in some part per-
sisting to this day, certain groups of Jews have under-
estimated the gravity of the Hitler threat.

Again, it should be recalled that the German Jews took
it for granted almost with unanimity that Hitlerism or
Nazism was a passing phenomenon. After declaring that
his access to power was incredible, they crowned their
blunder by assuming that he would speedily vanish. German Jewry made no preparations as against the advent of
Nazism and indeed up to the recent mournful utterances
of Dr. Stahl before the Jewish Community of Berlin,
there had been no genuine and unafraid facing of ultimate and tragic facts by German Jewry. Such facing as
came to light when the sagest of American Jews on March
13, 1933 a week and a day after the Hitler "election," declared "Jews must leave Germany." People scoffed at the

impracticableness of this prediction rather than counsel. It is, alas, coming to pass. Had there, for example, been any concerted, wise facing of the facts by Jews in Germany, there never would have been one penny of foreign funds expended in Germany for relief to Jews. Morover, every well-to-do family that migrated to Palestine should have been invited or even compelled to take a poorer Jewish family with it, so that instead of leaving funds in Germany or transmitting them elsewhere, instead of 50,000 German Jews going to Palestine, the number might have reached 100,000.

I do not hold that the German Jews should have been expected to foresee all the more tragic and the remoter consequences of the Hitler regime. Still a word must be said about those who, prior to March, 1933, maintained that the fulfillment would not be as evil as the promise. "The threat is grave but it cannot be carried out." The truth is that the fulfillment is a thousand times graver than any threat of the pre-Hitler days. I am reminded of that German official who, in 1918, was asked by an English diplomat, "And if you had conquered France, how would you have treated the inhabitants after exchanging a million of the French population with as many of the German?" His reply was *"dann haetten wir die Liebenswuerdigkeit tuechtig und gruendlich organiziert."* Verily the Nazis have in supremely thorough and competent fashion translated a campaign of hatred and vilification into the law and statute of their country. The Nuremberg Code stands as the incarnation of a nation's descent to the deeps of racial injustice and oppression of a minority.

WHAT, of course, could not have been foreseen was that Germany would be permitted to disregard and to violate the Versailles Peace Treaty at every point, the most conspicuous example of such unchallenged violation being the surrender of Danzig to Nazism at its worst. Something more has happened within five years that is of moment not only to Jews in Germany but to Jews everywhere and that is the spread through the devilish instrumentality of the Ministry of Propaganda and Enlightenment of Nazi propaganda in all the lands of Europe and indeed in Asia, Africa, North, Central and South America. Tragic as has been the cold "Anschluss," virtually unrebuked by the democratic powers which long stood as Austria's guardians, there has been something worse than the annexation of Austria over a period of five empoisoning years, namely, the permeation of Eastern and Central Europe by Nazi propaganda. The device of the "Ghetto Benches" would never have been urged had it not been for bribery by Nazi funds and empoisonment by Nazi propaganda. Even the temporary accession of a pair of desperate and dissolute creatures such as Goga and Cuza to power in Rumania could not have been had not Rumania been a prey of Nazism for some years.

One thing more requires mention. From the beginning, as that valiant anti-Nazi battler, Dr. Henry Leiper, has pointed out, the Christian communions of Germany imagined themselves to be secure and that Nazism was nothing more than yet another symptom of raging anti-Semitism. The writer of these lines predicted in the home of Harry Emerson Fosdick in October, 1933, that, even though anti-Jewish Nazism screened itself behind the mask of racialism, in time the Protestant and Catholic churches would become the victims of the Nazi scourge. For the most part there was unbelief on the part of those who took it for granted that Nazism could not, would not dare to touch either of the mighty Christian bodies of Germany. Needless to say, my prediction has come true.

The Catholic and the Protestant churches alike of Germany are in danger of having their influence minimized by the new paganism which has the sanction not only of Alfred Rosenberg but of most of the leaders of Nazi Germany. In a word, Nazism is Aryan-racialism against Semitic Jews. With its protean capacity for hatred and injustice, it takes the form of a paganish revival against the great Christian church and communities of Europe.

Against the ever-growing might of Nazism in Germany, which unhappily has come into alliance with Rome and Tokyo, there has been no mighty uprising, whether political or religious or moral. Socialists and Communists and the free Labor Front of other countries such as England, France and America have uttered their imprecations, but there has been no union of the church bodies of the Western world against Nazi paganism. Individual Christian leaders have spoken with power and inspiration under the early leadership of the golden-tongued Parkes Cadman, but there has to this hour been no voluntary union of the religious forces of mankind against Nazi paganism —it may be because Jews were its first victims.

Even more disappointing has been the constant yielding of the democratic powers to Nazi Germany's demands. The last two days in the House of Commons witnessed the almost unchecked triumph of the Nazi-Fascist axis. A handful of us, who have not wholly lost faith in the triumph of decency in the world, have felt it our duty to unite in a boycott against Nazi goods and services, a boycott being a moral revolt against wrong, making use of economic instruments. Timorous Jews and queerish Christians seem to feel that we are not justified in boycotting the foes of the human race.

Out of it all emerges the truth that we Jews have been taught that, unless we choose to go down to dishonor and even death, we will have to rethink our problem through. We will have to face what Nazism means to ourselves. The world will not think or act for the Jewish people unless the Jewish people think and act for themselves. We are not minors who require non-Jewish guardianship and even if we required it, we would not have an effective, dependable saving guardianship outside of ourselves. It may yet be that good will come out of the Nazi plague, the good of a democratic awakening, the good of a Jewish renaissance. The democracies may yet conclude that they will either stay the power of Nazism and Fascism or be destroyed. Jews may yet come to understand that their position in the world is imperiled as never before in history. The alliance that alone might save them must be an alliance of the democratic forces challenging and battling against Nazism and Fascism, whether in Berlin, in Rome or in Tokyo, and Jews everywhere coming to understand that political tyranny anywhere means death, that political freedom and international justice alone can save them and make life worth saving for Jews and all peoples.

— 1938

The Tragic Fate of Austria

THE Jewish world had naturally imagined that January, 1938, would long be memorable not only because of the suddenness with which Rumania went Fascist, but came throughout some lamentable weeks under the domination of that ignoble pair of brothers, Goga-Cuza. But that month has yielded in mournful interest to a week in March which, culminating on the blackest of Fridays, March 11, witnessed a *coup d'etat* unprecedented in the annals of history. After the most shameless blackmailing threats at Berchtesgaden to Chancellor Schuschnigg, Hitler issued a series of ultimata to the proud old Austrian Reich, which, for a time in any event, has ceased to be. With a velocity which is to be explained not chiefly by resourceful mobility but by never-ending preparedness, Hitler and his hosts fell upon the surprised Austrians, raped their Reich, exiled their heads, imprisoned multitudes of their political leaders and made of a free and sovereign Austria yet another province of the Nazi Reich.

The moment the Nazis fell upon Vienna, they set the seal upon Austrian Nazification by issuing special Aryan decrees against Austrian Jews and, it is now known, performing typical Nazi acts against Jewish notables of Vienna. Within the last week many eminent Austrian Jews have committed suicide. The President and Secretary of the Jewish Community, the President and Secretary of the Zionist Organization and Professor Frankfurter have been imprisoned. The Institutions of the Jewish community, including the Zionist office have been closed; Jewish newspapers have been prohibited; Zionist funds confiscated; prominent and venerable Jews have been forced to clean the streets. Jews are being dealt with in Vienna more brutally than in the worst days of Nazi Germany.

France and England mildly protested against a deed such as men have not hitherto known and Ribbentrop's predecessor, von Neurath, scornfully replied as did Hitler. Thus has a deed been consummated which would stagger people in a world that had not grown accustomed to Hitler ferocities and Nazi brutalities.

What the ultimate political consequences are to be, who can foretell? But certain it is that overnight the area of Jewish misery has been widened and it is become pitiable beyond telling. An ancient and noble Jewish Community, home of Theodor Herzl and Sigmund Freud, two of the greatest Jews of a millenium, has been swallowed up within the Nazi maw. However Aryans in Austria might have chosen at the Nazi plebiscite, Jews may not vote and are by the arbitrament of one of the supreme lawlessnesses of history transformed into Jewish non-citizens of the Nazi Reich in the Austrian province of which they have lived for 1,500 years.

Socially, that is humanly, the German-Jewish problem is doubled in magnitude for all Jews, who still live in free lands. For there are almost as many Jews in Austria—including the so-called converted and the children and grandchildren of intermarriage, all of whom alike are flung back into the lap of the Jewish community—as survive in Germany. So that problem is literally doubled. That compels a new and immensely heightened activity on behalf of German-speaking Jews. We shall have to cease to play around the periphery of the Jewish need in Europe which, on the morrow, may include the Jewries of Poland, Lithuania and Rumania, to say nothing of Hungary and Czechoslovakia as yet inviolate. And the beggarly dealing with a great problem by American Jewry, which has the resources but lacks the will to be effective, must cease at once. In the next place, there must be no echo among Jews of the cry *"Juden Heraus!"* Infinitely shameful and humiliating though it be for Jews to remain in lands in which they are unwanted by rulers, they cannot, dare not, pick up the wanderer's staff at every unfriendly nod from an upstart government or a mad dictator. Let Jews in other lands learn from Jews in Polish universities how *to stand* without surrender, how to refuse to obey laws that violate every human dignity and decency.

And yet it is not for Jews to bethink themselves touching problems that cannot remain unanswered. The manner of Austria's rape and the accompanying method of

Jewish destruction in Austria would prove anew that Fascism in its assault upon democracy is bound early or late to make use of anti-Semitism as one of its most beguiling and for its supporters rewarding instruments. If the crimes and processes of freedom were against us, we might be tempted to lose hope. But insofar as democracy and its program are threatened by the forces that would destroy us, we may take heart. For human freedom and the love of human justice will not perish in battle with enemies whose only right is might.

THE most important thing to be remembered at this moment is that the invasion and overcoming of Austria by the Nazi Reich constitute a peril to the whole of Central and Eastern Europe and any circumstance which imperils the status quo in Central and Eastern Europe is by the same token a provocation of war. It may be that England and France will not find the invasion of Austria a *casus belli*. But neither may it be forgotten that Austria may be followed by Hungary or Czechoslovakia and that democracies cannot forever be expected to remain unprovoked and unchallenging in reply to international defiance and brigandage.

Moreover, when a little more than a month ago the Rumanian government lapsed for an hour into the anarchy of anti-Semitism, Britain and France, not without a certain measure of non-British and non-French support, made sharp and immediate protest to Rumania and brought their case against the violation of minority treaties to the League of Nations. Why should not the same countries bring to the League of Nations, though the German Reich be not a part thereof, the same protest against wanton and criminal disregard of the treaties which embody minority rights as shall parallel, indeed equal, the force of democratic protest against Rumania.

Moreover, though one be loath to say it, there is at present in Rumania a lull in the matter of anti-Semitic persecution only because Rumania and Austria have stood out sharply against a background of relative quiet. If minority treaties can be trampled upon in Austria by the Nazi Reich, they may soon be trampled upon in Poland by its Government. Which is only another way of saying that the crime of Nazism in Austria is only in the least part a crime against Jews, even though Jews suffer most.

Austria has been an empire of light and leading for the civilized world and Jews have been among those privileged to carry high the torch of Central European civilization. The special attack upon the non-Aryans of Austria is nothing more than the measured brutality of the Nazi Reich against the Austria which kept undimmed the light of German civilization and German idealism. To the artistic, intellectual and spiritual wealth of Austria Jews made a significant contribution. They are now being harassed and punished and destroyed because they have supported the Austrian attempt to maintain unbroken the traditions of German not Nazi culture and life.

But we have another truth to face. From New York to Sydney, from Warsaw to San Francisco, Jews must plan to build their National Home. The foundations have been well and truly laid by our noble and glorious youth in the land hallowed as truly by hopes as by memories. Despite a multitude of differences and handicaps, a great beginning has been made. Nearly half a million Jews dwell in the Jewish land under human and social conditions which have in them the essence of prophetic fulfillment. Woe betide us if lulled as were the German and Austrian Jews by a false sense of security we become indifferent to the fate of our brother Jews in, alas, many lands, and fail to do what in us lies to meet threats to our collective integrity with the dignity of self-reverence, and imperilment to our very being with the resolve to suffer and endure, and after that to keep the Jewish spirit pure by recreation of Jewish life at its highest in the Jewish land.

— 1938

America Has Spoken

THE reaction of the American people to the recent barbarities in the Nazi Reich has been exactly what one might have expected from a great and democratic people. America has recoiled with horror and with loathing from the things that have been done in pitilessly brutal reprisal against the Jews of Germany. This loathing of Germany's shame has been embodied in the protest of him who is in truth not merely the President of the United States but the voice of America's conscience. It has been moving and heartening alike from the viewpoint of civilization to note that after infinitely patient waiting for nearly six years in the hope that reason might prevail over savagery, the Christian churches and peoples of America have spoken with one voice against the crime of a great people against its own loyal and law-abiding Jewish population.

If the American Jewish Congress has not summoned great meetings, as it did in 1933 and in 1934 and again and again, it has been because it was felt that what had happened in Germany since the lamentable murder of a German official by a grief-crazed Jewish lad, proved to the whole civilized world beyond the peradventure of a doubt, that this had ceased to be, if ever it was, a Jewish question, that this had ceased to be, if ever it solely was, a German question. What has happened in the last fortnight in the German Reich and is happening is obviously become one of the gravest problems of civilization.

For the first time in the six years of the Nazi horror the masses that spoke out included Americans of every faith and race and tongue. So that all that we American Jews found needful to do was and is to take our share in the sorrows and the protests of the whole American people. The leading statesmen, the princes of the church, the most eminent of our journalists, the greatest of our educators have spoken. We Jews echo and we thank God for the words of former President Hoover, of Governor Alfred Landon, of our own Al Smith, of Senator Robert Wagner, of William Green, of Bishop Manning, of Harry Emerson Fosdick, of John Haynes Holmes, of the most Reverend Archbishop Curley of the Catholic Church and of a great number of the most distinguished Americans who have lifted up their voices and helped Germany to understand that American civilization stands as one in detestation and condemnation of Nazi brutality against a people, despoiling them of their possessions, robbing them of their status, violating and desecrating their holy places beyond which not even Nazi savagery can go.

Not the least problem now before the American people —as it has not previously been, is the problem of boycotting Nazi wares and services. This has ceased to be a problem. It ceased to be a problem for us five years ago. For five years we have been insisting that no self-respecting American ought to touch Nazi-made goods or Nazi services. For five years the American Jewish Congress, in conjunction with the American Federation of Labor and other liberty-prizing bodies, has wielded the non-violent weapon of the boycott against Germany. Today the whole American people realizes that it can no longer traffic in the commerce to and from the German Reich. Even as Jewish persecution in Germany has ceased to be a Jewish question, so the boycott in America must not for one hour remain a Jewish boycott. It must be a boycott of all Americans who loathe the things for which Nazism stands, not that Germans may be hurt, but that Germany may be set free. The way to liberate Germany is to cease to have commerce with the German Reich.

THERE are many questions which we American Jews must come to face. We know that the Jews of Germany and Austria and largely Czechoslovakia, are on the march and that an army of involuntary emigrants is leaving and must leave and should be enabled forever to leave Germany behind them. The mass evacuation of a people rooted in Germany's soil for a thousand years is one of the most loathsome crimes of history.

Not being a race of beggars, though we are wanderers, we must make clear to the world that we are resolved that we are not to become, nor to be dealt with as *a refugee people*, even though the German-speaking peoples are forcing our brother-Jews into exile. The refuges for Jews are the lands in which they have lived for centuries and millennia. We raise our voice today against every proposal and program which deals with Jewish migrants or exiles as if they were to be further penalized by being settled in uninhabited lands, lands of doubtful title, lands of uncertain capacity for colonization and resettlement.

We lift up our voice in most solemn protest against any and every thought of settling Jews in the German colonies of yesterday. Having lived under the blight and burden of the Swastika, no Jew must ever again be compelled to touch the soil over which the German flag has been lifted up. Moreover, we Jews do not believe in reprisal or in vindictiveness. We do not wish even the German people to believe that we desire to possess ourselves of lands of which they have by war been dispossessed. Moreover, the destruction of any Jewish-occupied, one-time German colony would become the supreme objective of Germany. We would have Jews live anywhere outside of the Nazi Reich, live under almost any conditions, but we will never give approval or sanction to any plan which dooms Jews to live again in a land defiled up to the days of peace by that government which has sought to destroy them. I would rather have my fellow-Jews die in Germany than live somehow, anyhow, in lands which bear the imprint of yesterday's occupation by Germany, in lands which may tomorrow be yielded back by England and France to Germany, as all other conceivable concessions are being made to the Nazi Reich.

With respect to the right of Jews to live in the lands of which they have been a part for many generations, one thing more remains to be said. If England truly and genuinely wishes to help German Jews to live, there are certain things that it can do. We do not speak of the Dominions, Canada, Australia, South Africa, for these must reach their own decisions, but we think of one mandated territory of England, namely Palestine. If the English Government wishes to help Jews, it will admit Jewish children into England as visitors. It will take such action as the President of the United States has taken with regard to temporary residence of German refugees. It will cooperate genuinely with the Intergovernmental Committee for Refugees, under the leadership in part of two great Americans, Ambassador Myron Taylor and Director General George Rublee, in establishing temporary, transient homes or hostels for Jews of Germany, tens of thousands of them, pending their ultimate distribution among the lands, the provinces, the dominions, nations and continents in which they will ultimately be integrated.

But the one great, indeed supreme, service that England can render the Jewish people, the whole Jewish people not merely German Jews, is at once, without a moment's delay, to grant the request of the Jewish population of Palestine that they be permitted to welcome ten thousand Jewish children out of Germany, another ten thousand Jewish adolescents, another eight or ten thousand relatives in German lands. In one word, England can do most today for German Jews by opening wide the doors of Palestine. World opinion, including American public opinion, will not only support the British Government, but the conscience of mankind will praise and bless the wisdom and the generosity, the statesmanship and the nobleness of England, if it say to the Arabs, to whom it can frankly speak: "This people is homeless. It wishes to go home. You must be big enough to welcome the homecoming Jews in Palestine." If Great Britain fails to take the largest steps to give home not shelter, home not refuge, to German Jews in Palestine, all else that it contemplates and proposes and announces will be in vain, and the very earnestness and sincerity of English concern with the German refugees will be questioned. This is the day for England to write a worthy postscript to the Balfour Declaration.

— 1938

Enemy of Human Freedom

FOR SEVEN YEARS OPINION has annually sought to convey a picture of the accumulating evil done by the Nazi regime. It may claim to have been among the first journals of the land to have discerned that the least grave, though in many senses the most foul, aspect of Hitlerism lay in its treatment of the German Jew. And still such treatment, far from being the objective of the Nazi regime, was little more than a bait held out to those susceptible to anti-Semitic passion to wreak themselves against the most defenseless group within the Reich.

OPINION so deeply felt at an early stage of the Nazi revolt against civilization that within some years Hitlerism would pit itself against all non-German races and against the whole of the Judeo-Hebreo-Christian world fellowship, that for five years it has followed the practice of arranging an annual symposium in which Christian and Jew should have part in setting forth the moral quality and the social status of the phenomenon commonly described as Hitlerism.

We never stood alone as victims of the Hitler odium. We were in the fullest and proudest company from the beginning. For such company included all women who chose to be free; the self-liberating trade union and workers' movement of Germany; every German idealist who had spoken and acted in the terms and on behalf of the movement of international peace and international integrity; the entire socialist movement long dominant in German politics; and every group that embodied the forward-looking and forward-moving hope of the German people that was.

And yet it was not long before the Catholics of Germany had the honor of winning the enmity of the Nazi regime. Rosenbergism, then ever more dominant than it is today, battled against the Catholic church and the youth within the Catholic Action movement with much of the ardor with which the unspeakable and forever speaking Goebbels enlisted all that was worst and foulest in German life against the security and the honor of German Jews. The name of Niemoeller is symptomatic of the wrath of Hitlerism against the Protestant churches because one indeflectibly loyal Christian group, under the spiritual leadership of Niemoeller, refused to do obeisance to a State which sought to exact such worship as followers of Christianity felt they would yield only to Divine Rule.

In recent years Hitlerism has chosen to surround itself with a world of foes beginning with Austria, Czechoslovakia, and Poland. And it may, without exaggeration, be said that today the German Reich stands on the one side, and earth's civilized peoples on the other, save for Stalin's Russia, which has been beguiled into the unholiest of alliances, and Italy, which grows more deeply neutral in protest against the Hitler-Stalin alliance. At last the world has come to recognize what Nazism means. For years certain circles in France, dazzled by the hope of gain, were half tolerant thereof. England for five years and more could not be brought to understand the movement, and the imminence of the peril which it was unbelievably bent upon courting. But England and France are not alone in stating that Hitler and civilization cannot coexist, that civilization must free itself of the Hitler menace, or else go down to cureless catastrophe.

There will be no more Munichs. The Munich of September, 1938, marked the last effort of the then unaware democracies of the West to traffic, at heaviest sacrifice of the national interests of others, with an unbelievable enemy of all civilization. In the meantime Poland has gone down to defeat, and the greatest sufferers within the old Poland are the Jews. Nearly a century ago General Grant returned his sword to General Lee. Hitlerism has undertaken to show the world that military defeat must be followed by the most awful visitations of fire and sword and plague. Inhumanity is written upon every item of every page of the German story of dispossession of Poland. Democracies that would be prepared to leave those monstrous evils uncorrected were little better than the regime they are bent upon challenging.

The question has ceased to be one of war versus peace, but is rather become a question whether unbridled might and unmoral power shall again rule over the destinies of men and nation. Insofar as England and France have taken up the gage, insofar as the two great democracies of Western Europe dared to say to Hitler after his threat to Poland, "Thus far shalt thou go and no further," it is for peoples who are, and for men who would remain free, their most sacred obligation to give moral, political, and material aid and furtherance to Britain and France. The wrongs of a world in which democracy will triumph may be corrected and cured, but the wrongs of a Nazi world would be cureless.

We Jews have no special stake in this war. Save possibly for the handful of Jews in the lands ruled and conquered by Germany, Jews are at one in their understanding of the truth. But Hitlerism is the enemy of human freedom, of human justice, of all those imponderable values and ideals which together constitute civilization. It is for that reason that every Jew on earth must take his place by the side of them that are resolved that Hitlerism and all that it is and means and portends shall perish from the earth, and that all those moral and social and spiritual ideals which it would destroy shall remain, as in truth they are, imperishable.

— 1940

The Crime of Crimes

EIGHT years since Hitler's so-called "election" as chancellor of Germany. It is not true to say that nearly eight years have "passed." Truer to say that eight years of fire and sword have seared the hearts of mankind, that these eight years have brought more hurt and grief to humanity than any similar period of time within a thousand years.

Recall to mind the state of the world before Hitler and contrast it with the state of the world that is today. In 1932, the world was ready to act on the Disarmament plan. It was the one proposal for world Disarmament in our lifetime which received serious attention throughout many nations and around which a conference in Geneva was built up, that gave high promise of the fulfillment of the long-time dream of Disarmament. In behalf of that program of Disarmament, the then President Hoover labored long and earnestly.

Hitler came and not only was the Disarmament dream shattered, but the world, its simple folk, at once and instinctively felt that the end of peace had come and that evil days lay before it.

The Nazi program sounded simple. But it was belied by every word he had written in Europe's best seller, "Mein Kampf." In that volume, he had laid down the theory of the master-race and the slave-race, speaking as contemptuously of the Latin race, including the Italians, his new Axis partner, as about the Slavic race, including Russians and Poles, as feeble, effete, and fit only to be ruled. Two immediate aims he named—the obliteration of Jews as of the inferior Semitic race, and the destruction of Marxian-Socialism. At once he robbed and crushed every Labor organization, which was an unmistakable sign of his deadly hatred of the normal and accepted instruments of democracy. As for Jews, he robbed them; he struck them down in their citizenship; he inflicted upon them every conceivable, and, up to that time, inconceivable humiliation, indignity and hurt, though Jews had lived and served Germany for a thousand years, including, in our own day, the names of Albert Ballin and Walter Rathenau and Albert Einstein.

There are men of ignorant unconcern with regard to the illimitable evil wrought by Hitler or who, in silent sympathy, almost welcome Hitlerism. These demand a Bill of Particulars concerning the Western world's indictment of Hitler and Hitlerism. Alas, nothing is easier than to single out a few of the more grievous blows which he has struck at the political and spiritual life of mankind. At one fell stroke, he smashed, as I have already said, the entire labor movement, stole its very considerable funds, including its insurance treasury. He compelled women to give up their high economic and political status and whipped them back into the kitchen and the nursery to feed his soldiers and to breed new recruits for his relentless armies. He not only ended the peace movement but exiled and doomed its leadership including such men as Gerlach and Bernstorff, whose crime had lain in seeking world peace through the League of Nations.

But over and beyond his destruction of those policies and programs which had made Germany one of the socially advanced countries of the last century, he sowed anew terrible policies which the world is harvesting today on blood-drenched battlefields. The world will not soon forget, though it will be eager to bury them in a sea of oblivion, the major and in a sense original items of the Nazi program.

He introduced what might be called intramural war, a war of a large element of the population against the smallest of its population groups—the war of a majority of the people against a minority, with the result that 99% of the Nazi population were incited to brutality, theft and murder against less than 1% of the population, its

Jewish minority. But as if that crime of crimes were not enough, in "Mein Kampf" he proclaimed and after 1933 he proceeded to put into effect the doctrine of racialism. This meant that only one race on earth was fit to rule and to exercise mastery, and all other races, whether Semitic or Slavic or Latin, must accept the status of inferior and ultimately enslaved races.

TODAY, eight years after Hitler came, Europe presents the picture of an armed camp in which great and historic peoples such as the Czechs and Poles, Scandinavians and Rumanians, Belgians, French and Dutch, are nothing more than enslaved victims of the "master race." And the third plank of the Hitler program was summarized in the term *Gleichschaltung*, which means regimentation, placing the minds and moods and ideas and hopes of a people on the basis of unexceptionable uniformity. Regimentation meant the abrogation of every freedom of the individual, the mocking cancelation of all the great spiritual and political gains of the nineteenth century, the transformation of a great, reasoning and free people into a mighty and militarily usable army of machines.

But all this was preliminary to the great offensive now under way against democracy, which did not choose to war upon him but upon which he is resolved to war to the death. In his mad passion to rule a regimented world, he feels oppressed and hampered by the challenge of free and democratic peoples and seems resolved that the world shall not remain half Fascist and half democratic. Nothing in Hitlerism is more truly and completely psychopathic than the intensity of his passion against what he and his confederate Mussolini regard as the accursed challenge of democracy.

Five years and more, the world has watchfully waited.

It did not even, for the most part, arm itself in a defense against him, who almost frankly announced his program of world conquest through the destruction of the greater Western democracies of which the English and our own alone survive today. With singular unintelligence, the world for the most part refused to heed the warning of his theories and his conduct alike, until he embarked upon a career of incredibly brutal conquest.

Austria was annexed in violation of written and spoken covenants. Czechoslovakia was overwhelmed in the Fall of 1938 and finally crushed and annexed in the spring of 1939, after all the pitiful drama of appeasement and conciliation had been played upon the Nazi boards by Englishmen almost ready to yield up even the self-revering honor of a mighty Commonwealth for the sake of peace. Nothing availed to stay the hand of him or them to whom neutrality was nothing more than child's play, sneered at and crushed like a house of cards. Armed as a nation never was in history, they violated treaties, they broke neutral nations, they imprisoned their peoples, they starved their populations and the Axis became, together with Japan and, alas, the Soviet Union in the dim shadow—a world alliance of bane and blight.

ONE unappeasing leader there was who almost from the beginning, as history will yet chronicle, understood and in an early day proclaimed the menace of the aggressor nations, of those dictatorships against which he felt civilized people, democracies of free men, should institute a moral quarantine. Had America heeded and followed his leadership, it might never have become necessary even to consider all-out aid to England, which is nothing more, perhaps, than an imperfect and inadequate substitute for such moral and political cooperation with all the democracies of Europe as would have stayed the march of the aggressors before it was too late.

England stands almost alone today, if a people can be considered alone which stands in the panoply of its majestic and unconquerable strength. *Not alone*, for there is little doubt that somehow and in a very real measure, if only it be not too late, our country will recognize the truth that the unthinkable invasion and downfall of England would mean menace and imperilment to our own American democracy. No day has seemed darker, no portent blacker than that of this hour.

And still on this tragic anniversary, I venture to prophecy that England will not fall, that democracy will not perish, that the immortal truth of Lincoln, "government of the people, by the people and for the people shall not perish from the earth" remains as true and valid today as it was when first spoken. Nay, more—after eight blood-filled, shame-laden, crime-accursed years of Hitlerism, Nazism and Fascism, we know as never before that it is for us to cherish, to safeguard the altar of democracy at which we Americans live and move and have our being.

— 1941

Answer "Extermination"

EVEN THE most tender-hearted of people have become inured to horrors which are in fact the daily staple of mankind. But certain things have lately come to pass, which have shocked the least sensitive souls. The Nazi hangman Heydrich was slain in or near Prague, and it may be that after the true gangster fashion he was killed by order of his superhangman Himmler. A man-hunt was ordered at once, and it is no overstatement that more than five hundred men and women, it may be a thousand, some

of the choicest spirits of Czechia, were murdered without
trial or proof. Many Jews were among that number and
all of them were stamped out as Communists. Some days
after the assassination of Heydrich, the Nazi press proudly
announced that having discovered that the slayers had
been sheltered in a little Czech village and inasmuch as
its dwellers could not be prevailed upon to disclose the
identity or whereabouts of the assassins the Nazi authorities had decided upon radical treatment of the village and
its inhabitants. The men were lined up and shot; the
women were doomed to the living death of concentration camps, and the children were dispatched to "educa-
tional institutions," all because they did not know or refused to betray the heroic souls which had sought asylum with them. Not since November 10, 1938, the date
of the burning of the synagogues throughout Germany
and Austria, or December 7, 1941, had a gasp of horror
gone around the world such as greeted the ghastly news
of Lidice. Mankind felt that a deed had been committed
to the shame of which men had not before stooped.

Worse if possible was still to come almost immediately
thereafter. The Reich calmly announced that 268 "Jews
and Communists" had been shot for having part in a
conspiracy, the story of which was flimsier than the flimsiest gossamer. But simultaneously Goebbels, who per-
forms every threat as truly as Hitler violated every promise, made a statement which is not the business of Jews
alone but of all the United Nations. He declared that if
such bombings as that of Cologne continue, Jews will be
held responsible and, it was added, the Jews of Europe
would be "utterly exterminated."

The world seemed rather less moved by this unspeakable threat than by the more dramatic extirpation of the
village of Lidice, even as it too long remained unmoved

by a myriad anti-Jewish atrocities of earlier years. Ought not this threat give the United and civilized nations pause? As far as it is a threat, its blackmailing term should be promptly answered by renewed and ever repeated vast-scale bombings. But at the same time the United Nations ought once and for all make it clear to the Nazis that they themselves and their own crimes—not the Jews —are responsible for bombing reprisals and that these bombings would continue until the German people had freed themselves from their enslaving masters. This threat against European Jewry the United Nations are not free to ignore. For one thing, because silence might be held to be assent to the charge of Jewish responsibility for a campaign of Nazi destruction, and again because Britain and our own country have never explicitly alluded to the inclusion of the Jewish people within and among those peoples battling for the Four Freedoms and under the security of the Atlantic Charter. Such a word of solemn warning may conceivably serve as a deterrent against added anti-Jewish Nazi infamies. Above all, in view of the unmeasured sufferings of Jews in all the lands of the Axis, it is become the part of inevasible duty for Britain and our own country to speak the word which is needed to lift the heart of world Jewry and to discharge a debt of honor to those who have suffered most and have least been helped.

— 1942

Deliverance Will Come

OVER and above all else we gather here tonight to dedicate ourselves to the loftiest hopes of our country, to renew unshakeable faith in the victory, early or late, of America and all the United Nations. To the achievement of such victory over the powers of evil and darkness, we who are Americans and Jews pledge anew all that we are, all that we have, all that we hope to be.

Tomorrow will be the eve of Tishe B'Ab, the destruction twice or thrice of the holy Temple of Jerusalem. To-night we meet not only to sorrow over an ancient grief but also over a limitless wrong of our own day, the Nazi threat to destroy the Jewish people. Great as is our sorrow, deepfelt as is our grief, we do not mourn the destruction of the Jewish people. The destruction of the Jewish people can never be. Its Temple may be destroyed, its people plundered and stricken and wounded, but the eternal people shall not be destroyed. What Pharaoh and Haman, Nebuchadnezar and Epiphanes, Titus and Hadrian, Torquemada and Pobiedonosteff, failed to effect— the extermination of the Jewish people—will never be achieved by Hitler, nor yet by a thousand Hitlers. President Roosevelt's message is true and right, "The Nazis will not succeed in exterminating their victims any more than they will succeed in enslaving mankind."

We would not be worthy of our Jewish fellowship if we did not lift up our voices in solemn lamentation and mournful protest over the oceanic wrongs done to our brother-Jews wherever Nazis live and rule. We would not be equal to our American citizenship if we did not to-night with one voice ask our great-hearted, liberty-loving fellow Americans to join with us in solemn condemnation of the infamy of the Axis in dooming unarmed and defenseless men, women and children by the hundred thousands to suffering, torture and death. Honor is the fate of them who are privileged to fight and die for a cause, but shame is the portion of such as torture and murder masses who are weaponless and defenseless. Our hearts went out to the people of the heroic little community of

Lidice, every member of which in one way or another was slain by Heydrich's avenging monsters. There have been a thousand and more Lidices in the life of the Jews of Central and Eastern Europe in the last year.

We are not met tonight to cry for vengeance. "Vengeance is mine," saith the Lord. But for purposes which befit Americans and Jews, we are asking our Government and the United Nations to serve notice upon the Nazi despots that the horror of Nazi mistreatment of civilians should cease, whether of Jews, Protestants or Catholics, whether Poles, Czechs or Greeks, and that as our President has put it, "The American people will hold the perpetrators to strict accountability in a day of reckoning which will surely come," for the crimes committed in their name and at their dictate. We wish, moreover, in and through this assembly to say to our fellow-Jews in the lands of Hitler horror—Afflicted of our people—you are not forgotten and under God your day of deliverance will come. We know that one million and more of you, our brothers, have died of Nazi inhumanity to man, that Jewish multitudes have been and are being exposed to spoilation, starvation, disease, enslavement, massacre, and execution. These ruthless atrocities are visited by the Hitler rule upon the Jews of whom Dr. Goebbels said in *Das Reich* within a few days, "The Jews must be annihilated in order to save Germany." The fact is that neither the Germans nor the Jews will be annihilated, but a civilized world will exterminate the Hitlers and Goebbels and Himmlers who are the scourge of mankind. The salvation of our people and all peoples who would be free can only come under God through a victory speedy and complete of the United Nations.

The greatest crime against the Jewish victims of Hitler would be to treat the crimes against the Jews differently from the treatment of crimes against French, or Czechs, or Poles, or Greeks. The warning of Churchill and Roosevelt, after the murder of the French hostages and the destruction of the Czechian Lidice, has been renewed tonight by President Roosevelt himself with regard to the unspeakable mass murder of Jews. The threat of Goebbels to exterminate the Jews in retaliation for an allied victory can only be answered by more and more victories of the United Nations.

Tonight we speak through prayer to and of the dead. To the living, the surviving, we offer our loving greeting, and in the spirit of Tishe B'Ab we cry: That which is mortal falls, that which is perishable dies, but the hopes and ideals God has implanted within us are undying. You stand not alone in your sorrow; let the faith of a whole world of free men sustain you, the faith of men who now understand as never before that you have suffered through the ages because you denied and rejected Hitlers when you might have gained peace by all the pleasant ways of compromise or appeasement or surrender.

This meeting has yet another purpose. Our brothers in Nazi lands have perished unarmed. That is the tragedy of it. Wherever the Nazis went they could not resist and were doomed to perish without a cause. But one land there is wherein the Jews will and can defend themselves. If Britain only be wise and just enough to use them as the unswerving, loyal allies that they are. For Britain's sake, for the sake of the United Nations, for the sake of honor among comrades and allies—half a million and more builders of Palestine must not suffer the fate of all other Jewish victims of the Nazis.

They must not be left unarmed and defenseless. If, heaven forefend, Rommel reach the outer gates of Palestine, he must be flung back by the heroic prowess and resistless fury of the Jewish defenders of the land. Today, two or three divisions of young Maccabeans might have helped to turn the tide in British favor on the western border of Egypt. A Jewish Home Guard to safeguard Jewish Palestine is as rightful and fitting and necessary as an English Home Guard in and of England. Jews in Palestine are ready to die in the defense of Palestine, but they must not be massacred. They can and will die, if die they must, but they will die like men and Jews and Maccabeans.

My people, I summon you to take your place among the United and Free Peoples of earth. I summon you to fight on every front, including the Second Front, against all tyrants and oppressors. I summon you to arise and march forward as Americans to the liberation of our brothers, to the defense of Zion, to the victory of our country for freedom and humanity.

— 1942

Accumulated Horrors

THE horror mounts from day to day. It may be that no especially new methods of Nazi extermination have lately been devised and practiced. But there is now an unbelievable accumulation of atrocities, the story of which has made the Holy Days a season of mourning, and the Synagogue in all lands little other than Heartbreak House. When a distinguished Polish woman of American birth carries about with her a piece of soap manufactured out of the corpses of Jewish victims in Poland, one knows that Dante's Inferno has been outdone in horror, and that all Jews who are forced to enter or leave Poland are dealt with in a more ruthless and merciless manner than humans have ever experienced. Well-grounded tales have it that Jewish corpses are being exhumed in order to make fertilizers, the last and bitterest indignity that can be offered to the human spirit and body.

Jews who have known of these things have borne themselves and guided the Jewish people with extraordinary restraint. But is not the time come again, even though it may not be for the last time, to appeal to the conscience of our country? The American people is never deaf to the cry of suffering. And history records no such mass suffering as has in these last months overwhelmed the Jewish populations of Hitler-dominated countries. The men and women of our nation get no more than fragmentary bits of the actual story. They do not know of mass executions, mounting it is believed at one time to tens of thousands. even the figures, fifty and one hundred thousand, are credibly mentioned by non-Jewish report. And the wheel of direst tragedy turns on, each turn breaking added hearts and maiming more bodies.

The President and the Prime Minister have spoken out clearly with regard to the retribution that is bound after the war's end to claim the doers of these dastardly deeds. The American people, by the Clergy, the University, the Press, its Government, should cry out so strongly against these enormities and savageries that the German people may be compelled to understand and to remember what is to be the fate of those who now violate the laws of humaneness and life's decencies.

It had been hoped that there has been some measure of exaggeration in the most hideous of these rumors. But as a high officer of our own State Department put it to representatives of the American Jewish Congress, "the rumor at worst might be explained as aggregation rather than exaggeration."

With respect to certain aspects of the problem our

Government has acted with vigor, namely, in relation to the children torn from their parents as the latter were deported to Eastern Europe. In this the State Department as it is well known, had the reinforcing support of high representatives of the Catholic Church, such as the Archbishops of Paris, Lyon and Toulouse, who have uttered their brave and self-imperiling protest against the crimes suffered by these innocents.

A word of equally high commendation is owing to the heads of the State Department, who have spoken in terms of unmistakable clarity with respect to the major enormities of the Vichy regime, most especially the impressment for slave labor into Germany of tens of thousands of French citizens. Vichy's part in the enslavement of Frenchmen may yet prove to be its fervently wished-for undoing.

American Jews cannot, alas, wholly or even largely, avert the evil from the souls and bodies of their brothers. But they can give them whatever help and relief are called for by the uniqueness of their need. They can and must persist in their emphasis that after the catastrophe of these years their brothers and sisters shall finish bitterly marred lives not as the objects of Caribbean experiment, but as self-respecting Jewish men and women within the security and dignity of an unassailably rightful home, Erétz Israel.

— 1942

United Nations vs. Mass Murder

NOT more than thrice in a generation, indeed in many generations, have the nations of the world made a public declaration concerning the Jewish people. It happened in November, 1917, when the Balfour Declaration came to

light, to kindle a great hope in the heart of Israel. A sub-
sequent and related declaration took the form of the San
Remo Treaty, which named Britain as the Mandatory
Power for Palestine. In these days, there has been a third
declaration by the nations of the world, speaking and acting in concert, led by the United States and Britain, with
the cooperation of the Governments-in-Exile and Free
France.

This last declaration for the first time constituted a
public recognition of the most dire tragedy in history, the
attempted extermination of a people, the whole Jewish
people of Europe, with partial success, alas, in the extermination of not less than one-third of the Jewish population of European lands, outside of the Soviet Union.

Jews the world over will hail this declaration. It is informed by a sense of the magnitude of the tragedy. It is
infused by a spirit of deep and true understanding of what
that means in sorrow to millions and in hurt to the moral
structure of human life. The declaration followed soon
after the recent conference of the representatives of a
group of Jewish organizations with the President, who
solemnly and sternly warned the aggressor nation, which
he would have quarantined six years ago, "The mills of
the Gods grind slowly, but they grind exceeding small."
No need there was of evoking that quality of high rage
against the criminals of Nazi Europe, which the President
of the United States has expressed in enduring terms time
and again. But the word of the President has now been
followed by the United Nations, including our own country, which have taken note of the mass murder of hundreds and hundreds of thousands of Jews by that system
which is resolved to exterminate all Jews. Thus far Hitler
has been woefully effective. The man who breaks every
promise seems able to enforce every threat, with the result

that Jews have suffered wrong and hurt and shame such as no people has ever endured. In order to destroy those whom Hitler rightfully regards as the protagonists and defenders of the hated system of moral and spiritual civilization, he has reverted to the barbarism of deporting, expropriating and slaying of men, women and children, all of them civilians, none of them free to defend himself.

While it is comforting in some slight measure to know that the world of freemen understands and sorrows at the side of the Jewish people, the reflection cannot be shut out that the declaration of the United Nations is lamentably belated. Made seven or eight years ago by England, France and the United States, France would not lie prostrate under the crushing heels of Hitler and Laval; England would not be sacrificing the finest of her sons upon the altar of national defense, and we would not have been dragged into a war of infinite cost and sacrifice, which timely, concerted, vigorous action on the part of the great nations of the West, together with Russia, in the name of collective security, could have averted.

The United Nations speak of retribution and of Courts promptly to be organized in order to try the criminals. But in addition to retribution something more is needed, very much more. Let the nations, such as England, nearest to Hitler's Europe, save them who can be saved, admitting to asylum those women and children and even men, who somehow can get themselves or be gotten out of Hitler-ruled lands. Without wishing to break the blockade or impair the defense of the United Nations, what has been done for the starving of Greece must, because it can, be done for the half and more than half starving Jews who have survived these unutterably bitter years. Not after the war, but now England and our own country and Russia and China must move not through an inadequate inter-governmental committee, but through its wisest leadership and at every cost to arrange, together with Latin America, that temporary refuge and even permanent asylum shall be found for the hundreds of thousands who will not wish to go back to the lands of famine and of slaughter.

Over and above all, England and our own country, in the lead, will have to face the fact that Jews, the largest number of them, will wish to go to Palestine, the new Palestine, the developing, growing, larger Palestine which needs them, and that its resettlement will mean hurt to none and benefit to all. But this cannot come about merely through the cancellation of that document of appeasement known as the White Paper. It will come about through the united insistence of the enlightened leaders of England and our own country, Churchill and Roosevelt, that the doors of Palestine shall be opened wide and shall remain open.

Jews who have endured most shall not go without reparation. Reprisal is not a term of the Jewish vocabulary. But reparation to the Jew should be the supreme aim of a Christian world, which will at last have freed itself from the horror and the hideousness of that organized abrogation of Christianity, known as Hitlerism or Fascism.

The world waits upon the leadership of its greatest. The Governments-in-Exile must and will stand with the American and British Governments. Let these now translate their justified rage into noble reparation. Let these now implement an utterance of noblest sympathy into deeds of abiding help to a people crushed by sorrow and yet ready to help rebuild every land in which it dwells and to rebuild the scene of its heart's desire, the land of its memories, its present achievements, its solacing hopes —Palestine.   — 1943

Hitlerism — and Beyond

WHAT better summary of the immeasurable evil that has been wrought throughout these awful ten years than the word, "There is not an evil in humanity which has not been worsened, and not a good that has not been weakened during these ten years of Hitler's rule." The former half of the statement is indubitably true. The second half may be challenged from the viewpoint of those who believe that the worst has already been, that thanks to the incredible effort and the unwithstandable unity of the Allied Nations, Hitlerism is to be driven from the face of the earth.

True enough, alas, good has been weakened, and it was the weakening of the good which made possible the tragic toleration of Hitlerism by those nations which ultimately found it necessary to withstand the illimitable evil that lies at its heart. Many of the best and most precious things of life have been assailed and for a time overcome, but it is not too much to say that the light is beginning to dawn, even for the most reluctant of them that finally came to resist Hitlerism. Now it is clear to all who see, who are not willfully blind, that an unresisted Hitlerism would have meant the destruction—it might have been for centuries, if not millenia—of every value for which men of faith and courage and aspiration have wrought and fought throughout the ages. May it not truly be said that for a time, when Hitler began to rage, there was a woeful toleration of the evil that he meant by those who would not understand. After the years of toleration and compromise a great dread rested upon individuals and peoples, lest the world succumb to or be overwhelmed by the threatening evil. Today, however, that is, alas, only after a decade of easy tolerance or of explicable

dread, the world of freemen has put aside alike its tolerance and its dread, substituting for these things the will
to achieve victory as against every power of enslavement
and degradation menacing mankind. Even better, the
wisest and the finest within the leadership of the nations
will not rest satisfied merely to overcome the evil that
confronted them. They are, in the word of one of the
truest builders of the democratic faith of our own country, "resolved to build a better world, a world of peace-
ful work, in which the millions still living can be free
from haunting fear and can play their part as citizens in
a new and universal democracy."

For ten years OPINION has published a symposium
comparable with that which distinguishes its Tenth Commemoration Issue. It had been believed that the scourge
would be stayed within a brief period. Therein it has
been disappointed, for ten years unutterably bitter and
unprecedentedly tragic have passed since Hindenburg
and Von Papen awarded the crown of leadership to Hitler. For the first time since Hitler's coming, there is good
hope of his going. The free and democratic peoples are
united, and no power under heaven can hold their resistless march. As has been their lot throughout the ages, Jews
have been the earliest and the greatest sufferers. Even this
price which Jews have paid will not be accounted too
great if the downfall of Hitler and the whole miserable
Nazi-Fascist company will come to mean as it should, that
if ever again an anti-Jewish movement be initiated, it and
its authors will be suspect wheresoever they might dwell.
Anti-Semitism becomes even more intolerable within our
borders than within the frontiers of a nation that has not
striven to accept the democratic way of life.

The century of the common man, without regard to
creed or race or color, is at hand. As Jews we have borne

the heaviest burden. We have faith that humankind will recognize as never before that Jews have become the victims of the Fascist terrorism because they are the unbowed protagonists of freedom, faith, democracy. The nations must be united in safeguarding the four freedoms for all men and peoples. The Jew today looks forward to a new world for all men, including himself. The Jew has always made his own permanent contribution to the upbuilding of a moral world. Freedom and equality for the Jew will liberate and inspire the Jew to renew his gifts and to redouble his service for the weal of all mankind.

— 1943

III

Zion – Homeland and Hope

Our Noblest Achievement

ONE is somehow tempted to link a New Year's Message with one's experiences in the closing months of the Jewish Year. I have returned this day from the Nineteenth Zionist Congress at Lucerne. Would that world Jewry might have caught a gleam of the spirit that ruled there! None of us was unmindful of the fate of the greatest number of our Jewish brothers, spiritually homeless, even when not politically disposessed. Least of all did we for a moment fail to remember that tragedy of tragedies, which is the status of German Jewry. But at Lucerne, save for some inevitable digressions hereafter to be dealt with, every thought, every effort, every resolve was dedicated to a single end, the upbuilding of the Jewish National Home. A people which, while looking upon the destruction of its altars can refrain from lamentations and can convert a Wailing Wall into one of the pillars of its ultimate and rightful home, has mastered the art of deathlessness.

Though the Congress all but limited itself to its constructive and creative tasks, the shadows of Nazi Germany hung over it like a pall. One could not even for an hour forget the lot of them to whom every day brought the tidings of some new refinement of torture, some new fiendishness of destructive malice. Still, these or their representatives at Lucerne did not whine nor even complain. Their fate was sealed and irrevocable. They craved but two boons—reprieve solely for their children, and the opportunity, if it might be, to pour their lives into the mould of the structure of the new Palestine. This, the true *Umschichtung*, the transformation of Germans of the Jewish faith into Jews of one faith and one fate, Jews who had come to understand that they had built mistakenly and insecurely in the past, that they must build securely and firmly for the future.

One could not but reflect that it were well for every Jewry to take to its heart the lesson that it must not wait upon fortune, good or ill, ere it understand that a people uprooted in its own life is the prey of every wind of circumstance and every storm of fate. Oh, the joy of having these lawlessly dispossessed and disfranchised fellow-Jews, who had forgotten Jerusalem and whose chiefest joy was Deutschthum, plan and dream of rebuilding their life as Jews, of weaving their life as Jews into the texture of the ancient and incomparably priceless pattern of Palestine!

Better, perhaps, no New Year's Message than one that shall convey a picture of a people who mourn without hope. And yet, if the truth be told without rhetoric or reservation, three-fourths and more of world Jewry are without hope or would be if they were not Jews. Such hope as they still cherish grows out of the unconsciously held and almost inexplicable faith in that genius of their history which the humble and pious call God, in the dormant but not dead conscience of humankind, in their own unshatterable will to live, in their changeless trust that they will not be forsaken by their fellow Jews in other lands, and least of all by American Jewry.

Concerning that world conscience to which I have referred, it has in recent months been appallingly apathetic. These last days of September may witness a moral debacle that shall prove another Adowa to every high hope of mankind. And still here and there it comes to light increasingly—witness the Berne condemnation of the fabricators of the Protocol lies and forgeries—that humanity cannot shut its ears to the cries of the wronged Jew nor turn its eyes from the sight of a people defamed, degraded, crucified, because it has dared to be a prophet of the light of tomorrow and tomorrow's larger liberty and loftier justice. The Soviet Union adjures if not compels the Jew to ignore his ancient faith and his changeless race. But the new Nazi Attilas declare that race to be accursed which derives from an ancient lineage of prophets, seers, apostles, and Rabbins, equally hateful in the eyes of the new pagans.

But my New Year's Message is addressed not to them that are in bondage but to such as are free. If these need not join in the grief of the enslaved, let them at least seek to share the rapture of the noblest achievement of their people in nineteen hundred years! For such the new Zion is. Waiving opinions and prejudices for a moment, Palestine is become Home, not shelter, Home, not refuge to half of all the German Jewish exiles of the two hideous Hitler years. And within Palestine a new life is visibly being born, a life in which every returning Jew, Polish or German, Rumanian or American, Austrian or English, may have an honorable and creative part. My concern is not for them that build but for ourselves, lest we have no part in the making of a new order of life in the land which our people made immortal.

My wish for my people is threefold. May our brothers who sit in darkness not fail to see the light of the freedom and righteousness that shall yet dawn for all the lovers and servants of liberty! May the builders of the new Palestine who nobly plan and sacrificially build have merited furtherance from the governments and peoples of civilization. May we, far removed from the burdens and the yoke of enslaved Jewish subjects and from the rapture of the enfranchised builders, know that the New Year can bring no choicer gift than eager, generous compassion for our brothers in bondage, no fairer boon than the resolution, with our strength, our substance, our lives to hold up the hands of them that in Zion build for themselves and for mankind.

— 1935

As I Saw Palestine — A Diary

Tuesday, July 9, 1935.
APPROACHING TRIESTE! Never gladder to leave (European) civilization behind me than I shall be tomorrow, when we set sail for Palestine. Learned to my horror from dependable sources in Paris of the pending Anglo-Hitler accord. For such it is, with Montagu Norman and Dr. Schacht as its agents. The Bank of England, thus runs my information, directly or indirectly, is to supply the funds which are to enable the Hitler Government to purchase the output of Vickers. Something for England's "Munitions Inquiry Commission" to look into. Immediate consequences of the Norman-Schacht deal too awful to contemplate. The Scandinavian States must and will re-arm, in part at the bidding and in part because of the challenge of Naziland. Graver still, Soviet Russia at the mercy of the German fleet that is to be with England's blessing, despite the memories of *Der Tag*. Good indeed to escape from Simon-pure European civilization, with England berating France for its passion for security, after reaching an accord with Germany, France and Italy, either at the bidding of the security experts or for the sake of profit, striking hands with Hitlerism which means that the mother of democracy and of parliamentary government traffics with the most potent foe democracy has known in generations. All, all too much for a politically untutored and inexpert American.

Trieste, Tuesday night, after a twenty-hour ride from Paris via Simplon and Milan. In Trieste, caught first

glimpse of Jewish life organized with a view of "facili-
tating"—equivocal term—the Jewish migrants. The last
word I heard in Paris *re* German exiles in Palestine rather
dispiriting—the story of a German Jewish exile in Tel-
Aviv operated on by Dr. D. His farewell injunction to his
surgeon being "Don't bury me among these people of Asia
Minor; send my body to my German Fatherland for
burial."

In Trieste, before embarking on the Gerusalemme,
noted the preparations made by and through the Jewish
agency for expediting Jewish emigrants on their way to
Palestine, officials in evidence, and customs and immigration representatives of the Italian Government courteous
and seeking to be helpful. When in 1913 we sailed for
Palestine from the same port, my wife and I were the
only Jews on the boat. But the Gerusalemme, quite apart
from its Italianized name, is a Jewish boat. It sets out to
serve Jewish traffic and even serves Palestine wines, and
from the huge captain to the tiniest cabin-boy, the crew
of the ship ministers patiently and helpfully to the Jewish
passengers in all classes.

Only a few Germans were among the passengers, but
these complained bitterly about the ruthless uprooting
of which they are the victims. After generations of life in
Germany, they find themselves flung out and life becomes
unlivable. One family of means and civilization told of
being allowed ten marks in cash for the journey in addition to passenger tickets and orders covering hotel ex-
penses—all this after a 40% tax had been levied upon their
possessions, the balance to be retained only in the form of
goods and wares to be exported from Germany. One German Jewess spoke in sorrow rather than in anger of old
Christian friends who refused to recognize and greet them
in public, though this is not uniformly true. Another told

in anger as well as sorrow of rows of graves of young men in the Munich Jewish Cemetery—all falsely labeled "shot in the course of flight." The same woman lamented, "Yes, Hitler is making an international people of us. I went to South Africa in the winter and saw my son; now I am bound for Palestine in order to be with my daughter in her time of child-bearing."

These were the shadows. But there was a brighter and happier side of the picture. For our ship carried some three hundred chalutzim and chalutzot, young Zionist pioneers who go to join the men and women who have borne the burden of colonization for more than a generation. These youthful pilgrims had the joy of home-coming. No sadness of farewell as they embarked. Our contingent chanced to be largely of the Poale-Mizrachi group, social liberals with a conservative religious viewpoint. Their crossing of the Mediterranean was but a stage of the pilgrimage which begins with months of intensive training in agriculture and industry, in what are known as the Hachsharahs—camps, which fit youth for self-sustaining life in Palestine.

The days seemed to be divided between dancing and discussion. And such dancing and such discussion, both vital and intense and endless. The Hora is not unlike the Virginia Reel of our youth—plus oriental fire and Hassidic fervor. As Emerson said to Margaret Fuller, in extenuation of his prolonged stay at an exhibition by the danseuse of their time, "This is not dancing! it is religion." One feels that these young beings are dancing out of the bondage of the ghetto into the freedom of the Homeland. Any excuse sufficed to start a dance—all group or folk dancing, which made the sensual gymnastics of the modern dance in the first cabin seem pale and vulgar.

When dancing flagged—and that rarely enough—discussion began. I have not heard discussion on a higher level, nor carried on in a fairer and more sportsmanlike way. Plenty of bantering and sheer fun and unimaginably keen dialectics, in Yiddish for the most part, with not a little Hebrew added, which had been acquired as a living tongue in the training camps. The raillery and good-nature throughout did not blunt the sharp edge of controversy between two groups, one of them straightaway Social Democrats who look upon religious precept as a quasi-capitalistic device, and Mizrachi workers, who aim simultaneously at two Kingdoms of Heaven, the one purely spiritual or religious, and the other social economic or this-worldly. Never a bitter word, though these for the most part young people were dead in earnest—their earnestness suffused with the high anticipative joy of beholding and dwelling in the land of promise and redemption. I remember a rather sharp discussion, the social-radical non-conformist winding up in some such terms as these: "Because we do not obey and fulfill all the 613 Commandments (*Taryag Mitzvot*) you would deny us the privilege of fulfilling one of them which we consider superior to the remaining 612—namely to settle in the land of Israel."

Sunday, July 14, 1935.

I can hardly member to have experienced a more joyous Sabbath than the Sabbath of July thirteenth on the Gerusalemme. All the tourist passengers marked the day by some change, little or big, for the better in the matter of attire. A Sabbath air pervaded the entire ship. The Evening Service was chanted quite acceptably in the crowded synagogue by the director of Ann Arbor Hillel, Bernard Heller, a number of his American colleagues being present, including Stern of Montreal and Fram of Detroit. After the Morning Service, the young pilgrims urged me to speak to them. I answered that I was bound for Palestine to learn and not to teach. A compromise was reached, they being free to ask questions on problems of common interest. And they did, with a vengeance, for two hours, until at last Rabbi Fram mercifully interceded on my behalf and I was permitted to go in peace, after most searching queries: Why have I spoken as I did in unsparing condemnation of Revisionism; Why no World Jewish Congress session this year; what can be done with Polish Jewry; whom did I favor for Presidency of the Jewish Agency; if Ben Gurion, why; if not Weizmann, why not? One young man, something of a zealot, personable, attractive, aflame, will be a real figure in Palestine life, perhaps supply what it needs, a compelling leadership to the religious hosts. The young people had been visibly affected and influenced. Faith and recent training had begun to do their work. As one looked upon them straightening out and up from under their ghetto burdens, and noted them joyously lifting up their heads and straining their eyes to catch a first glimpse of Eretz Israel, one recalled the precious word of Theodor Herzl: "Zionism must transform *arme Judenjungen* into *stolze junge Juden*." As one looked upon these youths, in the joy of their quest, one was moved to pray that these might be worthy of their pilgrimage and equal to their tasks and trials.

Perhaps nothing better illustrates the passionateness of the pursuit of the Palestinian Home than the circumstance that in addition to tourist and third-class, there is a so-called fourth-class, made up of passengers without rooms or berths, permitted to sleep under the stars. One such "Fourth-Class Passenger" family was the delight of most of their fellow-passengers. Mother and five children, Krull by name, including three pale-faced ringletted lads of ten, seven and five, always together though they had not learned how to play; the oldest an admirable, thoughtful boy who turned the tables in answer to my question "Would you like to become a Rabbi?" with the answer, *"A ehrlicher Yid will ich weren."* When pictures were taken of the brothers and a passenger sought to expose the "Arba Kanfot" of the youngest, the eldest forbade *"Es passt sech nicht."* Some of us learned that the family was without food, except for dry bread. We offered to purchase whatever food they might need. The Captain would not permit this, and supplied every want from the enviably superior Kosher cuisine. We sent them on their way rejoicing, with a sizable purse made up by a number of us, to the husband and father in Haifa.

All that we felt on the boat with regard to our young Jewish fellow passengers was intensified by a glimpse we caught at old Brindisi of Italy's young soldiery "marching as to war." Italians to slay and be slain in Ethiopia in order that more Italians may ultimately be born in the blood-conquered territory. How Brindisi itself had changed since 1913—hangars and sea-planes dominating the lovely city, and a striking huge memorial to the Nation's sailor dead. Oh, the menace of a nationalism wholly in the service of an economic imperialism, which disregards the elementary rights of lesser peoples; Ethiopia a pawn in the game of the so-called great powers.

On the second and third days of the journey, we sailed close to the Greek Isles and stayed at Cyprus long enough to hear the tale of woe of a dozen Jews, transhipped to Cyprus from Palestine by the Government, which denied them admission. On the eve of landing in Jaffa an Armenian teacher, M., formerly of Beirut and New York, knowing of my devotion to the Armenian cause, before, dur-

ing and after the war, graciously offered me a letter of
introduction to the Armenian Katholikos in Jerusalem,
of which, unhappily, I could not make use. We reminisced
about Armenian hopes and dreams. He had not heard
previously of President Wilson's profound concern over
the Armenian people, which moved him to say to me,
upon several occasions at the White House, for the last
time after the notable interview of Mack, Marshall and
myself together with other representatives of the Amer-
ical Jewish Congress, "Rabbi Wise, Armenia will be
Christian, Palestine will be Jewish!" Alas, that the former
half of his prophecy is unfulfilled; as for the latter half,
I was now to see for myself whether any real progress had
been made toward the fulfillment of the prophecy of one,
who in all the years of his presidential office cherished no
privilege higher than that of furthering the restoration
of the Jewish people to the Jewish land.

Monday, July 15, 1935.

THE LAST night aboard was most thrilling. For hours on
end the Chalutzim danced their joyous Hora—singing as
they danced, usually some half-ironical, half-defiant song
such as "Israel lives an Eternal People, though we have
troubles enough." One youth to whom I have already
alluded, broke loose from the ring of the Hora, and stayed
with me long enough to make clear, "Avodah is not
enough; there must be Torah, too." Work without the
law is not enough. Or, tilling the fields without study of
the Torah will not give back to us the land of Israel. A
few supporters surrounded him but there were genial
scoffers who laughingly shouted, "He will soon be one of
us, Poale-Zion, and he'll leave the Torah to the Rab-
bonim." A soul afire burnt through his zealot's eyes, as he
shouted "Lo, Lo, Lo"—the Hebrew for "No, Never."

The Gerusalemme was scheduled to arrive at Jaffa by six in the morning. Up before daybreak to catch the earliest possible glimpse of The Land which I had not seen since the summer of 1922. The coastline for forty or fifty miles moving southward to Jaffa is enchanting. At last we reached Jaffa, which remains the port though overshadowed by neighboring Tel-Aviv. We quietly descended into the waiting boat, instead of being dumped as we were in 1913, having been met by most courteous and helpful immigration representatives of the Jewish Agency, The Jewish National Fund, and the Tourist Information Bureau, Messrs. Gordon, Epstein and Schachnai.

At long last, after thirteen years of impatient waiting, we were in Palestine once again. Some moments at the Immigration Office where I looked for our youthful steamer comrades, but nearly all of them were bound for Haifa, which they would reach by late afternoon. Rushed to Madame Moschowitz' Pension, where together with our hosts, we hurriedly breakfasted on home grown fruits, milk and honey—only the tea and sugar being imported. A passing glimpse of Tel-Aviv, as we motored through the town on our way to Jerusalem. When first we went from Jaffa to Jerusalem in 1913, it was by train; in 1922 we went by train from Alexandria via Kantora-Lud; in 1935, over a perfect road, we motored in little more than an hour from Tel-Aviv to Jerusalem in a car emblazoned with the (Dodge) Shield of David.

Sunday, July 14, 1935.

IN THE OLD DAYS, the first thing which even a semi-pious Jew did upon reaching Palestine was to recite *Shehehhianu*. In the new day one's primary privilege, or obligation upon touching Jerusalem, I was solemnly informed, was to enter one's name in the Book of Visitors at Government House. That formality over, one is free, formally or informally, to wend one's way through the unforgettable old and the undreamed of new sections of Jerusalem. We were to be privileged to get a good though in part hurried impression of Palestine plus a glimpse of Syria. We were to look upon the indisputable miracle of Tel-Aviv, to be thrilled by the splendor that is Haifa, with its explicable appeal to the artist in Herzl who chose Carmel as his place of burial, we were to be fascinated by the utterly exotic charm of Damascus which struck me like a Hollywood imitation of Jerusalem. But Jerusalem still stands and will, I believe, forever stand alone. Best of all the city, which has trebled its population in a decade, has not lost its old-time loveliness. A myriad changes and additions have not affected its mystic uniqueness. The city set upon a hill still remains the standard by which to measure every other city of famed beauty, whether it be Italian Florence or Spanish Toledo or pre-Nazi Nuremberg or Austrian Salzburg or Galician Cracow or Lithuanian Vilna. Anyone who can walk from Bethlehem to Jerusalem without lifting tear-dimmed eyes to the hills of Zion, whence help and salvation have come to humankind as from no other source, is made of sterner stuff than the writer.

Not having seen Jerusalem in thirteen years, it was not easy to get one's bearings outside the "Old City," the Enwalled City. One remembered the old Montefiore mill and house, and the Rothschild Hospital and the transformed King David Street, and the slightly improved Meah Shearim, but all else was new and arresting. And I rejoiced to learn that despite everything the general appearance of Jerusalem, if not unchanged, is largely unspoiled. I wonder whether much of the credit for this is not due to the work of General Storrs, who strove valiantly and effectively to keep the old city inviolate. Upon visit-

ing New York some years ago, he telephoned to my home
in the terms, "Pontius Pilate offers his greetings to
'Caiaphas'." "Caiaphas" knew at once that the only successor of Pontius Pilate who could have been guilty of
that delightful insolence was General Ronald Storrs.

Some of the Jewish suburbs are somewhat disturbing
because they affect overmuch that dry-goods-box style of
architecture, which seems to a lover of the Norman and
Gothic in architectural art to be Germany's gravest pre-
Hitler blot upon civilization. I noted immediately that a
considerable number of stately mansions were to be seen
dotting the circumambient hills of Jerusalem. Upon inquiry I learned that these were Arab homes, homes of the
Effendis. I cannot remember a single home of spacious-
ness or distinction or showiness which is owned by a Jew.
This was only the first of many indices of the vastly improved economic status of the resident Arabs of Palestine.
The poor Arab workers or fellaheen live under incredibly
improved conditions since the advent of the Jewish tens
of thousands and since the money of Jewish settlers has
poured itself into the coffers of the land-owning Arabs, for
whom the convenient description of "displaced Arabs"
has in hostile fashion been invented. These Jewishly-en-
riched Arabs supply the sinews of war to the Arab agita-
tors against Jewish settlers.

The rest of the morning I spent at the office of the Jewish Agency, the only as yet impressive Jewish structure in
Jerusalem. Brief chats with George Landau, associated
with our beloved Henrietta Szold in the direction of the
German-Jewish Youth Aliyah; Leib Joffe, fine of face and
spirit, the head together with Hantke of the Keren Hayesod; Moshe Shertok, gifted and modest Under-secretary
of Political Affairs, faithful and indispensable co-adjutor
alike of Arlosoroff and Ben Gurion; and, finally, Dr.

Ruppin, who looks like an owl and has more than an
owl's reputed wisdom. I came to him with a score of problems pressing upon my heart. His sage counsel was, "Forget problems and see Palestine. Give yourself the joy of
looking upon the land and its people and their achievements and forget all problems until you return to America
or at least until you reach the Zionist Congress." I followed his counsel. From that moment I tried to see Palestine not as a partisan nor yet as a critic nor yet, what was
impossible, as a care-free tourist, but as a measurably dispassionate observer eager to see what, since 1922, had under the British Mandate been wrought by our fellow-Jews.

A DAIRY luncheon in a surprisingly delightful tea-shop,
Cos Al The, and after luncheon we went back to one of
our favorite places in Jerusalem, the Tombs of the Kings,
which has rather changed for the worse, having become
since we had been there an admission-paid quasi-museum
antiquity. But perhaps these changes must be, in the light
of the startling growth of Jerusalem from the city we first
knew twenty and more years ago. Hunted at a near-by
American pottery for some additional pieces of such pottery as we had come upon there in 1922 at the then High
Commissioner's home, but the simple, imperfectly glazed
withal exquisite pottery was nowhere to be found, re-
placed by a more or less conventionalized porcelain without a trace of the simple art of the potter.

Motored to Mt. Scopus, some ten or twelve minutes
drive past the war cemetery and the really impressive War
Memorial and, after that, by the site of the new Hadassah-
Rothschild Hospital, heritage from that Jewish prince,
Baron Edmund de Rothschild, and to be the work very
largely of the American Jewish Physicians Committee
working in conjunction with the Hebrew University and

Hadassah. Hadassah is itself the finest contribution of Jewish women in America to the service of their people and American Jewry's finest contribution to the upbuilding of Palestine. What vision and what daring to take over the old city hospital and plan a new, large, modern hospital which is to include a medical school within earshot of the University of which it is to become a part. May the site prove to be ample enough, as hospital sites rarely do, and may the titles to the land prove to be secure and unchangeable!

And at last, nearly twelve years after its founding, I was rewarded with a glimpse of the Hebrew University. I remember to have heard it discussed at Basle in 1898 and even before that by one of the earliest of its dreamers, Israel Abrahams, beloved successor to Schechter at Cambridge. Here it was only a beginning but not without the dignity of lofty promise. I chanced to meet a Pittsburgh friend, Morris Neaman, busily engaged in choosing or affirming the choice of a site for the Rosenbloom Memorial, in memory of the late Sol Rosenbloom, one of the earliest and most generous friends of the Hebrew University, especially its Institute of Jewish studies—for Rosenbloom, in whose memory the Hall is to be dedicated, was representative of the old-fashioned Jewish merchant-scholar, who never permitted worldly affairs to interfere with a life-long interest in Jewish learning. An admirable site, as indeed the whole of the University site is commanding. From its summit one looks westward to the Mediterranean, the city of Jerusalem at its feet, and eastward to far-off lonely Moab beyond the Dead Sea. I did not try to see the University buildings, knowing that I should have further opportunity to do so in the company of its Chancellor, drove back to the Damascus gate that we might have the long awaited joy of treading the narrow

paths of the inner city, which for one who loves it is
Jerusalem.

Our walk through the crowded, colorful lanes was in-
terrupted as an Arab guide sought to be helpful. I was
about to free myself from his persistent attentions and
intentions when a little Jewish lad called to me in Hebrew, "Don't let him accompany you. He will take you to
Christian, not to Jewish places." A miniature Arab-
Jewish battle would have ensued had I not succeeded in
shaking off both simultaneously with the help of quite
conscienceless Baksheesh.

The day was brought to a close with a quiet chat at the
King David Hotel, immeasurably superior to the old
Allenby-Fast Hostelry of former visits, with the intellec-
tually sprightly young editor of the *Palestine Post*, Ger-
shon Agronsky, formerly of the Jewish Telegraphic Agency. The *Post* is the only English daily in Palestine and is so
good that I shall manage to read it regularly in New York
upon my return. Agronsky has a thorough and even rare
understanding of the problems of Palestine, is widely
informed without being pedantic or oppressive.

Our first day in Palestine was done. It was all too thrilling to permit of sleep, so that the sleepless hours of the
first night gave opportunity for review of things seen and
heard. Nor did the habit of a life-time of early rising ever
serve me better, who day after day arose to behold the sun
rise from below Moab's horizon and gild the city of a
thousand dreams with the austere gold of dawn. I recalled
in the still watches of the night a sage word of Dr. Ruppin,
"I have always been against this talk of majorities. Within four years our Jewish population in Palestine has
increased from 175,000 to more than 350,000 and by the
end of the year, we should have nearly 400,000 and," he
added in coldly precise fashion, "unless somehow we are

impeded or interfered with, the next Zionist Congress two years hence should mark more than half a million Jews in Palestine, one-third of the total population." And I recalled as he spoke Justice Brandeis' ceaseless insistence in 1918 and 1919, "We must have 100,000 Jews in Palestine," and Dr. Weizmann's still more modest figure in December, 1918, in London in reply to a searching question leveled at him by de Haas, "I envisage a normal annual increase for the next ten years of five thousand."

Truly men build better than they know. When I added that we might well consider my proposal at the Zionist Congress of 1927 which Weizmann had rejected out of hand, namely that a Commission to be made up of Government representatives and ourselves review the bases of relationship between the Mandatory Government and the Jewish people, Ruppin dryly said, with his air of indisputable finality, "We are still suffering evil results from the work of the Survey Commission of 1927." I recalled, too, what Shertok had in our brief conversation said about the proposed or threatened Legislative Council. He outlined the plans in strictest confidence but there was no secret about his firm and well-considered objections, with which I am persuaded the High Commissioner cannot be unfamiliar. What is to happen after the Enactment it is not well to seek to forecast, but I cannot see how the Jewish population can adopt any course other than that of non-co-operation with respect to the Council, however loyally Palestine Jewry continue to co-operate in every other respect with the Mandatory Government.

In the course of my address at the Zionist Congress, I shall say: "Non-co-operation re the Legislative Council is not breaking with the Mandatory Power. A Legislative Council whensoever it may have been promised, was and is a violation of the spirit of the Balfour Declaration. It

has regard solely to the spirit of a subordinate and quali-
fying amendment, to the letter rather than the heart of
that Declaration. Putting it crudely and undiplomatic-
ally, we to whom England made a solemn pledge are compelled by the Legislative Council proposal to pay the
price of a new arrangement of Great Britain with her
Arab subjects, chiefly outside of Palestine."

I INTERRUPT the publication of my diary narrative of last
Summer's Palestine visit, because I feel moved to put to
paper some thoughts suggested by the final announcement, if final it be, of the establishment of the Palestine
Legislative Council.

The Legislative Council is even more significant as
symptom than as event. The gnawing pains which herald
carcinoma are not deadly in themselves but ominous of
fatal changes in the metabolism of the sufferer. The Legislative Council, however evil its consequences are to
prove, is of gravest portent because it tokens an appalling
maladjustment of relations between the Mandatory
Power and the Jewish people with whom rather than with
Jews in Palestine, the Balfour Covenant was made. In the
earliest days of the British military occupation, the lack of
accord between Downing Street professions and Government practices proved startling to a most distinguished
American visitor. Personally debarred by his high office
from formal intervention, the difficulty was nonetheless
shortly thereafter dealt with vigorously and the Palestine
military officials were made to feel that they were not
quite free to reverse in daily practice the decisions of the
Foreign Office.

Whether the High Commissioner is responsible for the
actual summoning to life of the still-born Legislative
Council of the Winston Churchill-Herbert Samuel pro-

gram, or whether it be true that Government House is doing the will of the Colonial Office, or whether the Colonial office and Government House together are executing the "larger policies" of the Foreign Office must remain purely conjectural. The important and lamentable thing is that Britain's partner in the great Palestine enterprise, the Jewish people, is *not consulted* but *merely informed* about purposes and programs which are of deepest consequence to the Jewish National Home. The High Commissioner is urbanity itself up to the Summer months, in dealing with the representatives of the Jewish Agency, notably Ben Gurion and Moshe Shertok. But the Council was virtually *accompli* before any High Commissioner's courteous conversations with these representatives of the Jewish Agency Executive.

In many ways, the Mandatory Government has deserved the co-operation of the Jewish people in and out of Palestine and has gained such full and unreserved co-operation beyond its deserving. The never-failing courtesy of the High Commissioner in personal relations with members of the Agency Executive does not alter the fact that the course pursued in perfecting and formulating the Legislative Council plans would have been virtually the same if there had been no Balfour Declaration and no League of Nations Mandate. It must not for a moment be overlooked that, much as Jews have gained, Britain has gained far more. We have gained through infinite effort that which England has solemnly declared to be our own "of right and not by sufferance." While England has achieved a precious foothold on the England-India overland passage which strengthens its hold on Suez and at the same time makes it less dependent for communications and security upon the Canal. Moreover, Britain has gained a new dependency or Mandated colony which is not only completely self-supporting but by reason of Jewish investment of capital and effort, immensely profitable in every way to the British Empire, and not least among the imponderables is the good-will of an essentially loyal people whose gratitude outruns every present or prospective favor.

PEERING below the surface of things, there are personal factors in the equation, neutralized in the case of exceptional personalities such as Marshall Plumer, General Clayton, Sir Wyndham Deedes and General Sir Arthur Wauchope, which it is unwise and even unsafe to ignore. And the very virtue of the British is here involved and tends to injure the Jewish dwellers in Palestine. With certain striking exceptions, the British deal with native populations in such a way as to do justice and to merit goodwill. But those populations are native and they are (or must be) ruled. Jews are not natives in Palestine: they are, to improvise a term, ex-natives. Arabs seem native, though great hosts of them have trekked into Palestine from neighboring lands in recent decades. If Jews in Palestine, apart from the fifty thousand who pre-date the war, were profit-seeking visitors to Palestine bent upon speediest self-enrichment and earliest return to other lands, certain British attitudes would be explicable. Or if Jews were coming to Palestine to exploit Arab labor whilst leading lives of ease and leisure, certain things were understandable. Or if the status of the Arabs were steadily falling while personal Jewish fortunes were mounting, the British sense of fair play might well be roused in behalf of the Arabs.

None of these things is true. Instead of that Jews have enriched, indeed recreated the land, have vastly benefited the Arab and Christian populations, have brought back to life and strength an outworn land which had become half-museum and half-battlefield. No free men have ever labored more faithfully and steadfastly than have the earlier and later Chalutzim of Palestine so that there is no reason for thinking of exploited Arab and exploiting Jew. In many ways particularly in relation to land purchases, the Jew has been ruthlessly exploited.

Officials in Palestine must cease to view and to treat the Jewish settlers in and of Palestine as if they were European invaders and exploiters. They are exiles suffered to return to the land, access to which had been denied them throughout the centuries. They return to their land neither themselves to possess nor yet to dispossess others, but to rebuild the Homeland for which they are ready to make every sacrifice including, if it must be, that of life itself.

Much might be said of the tragic homelessness of the returning Jewish pilgrims. But, I doubt not, England took account of this item of such Jewish homelessness, though in 1917 it had not begun to reach its present tragic proportions. Unhappily for them, Jews are too much regarded by British officialdom as if they had come for a pleasure jaunt or a business expedition. They are pre-Arab natives of the land whom the nations of the world under the leadership of Great Britain resolved in the spirit of the World War Allies to restore to their never-surrendered national home.

And there is something that goes deeper still. Even holding in abeyance the debatable term State, Great Britain does not deal with Jews on the level of nationhood. If there be objection to the term, let us substitute nationality. Paradoxically enough, ours is in British eyes neither the favored status of a native population nor yet the position of a people with whom covenanted arrangements must be scrupulously observed. In a word, the curse of the ghetto is upon us even in Palestine. What we there are and have and seek to be depends too largely upon the good- or ill-will of an alien sovereign power, and there has been in the past too much assent on our part to such inferior status on the part of Jews. If Palestine is to be another land in which decisions can be reached for Jews apart from their own will and decision, then the Jewish National Home becomes no more than a taunting mockery. Far beyond the importance of being afflicted or unafflicted with a Legislative Council, which is the setting up of an instrumentality of racial unrest, is the need for Jews reaching an understanding with the Mandatory Power. And the understanding must embrace these facts: Jews are not a group of foreign and competing traders in Palestine; Jews are not in Palestine to serve the political or military or fiscal needs of Britain; Jews are in Palestine of historic right, recognized and confirmed by the nations of earth. Colonial Office and Government House must alike see that the time has come to end the policy from which the Legislative Council derives, the policy which every six months deals in insultingly niggardly fashion with the catastrophic needs of Jewish immigration, which in a word fails to recognize the Jewish partner in the Palestine enterprise, avowedly undertaken by Britain to the end that at last Jews might there have a Jewish National Home.

— 1935

Palestine — After Forty Years

PALESTINE—after forty years—is not to be measured by the increase of nearly four hundred thousand in its Jewish population nor yet by the investment of more than forty or even twice forty million Pounds in its Jewish development. It must be viewed and evaluated in a wholly different way with reference to the life of world Jewry which made Zionism possible, with reference to world affairs which have been profoundly affected and even altered by Zion's rise and development.

The compelling genius of Herzl is clearly revealed in the single circumstance that twenty years after his appearance upon the Jewish horizon, the Balfour Declaration was issued. That is to say, on behalf of the British War Cabinet, Balfour urged the Declaration of Britain's purpose to facilitate the establishment of the Jewish National Home in Palestine. Such was the persuasiveness of his appeal and the persuasiveness of his influence that it may in a very real sense be said that Herzl guided and inspired the deliberations of Weizmann, Samuel Tschlenow, Greenberg, Gaster, in London as well as their American associates under the radiant leadership of Brandeis. Out of this evolved the declaration of British purpose strengthened by the then indispensable American support. And at the Paris Peace Table again Palestine not only stood in the foreground of the minds of the real leaders, America's Woodrow Wilson, England's Lloyd George and France's Clemenceau, but it had come to be felt that no settlement of world affairs could be permanent that left out of account the fate of a weirdly backward land and the destiny of its grotesquely homeless people. Indeed, some of the world's leading statesmen have not hesitated to express their conviction that the Peace Treaties' concern with and solution of the Palestine problem was one of the major achievements of the Paris Peace Conference.

What has happened since the Peace Conference and England's assumption of the Mandate which, one remains ready to assume, England sought and accepted on the grounds of international polity and obligation as well as for safeguarding of imperial interests. In the nearly twenty years that have elapsed since the acceptance of the Mandate, our fellow Jews have wrought an incredible miracle in every sense of development, and one grieves to add all this has been done in the main with a minimum of help and that minimal help grudgingly and unhandsomely extended by the Mandatory Government. Some of the British pro-consuls in Palestine, most especially Lord Plumer, and with the exception of Chancellor, have not been unfriendly in executing the terms of the mandate. But in a time of plain speaking, let it be recorded that all that Jewish devotion and toil and genius have wrought in Palestine has been almost wholly in the despite of British Palestine officialdom, which almost uniformly thwarted the Jewish rebuilders of Palestine and made their day by day work one of difficulty and irritation.

OPINION lays down two incontrovertible truths though there may follow the gnashing of the teeth of Syrian poets in Massachusetts and Colonial officials in Whitehall and in Government House, Jerusalem, and though Zionist officials, too, tremble, become nervous over our plain-speaking: The Jewish resettlement of Palestine up to this day has by and large wrought much for the Arabs, unbelievably much and ever more for the British. With Britain virtually out of Egypt, Haifa created anew by the labor and investment of Jewish pilgrims, becomes the major East-Mediterranean port of the Empire. But this is only one of a multitude of benefits conferred upon the Mandatory power by a people who transformed an arid waste into a populous, profitable dominion, almost alone among governments in having for years an annual surplus in its treasury. The Arabs of the long time Turkish colonies of Palestine have been politically liberated, educationally benefited, economically advantaged, by the settlement in the midst of Palestine of hundreds of thousands of Jews bringing with them for the most part the standards and the ways of life of Central and Western Europe.

Why then all the alarm? And why the endless clashing of viewpoints, British, Arab, Jewish? Because Britain seems prepared to foreswear itself if rumor be true, because in order to find a way out which would be the most colossal of all blunders, England seems to be prepared to say at one and the same time to Arabs and Jews—Arabs who at this hour after twenty years have rejected the Balfour Declaration, and to Jews, who for twenty years have creatively and beneficently settled the land—"A plague on both your houses."

That is what Partition or Division or Cantonization of Palestine means. It means scuttling, it means the easiest way out for today, that is bound to become the hardest and impossible way on the morrow. It means that the Colonial Office and its lesser traditions usurp the place of Balfour and deal with world Jews as if we were an invasive and troublesome group in Palestine instead of being its rightful rebuilders. Woe unto Britain, mighty though Britain be, if, foreswearing its solemnly plighted guarantee, Britain bear itself after the fashion of the Germany of 1914 and reduce a sacred obligation to a scrap of paper. Britain may imagine that dealing with a world in chaos it may disregard public opinion and the finer scruples of mankind, but let England understand that the Jewry of 1937 is not the Jewry of 1897; the spirit of Herzl has ruled for forty years, that Spirit which has transformed the desert of Palestine into the glory of Zionism. Let Britain understand that because of Theodor Herzl the Jews are no longer a disunited and incoherent mass of suppliants for relief, that because of Herzl there has come to Israel a consciousness of oneness, a sense of coherence, of unity of purpose with which England must reckon in the hour of Israel's greatest need.

Let the Fortieth Annual Convention of the Zionist Organization of America proclaim: That the Israel which faltered not in an hour without hope, will not yield one jot or tittle of its rightful aims and claims in this hour. Britain is a mighty empire, but there are forces in the universe mightier and more enduring than empire or dynasty. Without empty boast and without vain threat, let the historic Fortieth Convention of the Zionist Organization of America make clear that it will never assent to any denial of our inalienable and uncancellable rights to Jewish Palestine. Empires live in the terms of centuries. Millenia have witnessed Israel's suffering and shall yet crown the triumph of Israel's hope.

— 1937

Appeasement Over Palestine

OPINION has no desire to appear unduly belligerent, but it feels justified in serving notice on behalf of the Jewish people that, if the Prime Minister's word is, heaven forefend, to be the last word to be spoken in regard to Palestine by the Mandatory Power, then grave will be the ultimate consequences. Easy enough for people who dwell at ease outside of Zion to disparage the radicalism of those who speak of self-defense in Zion. But the ultimate truth is that if the Mandatory Power should so foreswear its primary and ultimate obligation as to say to Jews, when the 75,000 mark of immigration shall have been reached —"The Jewish National Home is completed; the University is established; the Philharmonic functions; no further Jewish immigration will be permitted!"—woe betide Palestine and Britain, and, one is almost tempted to add, at the risk of seeming rhetorical, honor itself!

Nothing could be clearer than that the 1939 White Paper was just as truly an item of appeasement as the Munich agreement between Chamberlain and Hitler. The analogy may be further pursued. Hitler, with whom Chamberlain drew the covenant, came to war upon Europe and civilization. The Grand Mufti and his Irakian and Egyptian fellow conspirators, at whose bidding the White Paper was drawn, joined and fought by the side of the Axis Powers. But the White Paper agreement with these forces of evil stands, and only some miracle of grace or shame is needed to restore them to that power which enabled them to harass and bedevil the populations of Palestine.

Tho *havlagah*—perfect self-restraint and limitless self-control—obtained during the bitter years of Arab assaults on Palestine after '36, the Mandatory Power dare not count upon the same mood. A people capable of self-restraint when called upon to sacrifice its primary right to life and to the things which make life good and honorable, is not fit to live. Let those who are fearful of Jewish outbreak and violence in the Spring of '44 appeal to the Prime Minister and President not to permit this crime of appeasement to be carried to its ultimate and devastating conclusion. England has not sovereign power in Palestine. The Mandatory Power has nothing more than the responsibility of trusteeship. However sickening has been the moral malfeasance of the Colonial Office underlings in the last twenty years, no one who respects England—as the writer does—can believe that England will stoop to the shame of carrying out its covenant with the Grand Mufti at the price of civil conflict. For such there will be in Palestine. English bullets might for a time prevail in that conflict. The responsibility will rest not with them that revolt but with a government which moves from

the shame of the White Paper to the crime of its enforcement. Let America bethink itself, quite apart from the
obligation which Winston Churchill owes his word of
1923, his word which was a deed in 1939.

— 1943

Cancel the White Paper

THERE may be some Zionists thoughtless enough to hail
with approval the recent statement in the House of Commons by the Colonial Secretary that there will not be, as
there might have been, an immediate enforcement of the
White Paper March 31, 1944, but that after due consideration, and out of considerations of equity, the Government
had decided to postpone the White Paper's deadline on
Jewish immigration into Palestine, and allow the entry of
31,000 Jews, the remainder of the total of 75,000 permitted to enter the country within the five-year period to
terminate in March. In other words, excepting for the
extension of the time period, the White Paper is to go into
effect as scheduled, and without any regard to what has
happened from 1933 to 1939, and from 1939 to 1943—
namely, throughout the pre-war years, which saw the beginning of Jewish dislocation and exile whithersoever
Hitlerism could reach out, and throughout the unutterable war years, which have seen Jews uprooted from all
of Europe, save from England and Russia. It is only fair
to acknowledge that the English Government has performed an act of elementary decency in postponing the
deadline, though the failure on the part of the English
Government to be equal to this elementary courtesy
would have been regarded as a grave moral breach by
civilized individuals and nations throughout the world.

The statement by the Colonial Secretary offers no solu-

tion of a not insoluble problem. It is not the time factor
which is at stake. Things eternal are at stake; things which
cannot be timed are at stake—the honor of the British
Government; the uncancellable right of the Jew to regain
Palestine as his National Home; the pledge implicit and
explicit of the Balfour Declaration, of the Britain of Balfour's day, to the Jew, since confirmed by the British Mandate and ratified by the approval and the conscience of the
British people. The White Paper must be cancelled.
There is no other way. The White Paper means much
more than limitations affecting Jewish settlers in Palestine. It involves inhibitions with regard to land purchase.
It means the impossibility of Jews coming to be the majority population of the land. The White Paper uncan-
celled will be a deathblow to the Jewish National Home.

Moreover, it must be said, an England which is politically realistic surely understands that the way to bring
about strife and bloodshed in Palestine is to say to the
Yishuv, as Secretary Stanley virtually does, that after these
31,000 Jews have entered into Palestine, its doors will be
shut to Jews. This can never be! Jews will die in and for
Palestine, but they will not be denied the right to enter
Palestine. England knows it; the Arabs know it; and the
Arabs will accept it when England once gives assurance
of her willingness not only to cancel the White Paper,
which cancellation is not enough, but to give to the Jew
the right implicit in the Balfour Declaration to establish
the Jewish National Home.

— 1943

IV

Contemporaries and Comrades

Julius Rosenwald

JULIUS ROSENWALD was the first American Jew to have given in wide and catholic fashion. Schiff gave thoughtfully to Jewish causes and with measured generosity to non-Jewish causes. Nathan Straus gave much more wisely than men imagined it to be possible for this impulsive and great-hearted lover of mankind to give, who gave out of limited means but with unmeasured love.

The Rosenwald philanthropies grew and developed in rather close imitation of the Rockefeller-Carnegie patterns. We have heard it said that most American picture collectors begin with a Gerome and end with a Greco, or begin with a Bouguereau and end with a Botticelli. Rosenwald began bravely on his own with untiring personal effort in the federating of Chicago's Jewish charities; at the end came the Rosenwald Foundations.

Rosenwald did big things in a big way, princely, in truth, with nothing less than princely generosity. The Chicago Industrial Museum will yet prove an enriching asset to the Chicago of tomorrow. He set the example of ample giving for Jewish causes such an European Relief Work under Jewish Distribution Committee auspices and the dubious adventure of Russian colonization. He set the example, but none among American Jewish multi-millionaires so rich as to do him the homage of emulation.

Now that Rosenwald's life is beyond the reach of human praise and his remembrance is sure, it is meet to consider a singular aspect of a career of almost ecumenical benevolence. One thinks of the appeal of Henry V to his soldiers lest one find it needful to say "I was not there." For Rosenwald's time has witnessed the birth and rise and even coming to fruition of the finest of Jewish enterprises —and Rosenwald was not there. It is not quite true to say that he chose not to be there. The choice was made for him, in large part, by the influence of Jewish Reform theology and theologians. This theology long insisted upon the least troubling of the Jewish differentiae, namely Monotheism, and it denied the core and center of Israel's being, namely the changeless hope of Israel's life in Israel's land. This lamentable impact of Reform Judaism made for minimum Jewishness outside of the Synagogue and by contrast for exaggerated Americanism at all times.

Baron Edmund de Rothschild beyond all others has been the sustaining furtherer of Jewish colonization in Palestine. To his great work Nathan Straus added a colorful and personal touch. Schiff was wrestling with the problem of Palestine when he passed. To put it more accurately, Palestine was taking hold upon the Jewish heart and imagination of Schiff—but it was too late.

For reasons which are not without parity, the eyes of Baron de Hirsch and Julius Rosenwald were turned from Palestine. De Hirsch gazed upon a far-off South American land, safe and fruitful as it seemed in comparison with the more daring enterprise of Palestine. Rosenwald was captivated and captured by amateur but enormously skillful publicity methods in behalf of Russo-Jewish colonization. Documentary evidence will yet avail to show that the astutest of the protagonists of this colonization were more concerned about Russia than about Jews. The record is closed. And Jewish effort even in Russia goes bravely and unweariedly on in the direction of Palestine. Let a poll today be taken of the non-Communist Jews in Soviet Russia and the vast majority of them would, if free, choose to betake themselves to Palestine.

And Palestine will yet be rebuilt! Blessed are they who will have claimed a part in its rebuilding. That amid

Rosenwald's vast and unnumbered generosities no place was found for the Palestine ideal is indeed cause for sorrow. For Rosenwald was much more than a merely dutiful and unimaginative giver. He faced the problems of Negro education, housing, and hospitalization with wisdom and statesmanship; he met them with generosity and consecration of purpose. Would for his own sake that Rosenwald had known the ineffable joy of helping his homeless people homeward, once again to serve, to create, to bless, after the inevitable tradition of land and people together.

— 1932

A Jew Speaks

FEW LIVING men find themselves "anthologized." For an anthology, like beatification, is almost of necessity a post-mortem testimonial. And even fewer solely literary figures are "crowned" with an anthology, which, when awarded to the living, ordinarily aims to transmute the ephemera of non-literary figures into literature. And yet, despite the usage of anthologies, one is not surprised to come upon an attempt to bring together what the compiler and editor of "A Jew Speaks" calls the Jewish writings of Ludwig Lewisohn.

It may be that another anthology might be made up of other aspects of the genius of Lewisohn. But this anthology has come upon the central and incontestable truth that through all the writings of Lewisohn it is a Jew that speaks. If there be any who have not closely followed Lewisohnia, they will rejoice to come in this volume upon as finely sustained and deeply significant Jewish writing as has come from any pen in decades.

This anthology is more than conpendium: it outlines

the evolution of a Jewish soul, of one who seemed almost
ready to be swallowed up by the seas of assimilation and,
after being tossed and buffeted about by the waves of
intellectual jingoism and spiritual chauvinism, has found
shelter rather than security in "The Island Within" of
his awakening Jewish consciousness. "A Jew Speaks"
shows forth the clarity of Lewisohn's understanding of
the Jewish problem and his little less than incredible
grasp of its intricacies and complexities. The compiler
stresses too strongly the autobiographical and introspec-
tive character of Lewisohn's writings. This is the innermost become the outermost, a process of inevitable identification with the thinking and feeling and questing of
his people, Israel.

Hence the work goes beyond mere anthology of the
Jewish writings of one man. It is *the* Jew who speaks, not
merely *a* Jew! The Jew become self-conscious, or Lewisohn become Jewishly self-conscious; the Jew neither
arrogant nor abashed, who feels as a Jew and sets down
without compromise or evasion what a Jew feels or ought
to feel. Not since Heine's "Reisebilder" has there been
written a more simply eloquent and passionately direct
utterance of the Jewish case than is to be found in these
pages.

George Eliot was moved by a Hamburg Jew, her husband Lewes, to react to the sombre and vivid pages of
Zunz and thereafter Daniel Deronda stepped upon the
stage of Jewish figures of fiction. The influence of the
body of the writings of Lewisohn will be found to be no
less meaningful and permanent. Not only will "The Last
Days of Shylock," on which the compiler has heavily
leaned, long live, but "A Jew Speaks" is destined, I believe, to endure as a source-book of Jewish understanding.
It is another Emek-he-Bachah, "Vale of Weeping"; but

these are the tears of one who sorrows not without hope or pride. The proud and stirring, withal Jewishly considerate, concept of Zion which is set down in these pages in Lewisohn's name is bound to have an invigorating and enduring effect upon Jewish life and thought. For our generation and indeed for generations, Lewisohn's name in pages that will live as poetry lives and because poetry lives, has made clear as has none other the viewpoint of the Jew—not retreating within the sheltered ease of a perhaps obsolescent sectary but eagerly claiming his part and lot in those processes of Jewish rebirth or remaking out of which is to evolve the Jew who finds himself and his soul.

— 1931

Mr. Justice Cardozo

TODAY I witnessed a scene that will long live in memory. The hall of the United States Supreme Court in Washington was crowded with members of the New York Bar, the families of the Judges of the Court, and a little group of folk weirdly reminiscent of the Portuguese Synagogue of New York. The Court entered, led by an almost martial figure, that of Chief Justice Hughes. Third to enter, though second in point of seniority, was Justice Brandeis, easily the most striking figure in the great procession. One seat remained unfilled, that vacated by Justice Holmes. To it, shifted by law of seniority to the extreme left of the Chief Justice's seat, all eyes were drawn.

But Judge Cardozo was not there, for he was standing at the foot of the tribunal. The Chief Justice arose and with characteristic briskness announced the appointment of Benjamin Nathan Cardozo as Associate Justice of the Court, and directed the Marshal to administer the oath

of office to him. Happily, the scene was not marred by a
perfunctory and mechanical reading of the oath. The
rich, slightly tremulous, silver-clear voice of Justice Cardozo rang out in what sounded less like a set oath than a
solemnly conceived affirmation of faith and purpose, "to
do equal right to the poor and to the rich." Another moment and the new Associate Justice of the Court had taken
his seat, and the Court addressed itself to its business.

It was a moment for high exultation, looking for the
first time upon Brandeis and Cardozo as members of the
same tribunal, beyond all question the foremost judicial
tribunal on earth. Brandeis, sitting at the side of the Chief
Justice, a deeply arresting figure, concealed rather than
framed by a too capacious robe! Brandeis, mighty advo-
cate of the people, a people's conscience and a people's
voice, of whom President Wilson had said to me in Paris
in answer to a suggestion I had made: "I need Brandeis
everywhere, but I must leave him somewhere!" Brandeis,
dedicating his unrivaled learning and the power of an extraordinary mind to the work of the Court, but reserving
something of the finest of his thinking and dreaming and
being for his people, his people's hope even more than his
people's need. Brandeis, whom intrenched power and its
minions of every kind including the academic had once
arrogantly and brutally sought to keep from a post threatening to its security!

And now—may it be for years to come—Cardozo is to
sit at his side, Cardozo, one of the few great products of
the Sephardic Jewish settlement in this country, that is,
the Spanish and Portuguese Jewish refugees, who three
centuries ago gave Spinoza to Holland and after a quarto-
millennial gap gave Cardozo to America. I thought of
Cardozo's forebears, exiled from Spain, and after ten generations and more, one of the sons of those exiled Spanish-

Portuguese Jews is called to its Supreme Court by the unanimous voice of a nation, in the remote continent which Spain had discovered and made possible as a home for men. And I mused that both Brandeis and Cardozo were *inevitable*. Brandeis, because Wilson, his fellow-Liberal, recognized the mettle of this man who is at one and the same time the jurist and the prophet; Cardozo, inevitable by common consent and nothing less than universal acclaim. Someone in Washington today, who would hardly be suspected of familiarity with Gilbert and Sullivan, described his unprecedented acclaim in the line of "Iolanthe" as "A frenzy of love and devotion."

The echoes of Cardozo's voice had barely died out as I looked upon that fine face again, and for the last time my glance reverted to Justice Brandeis. Brandeis and Cardozo! Two sons of a people that live by law, whose highest fealty is to Torah, the living, and liberating Law. And my revery was disturbed as a neighbor said, "Great for Cardozo, but greater for the President." And one of the wisest, noblest servants of the Republic made answer, "And greatest of all for the Supreme Court!"

— 1932

A Weirdly Unerring Youth

I HAVE a word of testimony to offer with respect to the case of Governor Fuller vs. Professor Frankfurter. That case did not arise from an attack by Professor Frankfurter when, at the Republican Convention of 1928, the name of Fuller was being considered for the office of Vice-President. The case arose when, upon the announcement of Governor Ely's unsought appointment of Professor Felix Frankfurter to the highest court of Massachusetts, Governor Fuller delivered himself of a wild harangue against

Professor Frankfurter. That harangue was so ludicrously extravagant as to be self-cancelling.

But Governor Fuller, it may be, does not stand alone. He is representative of a group whose sense of guilt, subconscious of course, re Sacco-Vanzetti inexorably moves them to cry out against him who beyond any other focused the attention of men upon the case. It was Frankfurter who made it impossible for Governor Fuller and his personally conducted commission to do away with these men without facing an intelligent and instructed public opinion. Stooping for a moment to the manners and the diction of former Governor Fuller, he "might have gotten away with the judicial murder" of Sacco-Vanzetti, had it not been for Felix Frankfurter. That is to say, Felix Frankfurter robbed the final act of the last shred of its pretended judicial character.

In the light of the testimony which has voluntarily been offered in unique appraisal of Frankfurter by some of the noblest minds of the nation, including Oliver Wendell Holmes, it seems quite unnecessary to adduce further testimony. But the bit of testimony which I offer is of some moment. It will be remembered that President Wilson commissioned Frankfurter to make a survey of the Mooney-Billings case in California. Shortly after the Frankfurter Commission's report which availed to avert the execution of Mooney, I was at the White House. President Wilson was speaking quite freely in characterization of the group of brilliant younger men who had entered the service of the departments at Washington. He alluded to Frankfurter's various and uniformly effective services in the War Department, summing up a characterization of affectionate portrayal in the world: "Frankfurter—a weirdly unerring youth."

Frankfurter's has been one of the finest minds at the

American Bar, which knows no braver heart than his. If pride in wrong-doing and fanatical passions fanned by the winds of sub-conscious guilt did not prevail, Massachusetts would rise up in grateful homage to Governor Ely for his high-minded courage in naming to the Supreme Court of the State one of the great lawyers of its history. All that is needed is that Governor Rolph add his less unamiable sibilence to that of Governor Fuller at the hearing of the Judicial Council of Massachusetts, which is empowered to approve or reject the nomination of Professor Frankfurter. This appointment ought to be regarded as Massachusetts' expiation. Frankfurter's vindication is bound up with no appointment, judicial or other. "This weirdly unerring youth," as President Wilson described his young friend, is no longer a youth. At fifty he has fully reached the maturity of his extraordinary powers of mind. He belongs to a very select company of the creative legal minds of the nation. Holmes and Brandeis, Cardozo and Learned Hand know him for one of their own. If his appointment be confirmed, such confirmation will mean grievous loss to the realm of legal study throughout the nation. Students and scholars of the law know and honor him as one of the greatest of law-teachers. Frankfurter is an awakener, an extraordinarily invigorating and effective spirit as a teacher of younger men.

The Judicial Council of Massachusetts is to face its test. It cannot subtract an iota from the stature of this intellectual and spiritual giant. It can, however, take a step in the direction of restoring the glory of that court which vanished with the passing of Holmes from its leadership.

— 1932

Judge Mack

ONE could hardly describe Judge Julian W. Mack as the
man whom nobody knows, but he might fairly be called
the man whom few really know but many deeply love.
Little known, despite an eminent career on the State and
Federal Bench and service beyond telling in a score of
causes for more than a generation! Little known, for he
has such genius for self-effacement, that of all the leaders
in American Jewish Life, Mack is the only one who is
not a prima donna. Little known, because, though most
men love to be president of something or other and hun-
grily covet the aura of leadership, Mack dislikes, indeed
truly detests, these actual or titular leaderships when
thrust upon him. Little known, because he thinks so continuously and admiringly of others, and so little save dep-
recatingly of self, that he has never quite come to his own
in any segment of the sphere of life. Little known, because
forever occupied with the task of furthering the fortunes
of friends or relieving the misfortunes of strangers!

Mack has a rich and various collection of nice passions
—law, work, friendship, young people, Zionism, education, liberalism. May "passions" fitly be used touching
this peculiarly dispassionate being? Yes! For every one of
these is a tremendous part of his life. He slights and ne-
glects none of them, though there are others who believe
that had he waived all else aside, he would not only be
famed as one of the best trial judges on the Federal Bench
but as one of the great jurists of our time.

Richly he serves through all of them. The law is perhaps his supreme passion. The law knows no truer ser-
vitor, and justice no truer priest. And what service he
rendered a generation ago in the Children's Court of
Chicago, which his understanding and forward-looking-

ness did most to create, and for two decades on one of the great courts of the nation! His judicial-mindedness is a matter of instinct re-enforced by self-discipline: It is ethical as well as intellectual. He can see more than both sides of a case. He envisions simultaneously six sides of a cube—a rather strabismic feat but not beyond his will and power.

Lest one imagine that Judge Mack is all sweetness and compassion, I must say that I have seen him rise—or fall —to volcanic rage. Never, it is true, against ineptness, of which he is perhaps a little too impatient, but often against untruthfulness. Lawyers and witnesses in his court have had occasion to plumb the profundities of his contempt for the liar. The fact is that unveracity acts upon him as the touch of the ivy leaf upon those susceptible to its poison. Untruth, insincerity, even deliberate inaccuracy have a toxic effect upon him in evoking the violence of his wrath. I have seen him not only flare up but blaze and flame with long-sustained wrath against the liar. Ecclesiastes' reassuring word that all men are liars does not seem to have habituated the soul of Mack to tolerance of untruth. This kindliest, friendliest of men can be Draconic in severity, but his terrible sternness is always against untruth and injustice. Unconsciously he obeys the Talmudic law—"Hate the sin, but not the sinner."

As for his liberalism, it is as real as everything about this basically genuine being. Liberals there are—and some of the best—who accept liberalism as an obligation of the educated and forward-looking man. Liberalism exerts no compulsion over him. It is the very breath of his being. His liberalism leads him intellectually and spiritually into strange and sometimes bizarre paths. But he is changelessly true to its gleam. There are more radical liberals than Mack, there are more vocal liberals, but there lives no more effective and truer liberal than he. That is,

if the liberal be the man who is open-minded, believes in
the reality of human advance, and welcomes every adventure of the human spirit in the direction of truer equality
and larger human liberties as something precious. And,
be it added, despite judicial place and judicial-mindedness, Mack's liberalism is not preserved *in vacuo*. Much
of his life and strength are spent in support of the causes
of liberalism, in day by day help to and heartening of its
advocates, in patient hearing of its prophets, in more than
generous help to its daring pioneers.

I CANNOT think of any German-Jew—an American eu-
phemism for a son of German-born parent or parents—(in
Mack's case, parent)—who has as completely liberated
himself from the prejudices which have dominated Jewry
in our life for two generations. And yet, this may not be
regarded as a virtue. His freedom herein is natural and
inevitable. Never was there room in his elsewise capacious
being for racial prejudice or sectarian dogmatism or national chauvinism or social "airishness." I know no Jew in
America of German descent who is as completely oblivi-
ous to the idiotically arbitrary lines drawn between East
and West-European Jewry, chiefly by Western, more especially by German, most particularly and arrogantly by
South German Jews. The god of the Termini is not of
Mack's Pantheon. He knows not boundaries nor frontiers of any kind, and his life has always been the richer
and fuller for this blissful indifference.

No portrait of Mack would be even half-complete that
did not take account of the Zionist phase of his career,
which dates back nearly twenty years to the inspiration of
Schmarya Levin, Henrietta Szold, and Aaron Aronson.
For this phase, singularly enough, he had been prepared
in part by one himself a non-Zionist, Rabbi Hirsch, whose

teaching at Chicago's Sinai of the peoplehood of Israel
prepared the soil of his being for the reception of the
Zionist seed, which was to be planted much later. Judge
Mack's greatest Jewish service has been rendered in and
to Zionism. It is become a chapter of the Zionist record.
Suffice it to say here that this chapter will tell of ceaseless
devotion, of large generosity, of wise counsel, of loyal
comradeship, not marred by anything that he has said or
done but troubled at times by the ceaseless contentious-
ness and strife obtaining among certain Zionist groups.

In truth, the Zionist phase is, save for his professional
work as lawyer and judge, the most spacious phase of his
career and will probably be longest remembered. For
here, quite apart from the titular dignities which have
abundantly fallen to his lot and his disinclination to do
battle against persons, he has led. He has bent his mind, as
lawyers rarely do in relation to public affairs, upon the
business of Zionism, applying his unusual intellectual
powers to its many and complex problems with unwearied
steadfastness and the uttermost of devotion. Men and
causes alike evoke the instinctive loyalty of his soul. And
yet Zionism stands alone even in the category of things
cherished by him. For Zionism has evoked his best, and
Mack's best has meant an incalculable furtherance of the
cause.

A way of evaluating Judge Mack's contribution to
Zionism was afforded at the strenuous 1931 Zionist Congress at Basle. No man did as much as he to evolve order
out of the chaos of that divided assembly. He had the most
definite views on the chief problems before the Congress
and the delegates knew exactly what those views were. But
never did his incapacity for bitter and unyielding partisanship serve him and a cause better than at Basle. He listened patiently to all—a rare accomplishment among

Jews, the writer ruefully admits! As always in his case, he
was most patient with and understanding of those who
most differed from him. He was the soul of friendliness to
all groups from ultra-Revisionist to ultra-Radical, who
were as one in placing their trust in the man, his wisdom,
his fairness, his character. It was his inexhaustible patience, his unfailing resourcefulness which more than all
else saved the Congress from the party stalemate that
threatened disaster. The solution that finally held things
together would hardly have been possible without him.

While his modesty and self-depreciation, which have an
almost psychic flavor, have stood and will always stand in
the way of authoritative leadership on his part in American Jewry, it is only fair to add that there is something
more than selflessness and a very fanaticism of self-dero-
gation that stand in the way of such leadership.

Most loyal and devoted of followers, he is not a born
leader. He does not like to fight. He can fight when fight
he must, but he does it without heart or gusto. The Hora-
tian *guadium certaminis* is not for him. He can battle like
a lion *for* a man or *for* a cause. The leonine deserts him
utterly when he enlists *against*. It may be that his fatal,
withal infinitely lovable, inability to fight *against* a man
or cause is allied with or derives from his humility. The
latter is never a mask or a pose, nor even just virtue,
though it be, in truth, the defect of his virtues. Though he
commands vast stores of courage when these are needed,
he is almost constantly guilty of that rarest of virtues in
an age of aggressive self-confidence, namely, self-distrust.
For one reason or another, he is lacking in that ultimate
self-trust without which instinctive, authentic leadership
such as that of Brandeis cannot be.

Most of us remember Bolitho's thrilling volume,
"Twelve Against the Gods." Mack is never against the

gods nor against men. No Athenasian he, *contra mundum!* Not that he is ever lacking in courage and strength and self-reliance, this bravest and most selfless of followers! But, constitutionally, temperamentally, he cannot bring himself to be *"forninst."* He is, despite his name, as unIrish and unbellicose as a man can be. He is a man of peace, a seeker and maker of peace. For peace he will yield all save truth and justice.

— 1932

The First Lord Melchett

IN reading the masterly biography of the First Lord Melchett by Hector Bolitho, one gets the impression that the author approached his subject with no little misgiving, somewhat after the fashion in which a portrait painter approaches an unattractive sitter. But Melchett grew upon his biographer and grows upon the reader. This burly industrialist and bluff statesman becomes of all things a pathetic figure, by reason of the futilities of political life and the frustrations of industrial leadership complicated in the end by the newly awakened and tragic sense of "not belonging" as the modern jargon runs. This sense, which perhaps because of the coarseness of the Lloyd George comment on Melchett going over to the Tories, might have brought a great career to a gloomy and embittered end, had it not been for one happy and redeeming circumstance. This circumstance not merely wrought a redemptive change in a cruelly enshadowed and embittered life, but lent direction and inspiration to its closing years through bringing them into close association with the life of his people and its greatest task.

In the three closing swiftly moving chapters of this uniformly interesting volume, Bolitho tells that story

from which evolves a figure freeing itself from the disillu-
sionments of the political scene and the heartbreak of the
industrial conflict and finding at last innermost security
in complete identification with his people's loftiest hope
and most exigent task. Had Zionism been as easy, let us
say, as anti-Zionism, Mond-Melchett would have had
none of it. The *impossible* of it challenged him and that
stern challenge one cannot help believing was more compelling to his Jewish soul than its belated nostalgia or
Weizmann's alluring summons.

One wishes that the author had gone somewhat farther
afield in consulting the sources of Mond's Zionist motivation and devotion. Had he done so, he would have
learned the amazing truth that Melchett became an un-
compromising maximalist in Zionist affairs. His biographer ought to have gathered from wider and more impar-
tial sources that during the fateful days of Arab pogroms
in August-September '29, unchecked for the most part
because of Palestine Government timorousness or indifference, Lord Melchett spoke up and out with characteristic vigor and brusqueness while, strange to say, Zionist
leadership was still groping and hesitant.

Upon one other great occasion only little more than a
year before his passing, when Sidney Webb, forswearing
the ideals of a life-time, gave the thinly disguised im-
primatur of the Passfieldian name to the infamous White
Paper, it was Melchett again more than any other Zionist
leader who uttered his soul in unfettered rage. Scornful
of the niceties of political usage, he spoke like a man and
a Jew with a directness that must have appeared volcanic
to the urbane and unruffled spirit of Sir Herbert Samuel,
that was inspiriting to the leadership from which Mond
once had learned. Nor was Mond satisfied with the half-
promise and equivocations of the later MacDonald letter

which will be endangering to Zionist hopes until it go the way of the Passfield White Paper.

Bolitho's book is an illuminating biography of a strange and heroic figure. Even as Herzl and Nordau will be acclaimed by the gratitude of their people when their literary achievements will have faded out of the human record, even as Balfour's declaration of faith in his country's relation to the rightful demands of Israel for Palestine will be held in honor long after his metaphysical doubts shall have been resolved or ignored, so Melchett, empire builder and statesman, will be cherished in remembrance and honor by his fellow-builders in Zion long after all else of his many achievements shall have vanished from mortal memory.

— 1933

"Professional Jew"

WHEN after a generation—it may be a century before the echoes of Jewish strife are stilled—an objective appraisal of present-day Jewish history is attempted, Leo Motzkin will rank very high among the servants of his people.

His life and his death raise some interesting questions. Among amateur Jews (even when they are not, in the caustic phrase of Professor Kallen, uniformly amateur Gentiles), there is the tendency to view contemptuously the "professional Jew." Motzkin, in a certain sense, was a professional Jew as are few men. Comfortable vulgarians will say of him that he made a living out of the Jewish people. The truth is, though myopic Jews cannot understand it, that his lifelong calling was the service of his people and that he had, would have, no other calling. He never really had a living or even asked for it. For himself and his own, he accepted the barest subsistence, ceaselessly harassed by burdens of indebtedness which he assumed in the prosecution of his redemptive Jewish work. They who, after amassing substance, spare some hours for the Jewish people, cannot understand one who never spared himself in the service of things Jewish, and in the sub-conscious quest of self-exoneration or in any event self-extenuation, these Jews take hold upon and use the unclean weapon of objurgation, "professional Jew."

What the London Conference recently talked about for three days and more, at great expense to the delegates or their organizations, Motzkin did for over a decade with virtually no resources. He, who was one of the humblest of men, would deprecate any bracketing of his name with that of Herzl. But the fact remains that in a lesser or less conspicuous way, Motzkin suffered the same fate as the majestic Herzl, each forced to do a great work with a mini-mum of help from them that stood indifferently or con-temptuously aloof. In no year since 1919 did Motzkin command for the war he led on behalf of the Jewish mi-nority groups any such sum as was expended in connec-tion with the recent London Conference, as is expended day by day upon a myriad superfluities and luxuries by Jews, individually and collectively. Forasmuch as Motz-kin toiled with the most modest means at his command, save for intermittent help from the American Jewish Con-gress and sustained only by a few well-to-do East European Jews in France, he did superhuman things. Motzkin's achievements would have been creditable to statesman-ship commanding adequate resources. To have wrought as Motzkin did was nothing less than a miracle of Jewish devotion. Many so-called Jewish statesmen are intellec-tually and politically *Batlanim* in their meddling, pid-dling ineffectiveness. This selfless, unfailingly good-hu-mored *Batlan* was a true Jewish statesman.

In his own way Motzkin was as unique a Jewish figure as Ussishkin. The writer said of the latter, at the Prague Zionist Congress celebration in his honor, that Ussishkin was almost the only Jew born in Eastern Europe who did not seek to become or at least to seem a Westerner, but moved straight to his Palestinian goal without the faintest deviation in the direction of western assimilation. Not less unique was Motzkin, who was neither Easterner nor Westerner. He was resident in both. But he was at home nowhere save in Palestine, whither his dust is reverently to be borne. All his life in *Flucht*, he was, to cite the noble phrase of Chancellor Hitler, "the international gypsy" par excellence. In *Flucht*, but never from and ever to his people, a watchman on the heights, hastening hither and thither wherever Jewish rights were invaded or Jewish lives threatened.

But the enduring monument of Motzkin was the Paris Jewish Conference, of which far beyond any other, even its successive presidents, Mack, Marshall, Sokolow, he was the creator and inspirer. In those pre-Hitler days, tepid and timid Jews looked askance at this man, who, in the name of Jewish self-respect, fought with boundless energy and resistless enthusiasm for the loftiest ends of Jewish aspiration. The grandees, especially from England and France, stood aside and smiled benignly at this queer little man. After ten years, Motzkin beheld the tragic fulfillment of his rightful claims, most of all in Germany, where Jews today would find minority status elysian compared with the horror of their status-less existence in Naziland. The mocking impatience of the Jewish grandees with Motzkin was their shame not his, his vindication and their condemnation.

More than any Jew of his time, Motzkin served greatly in the two hemispheres of the Jewish globe—in the Galuth

and for Eretz Israel. This Zionist of Zionists never lost
sight of the grim realities of the Jewish Diaspora, the
tragedy of which etched itself into his heart in his youthful days in Russia. Touching Palestine, he was an uncom-
promising maximilist. As for his people in the lands of
oppression and persecution, he was the hardest-headed
and most realistic of meliorists.

But there was a third great service which he performed.
In the midst of the warring factions of Zionism, he was
the conciliator and mediator who never sacrificed his self-
respect in the interest of peace, nor forfeited the reverence
of the warring groups as these sought his mediatorial leadership. His will to Jewish peace did not affect or qualify
his own superb courage. He listened patiently to those in
control, but his heart was ever with the less privileged
and the less potent, even in the most democratic of movements.

If the writer had to sum up the career of Leo Motzkin
in one sentence, it would run in some such terms as these:
Motzkin was of the Jewish people, he lived and fought in
the name of a mandate which he sought from the Jewish
people, and he toiled for the Jewish people as bravely, as
greatly as any man, as any Jew, of his generation.

— 1933

George Alexander Kohut — A Tribute

MOURNING is often little more than official. It is seldom
the portion of the famous to evoke sincere grief at their
passing. Perhaps it is a penalty of eminence that it may
be attained only by such as hold themselves aloof from
and unrelated to the daily ways of men. In all the years of
a long ministry, I have not looked upon truer sorrow than
waited upon the passing of one, who in a technical sense

was a person in private life, Dr. George Alexander Kohut.

George Kohut, as he was familiarly and affectionately styled, was for years before his passing one of the most distinguished figures in contemporary Jewish life — though he would blushingly have challenged this claim. At a tender age which finds most lads pre-occupied with games, his unique filial piety had already made him the comrade and co-worker of his father, the great Alexander Kohut. As a result, from the time he was a stripling, he became the friend and familiar of his father's contemporaries and friends. To name only a few, Gottheil and Kohler, Mendes and Jastrow, Szold and Schechter in America, and in Europe, Steinschneider of Berlin, Loew of Szegedin, Rector Schwartz of Vienna, Kaufman, Bacher, Blau of Budapest, to cite only men of his father's generation rather than his own.

Being pre-Freudian in years, George Kohut's life was unmarred by his idolatrous tenderness to his father. It will always remain difficult to determine whether George Kohut's never-ending devotion to Jewish learning was his tribute, conscious or unconscious, to the memory of his father, whose blessed portion it was to evoke such piety, or whether George's piety grew in part in any event out of his instinctive and ceaseless reverence for the learned and his joyous discipleship to them.

In any event, this grievously handicapped youth, for such he was who never knew robust or even normal health, had by the time he was forty become a Semitic bibliographer of distinction and a Jewish historian of wide fame. Over and beyond his personal creativeness as a scholar of incredible industry and fine competence, he became the most generous friend and famed furtherer of Jewish learning in the Western world. Despite limited means—and these limitations none quicker than he to

ignore—he devised and executed munificent plans that
would have done credit to a Schiff or a Rothschild. The
Alexander Kohut Memorial Foundations in places as
widely separated in every sense as Vienna and Yale, Berlin
and New York, testify to something more than his large-
ness of conception and largesse in execution. All of his
daring Maecenas-like plans for the support of *Jüdische
Wissenschaft* were bound up with his exquisitely Jewish
concern for the scholar, his dreams and his needs.

Years ago I had occasion to note within a few months in
places as remote from each other as Texas and Vienna,
how the personality of George Kohut had impacted upon
two worlds. He had left Dallas and the pulpit of his temple a generation before my visit, but "The Little Minister," as his people still called him, remained enshrined
in the unfading love of his people. As for Vienna, there
he was a prized institution rather than a person, the symbol of the new world's generous concern for the literary
and scholarly achievements and personalities of the old
world. And Vienna, no more than Budapest and Berlin
and Breslau, cherishing George Kohut, who "thought in
gold and dreamed in silver" that Foundations might arise
and editions be published and the lowliest *ben Torah* be
furthered, and his contribution to Jewish learning be
made secure!

Never lived a more incurable Romantic, whose life was
compact of the graciousness and generosities and chiv-
alries which one is wont to associate with an elder day.
At nearly sixty, he retained the radiance of youth, this
figure of light and sweetness. He was not without wisdom
and foresight which he revealed in scores of ways and
works, but understanding and learning were never suffered to mar the purity of his instinctive reactions to every
opportunity for service, to every privilege of friendship.

Boundless was his capacity for enthusiasms, enthusiasms that lifted up his own heart and gladdened the hearts of multitudes. A witty woman applied to him a pet name that was a perfect characterization, "Rhapsodie Hongroise." If he rhapsodized in many fields, he was the supreme rhapsodist in the realm of friendship. Worshiper at many altars, his religion was friendship. Not that he gave his heart to all, for he could be as capricious in withholding as he was catholic in bestowing friendship, yet friendship was not so much a gift from him as the expression of his own personality. When he gave he gave all. None could give more—I cannot remember who gave as much. George Kohut's supreme passion in life was to befriend and to serve.

Some day the story of George Kohut's life must be told. The pen uniquely fitted to tell the story is that of his gifted and honored mother, Rebekah Kohut, whose biography of Dr. Kohut would add another to those beautiful chapters of *Jüdische Kulturgeschichte* which are embodied in the autobiographical "My Portion." George Kohut's correspondence with Jewish scholars from Steinschneider to Freidus, Guedemann to Chajes, Lewy and Maybaum to Elbogen and Perles, Irsael Abrahams, Ginsburg, Marx, Baron, Spiegel, will add much to the history of the development throughout forty years of Jewish learning.

George Kohut's work will go on. The Foundations he has established will continue their fruitful work in the field of learning and letters, but George Alexander Kohut, alas, is no longer among us. Life is poorer and colder without him and the warming radiance of his being. For us who knew and loved this figure of light, the Sun, in Homeric phrase, seems to have perished out of the heavens. The fullness of his life in all essentials, the immeasurable richness of his service and achievements in the field which chose and was chosen by him, these things will in time bring some healing to our hearts, and we need healing. For our hearts are sore bereft by his passing.

— 1934

"The Baron"

No JEW lives today whose death could more completely symbolize the passing of an era than does the death of Baron Edmond de Rothschild. For one thing, he was *ein echter Rothschild*, the last surviving grandson of Mayer Amschel. That world interest in the Rothschild family continues unabated is shown by the never-ending publication of Rothschild volumes and by the extraordinary interest in the pointless but far from unoffending "House of Rothschild" film. Again, he was the last of the Jewish Princes in the realm of finance, the group which included, preeminently, Baron Maurice de Hirsch, Jacob Schiff, Baron Nathaniel Rothschild, and his brother Leopold and Baron Edmond's elder brother Alphonse. Strangely enough, Baron Edmond never became a master of finance in the sense in which Schiff and de Hirsch and the London Rothschilds indubitably were. Jewry offered honor and gratitude to all of these—sometimes overmuch—but it reserved its deepest affection for "the Baron." The latter's unique place in the heart of world-Jewry was most nearly approximated by that which deservedly fell to the lot of Nathan Straus in our own country, least of the Jewish millionaires and largest in the measure of his beneficence. The very name by which Baron Edmond de Rothschild was known was in itself a token of a people's intimate love. Hirsch was a Baron, as were the English Rothschilds, the Austrian Guttmanns and Koenigswarters, and the Russian Ginzburgs. Edmond was *The Baron* and any mention of "the Baron" in a company of Jews anywhere for half a century pointed unmistakably to him.

About him, too, there was woven by the humble and naive Jewish masses the glamorous romance that was bound up for generations with the *Hofjuden* of other days. Jews rested their faith in this gift for service and beneficence, and they came to attribute to him superhuman power and, it goes without saying, they invested him with an unimaginable fortune. He never assumed or purported to be the Ambassador of Jewry in the sense in which others were every ready to volunteer. Whatever influence he exerted grew out of an unusual sense of homage to this man of fine sensitiveness, of lofty character, of simple piety. In one sense, he might have been described as a *Hofjude*. He had his own *Hof*, his own court of entourage, and the best in such a court was that noble and godly Grand Rabbi of France, Zadok Kahn. But, alas, there were others. The entourage of a Jewish philanthropist, even though he be as saintly as was the Baron, too often includes the selfish and the servile, who nominally link Prince and people together, who actually hold Prince and people apart from each other. Baron Edmond de Rothschild fared not too well in this respect. Some of the agents nearest to his ear were farthest from his understanding and his heart's desire—doing his will in form, but in substance wreaking their own purposes upon tasks nobly conceived and generously planned, but, because of them, less nobly executed. And the Princes never learn, are seldom disillusioned, for rare are they who are brave enough to seek to neutralize the petty and even treacherous agents of great doers of good.

Is it not passing strange—or shall we deem it inevitable—that the two greatest names, surely the most beloved,

in modern Jewish history, Theodore Herzl and Edmond
de Rothschild, are alike bound up with the building of
the Jewish National Home in Palestine? It seems such a
simple matter after fifty years and more to regard it as an
item of Baron de Rothschild's story that he began to interest himself half a century ago in colonization and re-settle-
ment plans in Palestine. But the truth is that it required
vision and statesmanship in the early eighties for Edmond
de Rothschild to undertake to settle homeless Jews in
Palestine, as truly as Herzl revealed vision and statesmanship when, fifteen years later, in a fury of Dreyfus despera-
tion sublimated by Jewish hope, he wrote (in Paris not
Vienna) *"Der Judenstaat."* Palestine of the eighties was
a Turk-ridden, tax-crushed, sterile, mediaeval Satrapy.
History will deal with the good and evil methods of the
administrators of Rothschild's daring experiment, will
evaluate the wisdom and bona fides of some of his procon-
suls, may even comment unfavorably on the weakening
effects upon the first generation of an absentee regime of
limitless resources and of those processes which would
have given rise to an intolerably Junkerish second generation, had it not been outnumbered and outweighed by the
intrepid Chaluzim. But who can doubt that to this gentle
and compassionate sage will fall the distinction of becoming associated in history with Herzl, as Herzl's unwitting
and almost unwilling forerunner, who builded for Herzl
better than he knew, though not more enduringly than
he willed!

And this juxtaposition of the names of Herzl and Edmond de Rothschild evokes tragic memories of yet another might-have-been. What might not these two together have achieved! It was not to be. It may have been
better that the Jewish people at the last should not have
been favored by an alien ruler, Abdul Hamid, whose

greed robbed him of Cyrus' glory, nor yet that it was unduly helped even by one of its own Princes! A people may not be served overmuch even by one of their own, save as he evokes their own capacity for self-help and resurrects their own will to self-determination. Nor would it be wholly fair to place all the blame upon Rothschild for the failure to achieve co-operation with Herzl. The ill-starred circumstance of the Ghetto-centuries inexorably kept apart two men who alike sought the honor and well-being of their people. Baron Edmond de Rothschild will live in the lore and in the love of his people who had become a legend to them in his own life-time. He sought not glory, but it claimed him, this kindly, simple, far-seeing Jew forever to be enshrined in the unfading remembrance of his people. With his millions and an unprecedented generosity, he did much to set the Jewish millions free. Baron de Hirsch gave more, but not himself. Baron Nathaniel Rothschild gave much and he did much—from above. Others among rich and powerful Jews gave largely *noblesse oblige*. "The Baron" gave his brotherly hand and his merciful heart to his own. Immortally he will live, who willed to share, to heal and to ennoble the life of his immortal people.

— 1934

Four Who Have Died

It would be difficult to think of a month in many years in which so many eminent figures have passed whose life was definitely related to the Jewish people though they were not of it. Three of the four figures were of world significance. The fourth was a creative factor in that new world which the Soviet Union is bringing to pass.

Jane Addams was a great American, as truly American as Charles William Eliot or Woodrow Wilson or Theo-

dore Roosevelt. One does not lightly liken any American
or any human to Abraham Lincoln, but Jane Addams,
whose father was one of Lincoln's closest friends, had
something of the simplicity and of the sheer human greatness which were Lincoln's. One might almost add rugged-
ness, except for the fact that Jane Addams with all her
strength in and for the right was one of the most gentle
and gracious of human beings. Throughout her life, this
woman of Illinois did as much as any American to insist
upon the value of foreign groups in the upbuilding of
America. Jane Addams seemed to have a peculiar understanding for the races that were farthest from her blood.
This quiet, serene woman could become and was a flame
in the battle against the wrong and injustice of tyranny.
One of the last acts of her life was to join the Council of
the Women's Division of the American Jewish Congress
in order to bear witness to her abhorence of the Nazi
crime.

Joseph Paul Pilsudski will live in history as one of the
elemental figures which created a new political world.
How great he was as military commander the experts will
determine or in any event debate. How wise a leader he
was of the post-war Polish Republic, it is not for us to ap-
praise at this time. There are those who believe that Pilsudski should have been firmer than he was in defending
the status of the Jewish population of Poland. The truth
is that, although dictatorships are rarely tender of the
rights of minority groups, Pilsudski deserves the credit of
having averted the translation into law of the anti-Jewish
practices which obtained too largely in Poland. If Pilsudski did not save the Jews of Poland, was it not in part
because of the political, economic, territorial, racial con-
fusion out of which Poland emerged but from which Poland has not yet liberated itself?

Lawrence of Arabia was one of the glamorous figures of his generation. An Oxford student become an Empire builder! Whether "T. E." was authorized to give to the Arabs such ample and wide-reaching assurances as he gave is a problem which only research into documentary material of the time will disclose. He was a fascinating as will as an heroic figure, who takes his place in the great tradition of Gordon and Livingstone and the Anglo-American Stanley and Doughty and Sir Walter Raleigh, a race which the far-flung British Imperium best knows how to breed. When will a great Englishman adventure on behalf of Jews as Lawrence adventured and wrought and fought for the Arab world? Only the name of Josiah Wedgwood springs to mind in answer.

Peter Smidovich of the Soviet Union was less of a world figure than Pilsudski and Lawrence and Jane Addams, but his was a compassionate and generous understanding of the needs of declassed Jewry in his country. Had some timid Jew of the Yevsektsia tried to handle the problem with which Smidovich dealt, no such progress would have been made toward the economic solution of the Jewish problem in the Soviet Union, as came to pass under Smidovich's far-seeing and courageous direction.

None of these belonged to us as a people, yet each of them was of choice or of necessity related to elementary Jewish questions. All four, unrelated in any other way, will have a place of remembrance in the annals of a people which is boundlessly grateful for the understanding of a Jane Addams, and not without gratitude for the more limited benefits which came to Israel through those who, being peripheral to Jewish life, have never quite grasped the heart of Jewry nor grappled with its central problems.

— 1935

Three Men I Knew

RECENT YEARS have taken a heavy toll from the leadership of world Israel, and most especially of the Zionist movement. For Bialik, Schmarya Levin and "Baron Edmond" have fallen.

Early in the month, Lord Allenby of Megiddo passed in London. His very name types the romance of his role in the World War, a role second only in popular interest to that of the fascinating and legendary Colonel Lawrence. Lawrence liberated the Arabs to the service of Britain, while Allenby freed Palestine from centuries of gravest misrule and placed it under the care, confirmed by the League of Nations, of the British commonwealth. Allenby will be enshrined in remembrance not only because he redeemed Palestine, but because his capture of Jerusalem was performed without hurting a stone within the city!

His later service as Administrator for his country of affairs in Egypt was admirable. But nothing could compare with that gleaming feat in Palestine. I remember at a luncheon in the office of the *London Times* in December, 1918, to have heard Lord Burnham tell the story of a younger officer of Allenby's staff who inquired on the eve of the Palestine campaign as to its "immediate objectives." Allenby's answer was: "Our immediate objectives are the capture of Jerusalem and the destruction of the Turkish army." Allenby achieved both. Truly, it might have seemed a month ago as if nothing could add to his fame and yet, shortly before his death, he uttered some words as Honorary Rector of a Scottish University which reveal that the mighty captain of war was no less truly a statesman of peace: "The lust for expansion is not yet quite dead; but the glory of war is departing. Its gains

are Dead Sea fruit. Its legacies bitter memories alone."
These words, and Jerusalem unmarred but redeemed be
his remembrance!

NAHUM SOKOLOW was as completely a Jewish personality as the nineteenth century produced, and he remained that throughout his days. He was a child of the
East-European ghetto. He was an amateur rather than
a professional scholar. His amazing vitality to the end
and his incredible versatility, these two were ghetto-de-
rived, for the ghetto child was toughened by fate's sternness and could turn his hand to any duty that claimed
him.

What a career! Editor of *Ha-Zephirah* while in the
early twenties and head of the World Zionist Organization and the Jewish Agency for Palestine fully half a century later, and everything done throughout these years
with unruffled ease and incontestible authority! The
flexibility of his mind was revealed in 1897, when Herzl
first summoned the hosts of Israel. The great among
East-European Jews answered, none more eagerly than
Sokolow. My first Zionist Congress was that at Basle, 1898.
Herzl was sore troubled, not only by foes outside but by
comrades and friends within. Herzl leaned heavily upon
Sokolow as mediator between the conflicting groups.

At the Paris Peace Conference of 1919, by the side of
Motzkin, Mack, Marshall, he became chairman of the
Committee of Jewish Delegations, and filled a role for
which he was uniquely fitted—mediator and reconciler
between East and West. He was essentially a man of peace,
whose incredible learning and command of tongues especially equipped him for the mediatorial office which
became his own. Since those days, nearly twenty years
ago, he served, despite advancing years, as head of all

Zionist work for a time, not nominally playing the part but serving with vigor, and even undertaking a journey by airplane to South Africa, which turned out to be a triumphal tour for the Keren Hayesod, and a pilgrimage of honor for himself.

Nor will his literary achievements soon be forgotten! Within a decade he wrote in English a brilliant history of Zionism in England, a work of prodigious learning and extraordinary penetration. Then came a volume on Spinoza for the Tercentenary Celebration, which in Hebrew set forth lucidly and adequately the philosophical doctrine of Spinoza the Jew. Wise and understanding, cultivated and gifted, Sokolow began his life as a brilliant *Wunderkind* of the Ghetto and remained to the end of his nearly eighty years a miracle of intellectual astuteness, of patient persuasiveness and of unweariable devotion to Israel as people of the past and of the future!

MEMORABLE among the losses of Israel in the month of May was the latest of all, the passing of Professor Richard Gottheil. Gottheil, with his honored father, Dr. Gustav Gottheil, long-time Rabbi of Temple Emanu El, stood at the cradle of American Zionism. That championship was of the highest value because father and son had stood within the ranks of Reform Judaism and yet proved ready to share the vision of Herzl when he summoned. Richard Gottheil was a fanatical Jew, not fanatical in the matter of minor conformities but with respect to his insistence upon major loyalties. He was fanatically wrathful against any and every Jewish disloyalty, and fanatically bitter against every Jew whose life and conduct were such as indicated that he was untouched by Jewish pride. Such was the dignity of this Jew that he could not even understand Jews who sought to escape their Jewish bonds and to slight or minimize their racial birthright.

In the earliest years of the Zionist movement, of which Gottheil wrote a competent history, this Jewish gentleman and university teacher was a tower of strength to the movement. He guarded it against its foes, he added to the number of its understanding friends. Friend of Herzl in a peculiar sense, comrade of Nordau, helper of Wolfsohn, he gained and held a place of honor in Zionist leadership throughout the difficult and formative years of the movement. In the annals of Zionism, his people's rebirth, his place is sure. To it he lent the prestige of an eminent Semitic scholar and the distinction of his high academic status. For some years prior to his passing, as President Nicholas Murray Butler pointed out at the service of farewell, he had come to be the senior and widely revered professor of Columbia University.

Richard Gottheil was a humble, God-fearing Jew who faced realities, whose sensitive nature was tortured by the Hitlerism of his father's native land, whose soul was saved from wracking despair by the grandeur of Israel's hope and the (for him) certitude of Israel's future. To Mrs. Richard Gottheil, no less fervent and serviceable as worker and leader in the Zionist movement, the tender sympathy of Zionist leadership and masses goes out in sorrow for him whose life was a *Kiddush ha-Shem*, which alone is immortal!

— 1936

Mr. Justice Brandeis' Eightieth Birthday

NOVEMBER 13 will be observed as a high and festive day by Jews the world over. For the day will mark the eightieth anniversary of the birth of Louis D. Brandeis. He is not the only Jew of eminence in our time. One thinks of such living contemporaries as Einstein and Freud, Bergson and Weizmann, Cardozo and Flexner. Yet, in a very real sense Brandeis stands alone—as Einstein clearly saw when, describing him as "a person of swift and clear insight, of keen conviction, wanting nothing but to serve society," he discerned that Brandeis served in the loneliness of great work.

Others with the authority of knowledge and competence will speak, as Professor Felix Frankfurter has in this issue of OPINION, of Brandeis' service as jurist and interpreter of American law. The American Bar, we are led to believe, would subscribe to the memorable summing up of Frankfurter, "a judge, who by common consent, is a great and abiding figure of the world's most powerful Court."

OPINION's concern is with, as the writer's knowledge is of, Brandeis the Jew. Reared as were many of the finest among the children of German-speaking Jews of the last century, in an atmosphere of more or less reverent agnosticism, Brandeis was not, nor more than Adler and Jacobi and Flexner, drawn within the walls of a synagogue of inadequate content. But a day and cause came in Brandeis' life which touched his innermost being. It was the day and the cause of Herzl, the cause of Jewish self-rehabilitation through effort and achievement. This, supplemented by the impact of Jacob de Haas, Henrietta Szold, Aaron Aaronson and Nahum Sokolow, brought Brandeis to the understanding of a great purpose and ultimately to identification with and leadership of the Zionist movement. For nearly a quarter of a century Brandeis has qualitatively given more to Zion than any Jew since Herzl. Not only has his generosity been boundless, but he has above all given of a great and richly stored mind to the mastery of the daily processes of the movement which after the Supreme Court has been his only client.

But more even than the unbelievable generosity and tireless study of the minutest details of the Palestine operation has been the spirit of high and consecrated devotion with which he has dedicated time and substance, insight and counsel, to the cause that revealed Brandeis the Jew to himself and made him a Jew immortal.

The writer of this word of revering congratulation to the *Resh Galuta* remembers two things said by President Wilson of the man whom he named to the supreme Court. And Wilson was not so much a master of phrase as of insight that lives. "Isn't it a pity, Mr. President, that a man as great as Mr. Justice Brandeis should be a Jew?" Instant was the reply: "But he would not be Mr. Brandeis if he were not a Jew." In January 1919 someone in Paris urged President Wilson, in attendance at the Peace Conference, to borrow Brandeis for a time from the Supreme Court and let him take over a task for which, as Wilson admitted, Brandeis was uniquely fitted. Wilson's comment was: "I need Brandeis everywhere, but I must leave him somewhere."

Only they who have been privileged to stand near to Justice Brandeis in the performance of an historic task will understand why what would seem extravagant praise touching any other is truth unadorned with respect to Brandeis, seer and prophet.

"Praised and beloved that none
    Of all thy great deeds done
    Flies higher than thy most equal spirit's flight."

— 1936

Thomas Masaryk — A Tribute

As I recall it, when Daniel Webster died, his passing was
lamented in the perfect tribute, "There is no Daniel
Webster left to die." In the month of September, another
Homeric figure was called by death, and a world plunged
into mourning might well express its sense of loss in the
terms, "there is no Masaryk left to die." Surely in all the
world there survives no other figure before whom detrac-
tion long was silenced and calumny transformed itself into
praise. Best of all, he was not a martial figure, though
he moved a nation to take up arms to liberate itself. He
was not an exciting personality such as were two other
octogenarians at the zenith of their mighty careers, Gladstone and Clemenceau. He had none of the oratorical
genius of Gladstone. He had nothing of the hypnotic
potency of France's Grandfather of Victory.

I remember to have come upon his name for the first
time in the course of a conversation with Theodore Herzl.
He mentioned Masaryk in the accents of superlative
praise. As to Mararyk, Herzl told me the story of the
Professor at Prague University and member of the Austro-Hungarian Imperial Parliament, who had volun-
teered to defend a dissolute Jew, Leopold Huelsner by
name, who had done away with a young woman in Polna.
What brought Mararyk into the case and to the defense
of this degenerate was not the question of his guilt or in-
nocence with respect to the murder charge, but the accusation that he was guilty of *ritual* murder. Against this
unspeakable but oft-recurrent accusation, the then Professor Mararyk fought with measureless courage withal
irritating serenity.

His enemies had their revenge. He forfeited his parliamentary seat, he was dismissed from his Professorship.

The case was fought with virulence which almost equalled the bitterness that surged about Captain Dreyfus. Not a little of the Austro-Hungarian ferocity against Masaryk was due to something which did not quite come to the surface, but nonetheless moved the enemies of Masaryk to the fury of hatred which they exhibited. Masaryk was intransigent about Bohemian (or, as we now say, Czecho-Slovakian) independence. His unafraid pioneering in that cause barbed and poisoned every shaft which Austria leveled at him.

We did not personally meet until Masaryk, not for the first time, visited America in 1907. I sought him out. He accepted my invitation to deliver the address at the first service of the Free Synagogue. My admiration for the man, my gratitude for his intervention in the Polna ritual murder trial, moved me to feel that the Synagogue and its work could have no more fitting inaugural nor surer dedication than at the lips of one who had taken every risk and faced every loss in order to stand against injustice to a people.

The congregation which gathered, no more than American Jewry generally, knew his name. In those days, his English speech was rather inadequate. As I listened to the man and we later chatted at the dinner table, I came to feel that his strength lay in character, the character of a man of steel-like will, who had no private ends to serve, who was solely a servant of a great cause. I felt that another of the heroes of my youth was come to life again, Mazzini. In Masaryk there was something of the same exaltation, utterly free from posturing, as if he were conscious that a people's rebirth depended upon him.

We did not meet again until the war years came. I saw him often and together with some others who came to be among his American friends, including Judge Julian W.

Mack and the late Jacob de Haas, I sought to help him
in his great task of winning American support for Czecho-
Slovakian independence. Colonel House became his wise
and resourceful friend. The diaries have not yet told what
was said when two Professors met, Wilson and Masaryk.
But one knows that Czecho-Slovakian liberation became
one of the articles in the Wilsonian creed and that President Wilson loyally supported Masaryk at the Paris Peace
Conference.

Czecho-Slovakia came into being and Masaryk became
its first President. No other was considered whilst he lived
and remained able to serve. Since the death of Wilson and
Clemenceau, Pilsudski and Balfour and the retirement of
Lloyd George and Paderewski, Masaryk has stood virtually alone among the decisive figures of the war years and
peace days. Not only did he lead rather than rule his people with the wisdom of statesmanship, but he held his
country true for nearly twenty years to the ideals of democratic government. Amid a sea of dictatorships, Czecho-
Slovakia, under the fatherly hand of Masaryk, remained
an island beacon of democratic self-rule. Little wonder
that his people would not let him step down from the
Presidency until two years ago, and then only after feeling
assured that his disciple, Dr. Benes, was equal to the for-
midable task of maintaining the Masaryk tradition.

I count it perhaps the greatest distinction that fell to
my lot, that when the Czecho-Slovakian government was
being set up and the problems of nationalities were being considered, Dr. Masaryk, through an American friend
whom I leave unnamed, invited me to go to Czecho-
Slovakia for a time and undertake the organization of
its Jewish community. My declination was motivated in
large part by the feeling that the Jews of Czecho-Slovakia,
including the old Moravia, whence two centuries earlier

my paternal ancestors migrated to Hungary, were abundantly able to manage their own affairs without interference even though invited by the Head of the State.

Masaryk requires no memorial. Free and sovereign Czecho-Slovakia is his living memorial. If only the surrounding dictatorships did not seek to overwhelm it because its democracy is challenge and reproach to them! We Americans do not lightly liken any man to Washington. And yet Masaryk, like Washington, was the Father of his country. Oh, that the land of Masaryk may endure as bulwark of freedom and democracy, even as the country of Washington!

—1937

Felix Warburg — A Tribute

ONE would find it difficult to remember a time when the death of a Jew evoked such genuine sorrow and such unanimity of praise as has the passing of Felix Warburg. Within a decade, only the death of Nathan Straus and Baron Edmond de Rothschild has so stirred world Jewry, Straus because men felt he cared for them, "Baron Edmond" because he munificently pioneered for Eretz Israel. About Warburg's death there is the instinctive feeling that no Jew has served his people as widely and variously for a generation as he did. They who believe that a man best serves his fellow-men by concentration, as did de Rothschild, forget that, virtually abandoning all else, Warburg concentrated on a score of causes, giving to every one of them not the attenuated make-believe interest of a dilettante, but deeply earnest and constantly generous concern. And such as cavil at the unwisdom of diffusion in well-doing are perhaps unable to understand the heart of one, who like Warburg was ecumenical in well-doing not because of choice or weakness, but because of a great love and deeply rooted compassion for all mankind.

Therefore it was that Warburg had part in the direction of almost innumerable causes. But within the area of human needs he most sedulously and tenderly cultivated the Jewish garden, a garden that flowered in fair dreams, a garden poisoned by tragic weeds. No need in this brief and tentative appreciation of Felix Warburg to dwell upon a lifetime of service to all those agencies, material and spiritual which seek to make good in some part the deficiencies of our social order. That he was not without the imaginative faculty, rare among dutiful humanitarians, came to light Jewishly in his assumption, together with Louis Marshall, of the leadership of the American non-Zionist section of the Jewish Agency for Palestine, and most especially in his valiant acceptance of the entire burden after Marshall's lamented passing.

The writer does not claim that he always saw eye to eye with Warburg in relation to Palestine and its problems. The latter never pretended to share the viewpoint of Jewish Nationalism, though he respected the integrity of those to whom Jewish Nationalism was central and essential in every Palestine rebuilding program. All the more honoring to him that he often, almost constantly, strove to moderate within his own (Jewish) entourage the anti-Nationalist ardor of such as "would help Palestine along with other places of refuge."

Marshall passed after he had climaxed a career of Jewish service by creating at the side of Dr. Chaim Weizmann the Jewish Agency. Melchett passed after he had manfully resisted the insidiously evil Passfield Report and joined with Weizmann and Warburg in resigning from the Agency by way of solemn and concerted protest. Warburg passes after one of the great moments of an all but unmatched career of service. Whether he chose aright in vigorously rejecting Palestine Partition, though (or because) bound up with Britain's offer of Jewish Statehood only history, which is another name for the wisdom of experience, can determine. But two months after the event we may pass judgment on Felix Warburg at Zurich and after. There he rendered an indivisible Palestine the service of organized and weighty opposition to Partition.

But his greater, in truth greatest, service to Palestine law in the forbearance and wisdom which moved him to assent loyally for the non-Zionists, whose dominant figure he was, to the earlier Zionist Congress resolution looking to further exploration and negotiation. Had Felix Warburg remained unyielding, the Agency would have been cancelled then and there or, in any event, rent asunder. And an appalling breach of Jewish life and forces throughout the world would have resulted. To Warburg goes the high and enduring honor of having averted a disastrous breach, and that immeasurably important service grew out of a life-long instinct, veritable genius, for conciliatoriness and above all out of an unshakable Jewish loyalty which rose to the vision of statesmanship.

JEWISHLY untroubled souls will murmur—and what a pity that Warburg should have spent himself so ungrudgingly! And they will add that if he had spared himself and not borne the strain of two especially hurried journeys in spring and summer for the Jewish Agency, he might still be living. But these super-cautious beings to whom life means chiefly the postponement or avoidance of death forget that had Warburg been so self-sparing, he would not have been Warburg and he would never have been the living, vibrant, loved figure that he became. Bet-

ter the life lived in uncalculated and even reckless use of
one's gifts and strength than to aim merely at length of
days!

And there is one word more to be said, the utterance of
which the death of Felix Warburg necessitates. Specula-
tion is already afoot as to his successor and the leadership
of American Jewry. Are these men of little faith and less
vision blind to the truth that Jewish leadership is not a
crown to be surrendered nor a heritage to be bequeathed?
Let some Jew serve for a generation, as did Warburg. Let
him include every continent of Jewish life within the area
of his concern and devotion, let him engross himself day
by day in the heart-breaking needs and problems of his
people, let him forget himself and remember only to share
his people's hopes and dreams and agonies, let world Israel
feel that he gives all that he is and has of mind and substance, of purpose and love, and it will come to revere and
cherish another great servant as it came to know Felix
Warburg for its own.

Leadership will not be conferred by committee or congress, by community or federation. Nor is leadership a
patent to be bestowed by favor or vote. Jewish leadership
derives from unconscious and universal recognition of a
man's utter dedication to his people's cause, all that they
are and ought to be, all that they dare dream and achieve
at their highest. Such dedication was the highest distinction of Felix Warburg. It determines his place in Jewish
annals. It is challenge to such as would harvest without
sowing, who would purchase leadership and immortality
at bargain rates. Warburg paid the full price of a life-long
devotion to Israel, which stands sorrowfully and gratefully at his fresh-made grave.

— 1937

Toscanini's Return

WAS the uproarious, indeed regal, welcome under National Broadcasting Company auspices to Toscanini solely for the Maestro? Was not the tribute to the master musician tinged by reverence for the man? Toscanini is not an artist who seeks adventitious help in fields related to the art in which he is supreme. But despite his humility and self-effacement, he reveals his Titanic stature anew in a widely discussed report of a meeting at Salzburg between himself and Furtwaengler. It is not, as the latter sought to twist it, a matter of whether a musician must not keep out of politics, but whether a totalitarian State does not trench even upon the realm of music. Witness Nazi Germany's prohibition of the playing of Mendelsohn's inferior Oratorios.

Somehow men have come to feel that the man Toscanini is, paraphrasing Emerson, greater than any of his (even greatest) work, that his unique genius as conductor is no more than the outward sympton of that inward greatness which is he. Nothing quite as capricious and unpredictable as human greatness! Sometimes it clothes itself in the unstriking form but utterly enlightening spirit of the prophetic Thomas Mann: again it arrays itself in the habiliments of Einstein, and his stellar quality: again it expresses itself in the evocative and re-creative power of a Toscanini. And these three symbols of human greatness are alike exiles from Nazi Germany, alike voluntary, too. For Mann and Einstein through silence and surrender, a la Gerhardt Hauptmann, might have made their peace with the regime. Unthinkable for all alike, for these are men whose greatness is crowned by that moral grandeur which is deathless.

— 1938

Cardozo and Montefiore

NOT IN a generation have we been so bereft as we became on the ninth day of July. For that forever sable-hued day beheld the passing of two of our greatest and noblest sons, Justice Benjamin Nathan Cardozo, American, and Dr. Claude Goldsmid Montefiore, Englishman. Both men died full of honors, Montefiore alone full of years; Anglo-Jewry had a month earlier reverently celebrated his eightieth birthday. They had met only once—in the writer's home—but they had much in common apart from their Sephardic or Spanish-Portuguese ancestry.

Alike in this! Each was a man of strong convictions gently expressed. Montefiore was a prophet-saint, who, with a touch of Jowettesque Paulinianism, was fearful of the spiritual involuntariness called forth by the imperatives of the Religious Law. Cardozo was a saint-prophet whose adherence to and interpretation of the law was in its essence prophetic of a future liberated for the processes of equitable service of all human needs.

Next to Disraeli, Montefiore's was the most distinguished Jewish career of two Anglo-Jewish generations. Overshadowed a little in his youth by his elder and brilliant brother, Leonard, of whom Lord Milner said to the writer, "had Leonard lived he would have been Prime Minister," the latter passed away at Newport in his early twenties. To Claude were left the traditions of a great Jewish name and the obligations of a huge English fortune. The Saint and his fortune were hit off in the matchless quatrain of Zangwill:

> Of men like you
> Earth holds but few,
> An angel with
> A revenue.

Anglo-Jewry barely knew another who lived as he did, who gave as he did, and for the most part by stealth. The too cheaply used term philanthropist little describes one, who in advance of his time, furthered unpopular causes in the realms of education and social service. His deepest loves were the causes of Jewish learning and liberal Judaism. As for the former, if he had done no more than together with Israel Abrahams to have founded and for twenty years to have edited the Jewish Quarterly Review, which died in the course of its trans-Atlantic voyage, that would have been merit enough. But he did much more, making possible the Lectureship in Rabbinics in Cambridge and, what is still more, its occupancy in succession by Solomon Schechter and Israel Abrahams. His Synoptic Gospels were epochal, though with the most exquisite humility he decried his own learning and was as apologetic as the veriest tyro is not.

His militancy was limited to his leadership of liberal Judaism, particularly after the Berkley Place Synagogue, with the passing of the Reverend Professor Marx, his tutor in religion, had grown stale. Here Montefiore was at his best. The movement, save for the leadership of a small company of devout liberals, himself and Lily Montagu, Harry Lewis and Israel Abrahams, was little more than a renewal of the fading reform movement in our own country. But Montefiore led it to the end of his days with high vision and the utter devoutness of his own changelessly mystic spirit, and without a trace of the spiritual smugness which is Jewish liberalism's undoing. The intensity of his loyalty to Israel's faith blinded him not to his people's fate over which he brooded with loving compassion, but to its will to be and to create, as a people in its own land, the one blind spot where all else was light and sweetness. If Montefiore invited Israel to ascend the

Mountain of the Lord, ever to lift its eyes unto the hills, he never failed to go before. The eloquence of his teaching was fortified by the nobleness of his life. He was examplar of all that is highest and finest in Israel's tradition.

CARDOZO was an unique figure in every sense. A scion of distinguished stock on both sides, going back paternally to Dayan Cardozo of Amsterdam, follower of the pseudo-messianic Shabbatai Zvi, he faced most harassing difficulties from his earliest youth. He could hardly have overcome them, had it not been for the wise and resolute guardianship of a brilliant and adoring elder sister, Nellie. She was the first to see that embarrassment over his father's tragic failure on the Supreme Court of the State should not be suffered to mar, let alone destroy, the exquisite texture of this shy and reticent spirit. Horatio Alger Jr. taught the lad, but Nellie conditioned him for life and its achievements until her passing a decade ago left him crushingly bereft. She felt from his earliest years what "Ben" was destined to become. His Alexander Hamilton-like record at Columbia University was the first fruit of her planting and of his own thirst for knowledge. After the law school years he came quickly and increasingly to win the respect of the New York Bar. As early as 1911, President Taft authorized me to invite Cardozo, "whom my brother Harry considers one of the finest lawyers in New York," to accept an appointment on the Federal Bench. This Cardozo found it needful to decline for a reason which may now be told: its salary being insufficient to bear the burden of two households, his own and that of another most gifted sister, Elizabeth, whose illness necessitated the maintenance of a separate establishment. But shortly thereafter a most fortunate civic reform movement elected him to the Supreme Court of the State, almost immediately thereafter he was promoted to the Court of Appeals as presiding Judge of which he later served and latterly became a member of the highest judicial tribunal in the world, our own Supreme Court.

Only a jurist-scholar such as Professor Frankfurter, his friend, can do justice to the equipment and the achievements of Cardozo. The record runs that Cardozo's contribution was greater than that of any other member of the Court who sat for so brief a period. The American Bar, which was virtually unanimous in urging his appointment, came to feel that in Cardozo the Court had found another of the giants of its history. Titan in intellectual prowess that he was, he never lost an atom of his humility, his sweetly childlike diffidence, his unconquerable self-distrust. The great among his colleagues such as Brandeis, Hughes and Stone, welcomed and rejoiced in the camradeship of his radiant personality.

To Hoover fell the distinction of naming Cardozo, to the discomfiture of the lesser breed of the Court and to the illimitable joy of the members of a calling which he deeply respected, to the service of which he gave the matchless gift of a grand manner in style and substance alike. Not gigantic as is the spirit of Brandeis, not diamond-faceted as was the quality of Holmes, not Damascene as is the mind of Hughes, he yet adorned whatever he touched and resolved doubts because of his courageous humility in the presence of incertitude, and above all did all that one man could do to make the legal processes the foundation of justice in a democracy. How speedily was fulfilled the prediction of an eminent United States Senator to President Hoover on the eve of Cardozo's appointment. "Mr. President, as John Adams is remembered for his appointment of John Marshall, you will be remembered for having named Cardozo."

As Jew he knew and followed one rule, utter loyalty to the tradition in which he was born rather than reared. I recall a most felicitous essay by Cardozo in characterization of Disraeli, whom he overrated. His cousin, Emma Lazarus, could not have failed by her gifts as a poet to have impinged upon the sensitive nature of his youthful years. His older friends knew he made an annual contribution to the Zionist funds, and once he spoke as he alone could speak with regard to the Hebrew University of Jerusalem, with which he associated himself. In religion today, he said, "the need is great that we should view the profession of the law as a manifestation, a flowering of strivings and phases of the human spirit that are essential and enduring . . . we must feel in our hearts and show in our lives that law is in touch with the eternities. . . . Law, human and divine, has been a craving of the Hebrew spirit."

His two last appearances on Jewish platforms were on the occasion of Rabbi Pereira Mendes' Eightieth Birthday Celebration and of the seventh annual Commencement of the Jewish Institute of Religion, when, despite certain reservations clearly put, he brought a classic message to the graduates to cherish the inmost and enduring values of life, a message pitched in an even loftier key than was Barrie's summons on a parallel occasion to Courage.

Emerson once said that a great man is greater than all his work. If Emerson could have known Cardozo, as he was the friend of Cardozo's cousin Emma Lazarus, he might have said, "This man is equal to his greatest work." They who knew Cardozo best will understand me. Great was his mind; greater was his heart. His mind a divine gift, was enhanced in value by rigid self-cultivation. But his heart was the supreme grace of the man. It was said of Theodore Roosevelt's father that to see him help his wife with her wrap was a liberal education; to see Cardozo watching over his sister Nellie with a never-wearying tenderness, with a love of inmost transfiguration in his beautiful face, was a benediction. So was his life. We thank God that he has been, that this American Jew has made his abiding contribution to his country, that what he was and wrought witnesses anew to what a Jew may under God and under freedom become.

— 1938

George Alexander Kohut

The above was written as a Foreword to a movingly beautiful biography of the late Dr. George Alexander Kohut. The volume entitled "His Father's House" was written by Rebekah Kohut, member of the Editorial Board of OPINION *in succession to the late Dr. Kohut, and is published by the Yale University Press.*

To ONE who during his life knew not the subject or the idolized central figure of this story it may sound like an unreasoned hymn of praise. To such as knew George Kohut, it will seem as natural and inevitable as was his personality. No one could have told the tale with the understanding and tenderness of Rebekah Kohut, friend, comrade, mother. But any one of a score or of scores of friends of George would have found objective appraisal of the radiance that was he as impossible as did the author of this book. Rebekah Kohut was so near to the subject of her sketch, throughout forty-five years was so much a part of his life, its agonies and its triumphs, that such objectivity as she attained is an achievement of no slight moment.

Certain elements in the life-story and background of George Kohut upon which of course the writer adverts must be held clearly in mind. George was a Jew with more than typical or average family feeling. In truth, he was never typical or average in any aspect of his life. The sense of family bond and responsibility, which is characteristic even of the modern Jew—and George was born on the eve of the last quarter of the nineteenth century—became in his life exaggerated to an almost pathological degree. This family feeling merits a word of rational explanation. Denied throughout centuries access to an outer world, his inner life with his God, his faith and his family became everything to the Jew, with all externals minimized. There was something more. Living in a world of meditation and the quest of truth, the learned student of His Law came to be regarded with special veneration as likeliest to know the Divine way. In the life of George Kohut, the family head was such a ben torah—a restless, selfless, devout and scholarly seeker after truth.

Added to all this, the father of George Kohut was a man whose world-wide fame in the realm of learning had left his simple, guileless soul unspoiled. On all these grounds, which were subconscious motivations rather than reasons, George, from his earliest youth, watched with paternal rather than filial solicitude the heroic struggle of his father to complete a great life-task, bound up with one of the precious items of Jewish science. So it was the son not only stood slavishly and with unashamed adoration at his father's side, but when his father died after a period of undaunted struggle, was ready at the age of twenty both to act as pater familias and to enter upon his life-work, paralleling, continuing and crowning his father's classic service to Jewish scholarship.

There were interludes of various kinds, including an unforgettable ministry at Dallas, Texas, the founding and leadership of admirable schools for youth. But his great heart was wedded to one task, and to it he remained unalterably true, the task of furthering and supporting Jewish learning, which expressed itself in substantial Alexander Kohut Foundations at home and abroad. These meant for him the seeking out of scholars like his father, enabling them through moral and material support to carry on their work of research, and finally bringing their works of erudition to publication. This miracle would for the most part have remained unwrought had it not been for George Kohut's tactful interposition, his generous cooperation, his brotherly help.

Thus at one and the same time George's filial yearning sought satisfaction and his scholarly interests found fulfillment in making numberless contributions to Jewish history and bibliography while acting as an institution for the endowment of research and support of scholars. Without having large means he yet gave largely, and when the whole story comes to be known, it will be found that the Kohuts, George and Rebekah, were one of the two or three American families most generous in their support of Juedische Wissenschaft.

A verbal portrait can no more reproduce George Kohut than a canvas could limn that delicate, mobile, often beautiful face. And this is especially true of one who was finer and in truth greater than all his works. It may be that no small part of his winsomeness lay in his exotic quality. Sturdily and passionately American, he was yet an unassimilable exotic, an old-world being who looked not like a child of the Hungarian or Moravian Ghetto but rather like a youthful Latin Grandee. He seemed as if he might have held converse at Fez with Maimonides in the twelfth century, sat patiently and helpfully at the side of the Tibbonides as they translated Judah ha Levi and Ibn Gabirol into Hebrew, as if he might have listened breathlessly to some Hebrew song at Cordoba in the days of its glory. Changeless European Jew of a thousand years ago, he was nonetheless an American of Americans, whose heart the World War nearly broke and whom the latest insurrection of mediaeval fury against his people and his race crushed, finding a victim in his otherwise indomitable spirit.

As I have read over again Rebekah Kohut's story, "His Father's House," I have felt deeply that, however reserved the manner and restrained the style, it imparts the glow of a heart that shared and enriched the experiences of lives greatly lived. But above all else, it is a fireside tale of a life lived at the hearth, quietly told to those who loved him. This book, adequate and precious though it be, can do no more, as its author well knew, than give a glimpse of an inward life, a life of love and service. George Kohut gave his own life to his own, to learning and to the learned. He loved scholars as a son, he cared for them as a father, he served them as a brother. His was a great soul in a great generation.

— 1938

A Servant of God

I FEEL it alike duty and privilege to dwell for a moment on the life of one who was not of my own faith or people. I did not so much honor him because he was a Bishop, as I revered and cherished him as a man. Our earliest meetings go back more than forty years, when he held a minor place in the pro-Cathedral of his, the Anglican,

Communion, in the heart of the crowded East Side Jewish district. He fought then, as he fought to the hour of his passing, for a fair chance in life for all men, that the underprivileged might not be denied elementary and inalienable rights.

Later, after I had completed my Oregon Ministry in 1907, he became missionary Bishop of Eastern Oregon. From Jews and Christians alike I heard much of the informality and friendliness of the new Bishop, whom people quickly came to love, but whom his fellow-Diocesans seemed unable to understand. A formalistic and conventional Bishop would quickly have been laughed away from the primitive altars of Eastern Oregon. But Paddock rode up and down the land, taking nothing seriously, least of all himself, save the precept and example of his Master. There, in Oregon, he began to wield a real influence. For in the frontier country a stuffed shirt cannot last and a vested ecclesiastic of whatever rank counts only in the measure of his manhood.

He was as undramatic as an honest man could be. But there was drama in the simple, kindly, unaffected way in which this young man performed his offices, concerned little, if at all, with the dignities and solemnities of his rank, but much with the folk to whom he ministered, simple beings whom he could truly serve because he gave them his heart.

I saw much of Bishop Paddock again in recent years, when, during a partial restoration of long-broken health, he gave himself with all his heart and soul and strength to the cause of the Loyalists in Spain. Once again he became a Crusader, but a Crusader without hatred or bitterness, a Crusader touched only by great love for those sons and daughters of Spain, whom he felt to be trebly wronged, wronged by the invading armies of alien lands, wronged by them that ought to have been their militant guardians, wronged, alas, in large part by such as should have faithfully shepherded them, though the heavens and even the hell of enslavement fell.

It was a grand climax to a simply beautiful life. He was not a politician, splitting hairs over purely political problems and groups. Perhaps Bishop Paddock was not even a statesman, how he would have shuddered at the title—for he cared little about the major and minor political dialectics and there was no guile in him.

But he cared deeply, terribly about folk, however far away and "alien." Mere geography could not estrange from him a fellow-soul, however remote from his own stock or faith. And so this gentle, brotherly being came under attack by such as would penitently have sought his forgiveness had they known the man, a modern Saint. If to be Saint is to be utterly true to one's faith and to live by it without compromise or faltering, Robert Paddock was just that.

Only the thought of his disarming and childlike modesty halts my pen as I offer my tribute of unashamed affection to the living memory of one who was courageous without pose, religious with affectation, tender without sloppiness and passionate without wrath. He has made clear to me, a Jew, how a Christian can and ought to live, faithful in the least and the greatest to his Master.

— 1939

Senator Borah — A Tribute

I REMEMBER my first meeting with Senator Borah. It was in connection with a visit which, while Rabbi of Portland, Oregon, I paid to Boise, Idaho, in 1902 or 1903. Borah was an intimate friend of the leading Jewish citizens of

Boise—the one-time Idaho Governor Alexander and Nathan Falk, Boise's leading merchant. Months later, to my delight, Mr. Borah came to me after a Friday evening service in the Synagogue and we renewed our acquaintance, which was continued up to the day of his election to the Senate from Idaho, and throughout the full generation of his matchless service to his State.

In fact, our friendship was unbroken throughout all these years. I was very unhappy over the vote which Senator Borah cast against the confirmation of Mr. Brandeis as Justice of the Supreme Court; the more, because I had gathered that he would not reach a decision about his vote until after I had had an opportunity to present to him afresh the Brandeis case, especially in relation to the timber problem, wherein Mr. Brandeis had made a notable contribution to the commonweal. Borah intimated with little hesitation that "the timber interests in my State are very strong, and they feel that Mr. Brandeis is very hostile to them." It was the only disappointment suffered throughout nearly forty years of friendly relation with Senator Borah.

I remember that on that same occasion Senator Borah spoke slightingly of President Wilson, who had named Brandeis, saying "The President does not care about Brandeis' confirmation. He sought the benefit from the Liberals of having named Brandeis, but he will do little or nothing to secure his confirmation, which he might easily do." The message was conveyed to President Wilson, whereupon the latter wrote that letter of glowing appreciation of Mr. Brandeis, to Senator Culberson, which was almost more honoring to Mr. Brandeis than the original designation.

I cannot forbear to remind readers of two memorable services which Senator Borah rendered in relation to Jew-

ish problems. I cherish the memory which I have re-
freshed by referring to the original text of Senator Borah's
address, delivered at the Madison Square Garden Protest
meeting in September, 1929, after the Arab riots. I have
often heard Senator Borah on and off the floor of the Senate, making some of the finest and noblest addresses that
it has fallen to my lot to hear. He never rose to a great occasion with surer and loftier eloquence than he did that
night—Felix Frankfurter presiding. He was courageous
enough to warn the twenty thousand Zionists assembled
against what he had always believed to be the incertitude
of the Zionist position, saying, "When the word went
forth that a home for the Jewish people was to be established in Palestine it was a matter of profound interest
not only to the Jewish people but to people throughout
the world. It seemed in accord with a beautiful and sacred tradition. The story of a marvelous race surged upon   •
our mind, enriching our thought. It seemed in accord
with the highest dictates of humanity and the highest and
loftiest principles of justice that this should be so."

After these words, however — after speaking of men
thrilled by this dramatic movement, to see a people taking position in the line of their forefathers—apparently
without premeditation, for he never read his speeches—
he burst into a paragraph that still haunts one' memory:
*"Is this to be a National Home or an international sham-
bles?* A home is not a place where one is tortured with
fear. A home is not a place where the assassin clutches at
your dreams. A home is not a place where helpless men
and women and children are subjected to the barbarisms
of the barbaric. This meeting, this movement should be
firmly resolved to see to it that in the future such obligations are met as will make it a home."

The audience was stabbed into silence by the graudeur

of Senator Borah's eloquence. And as he closed with the words "In the faces of this vast audience I see great anxiety, great worry and great sorrow. But I also read in your faces great purpose and great determination. Let that purpose and that determination be your pillar of fire by night and your pillar of cloud by day to lead you into possession of that which belongs to you as a race," the great audience, hungering for comfort and passionately eager for light, burst into a demonstration, which, Senator Borah years later told me, he would remember to his last day.

One must admit that Borah's attitude in respect to the advent of Hitler was surprising, though, for a reason to be made clear, it was not inexplicable. The Hitler regime, from the moment it came into power, had the shrewdness to surround Senator Borah with its representatives. The German propaganda sources fully understood the value of anything that Borah might say or leave unsaid. I remember as if it were yesterday a conversation which the late President of the American Jewish Congress, Bernard Deutsch, and I had with Senator Borah within a week of Hitler's "election." We earnestly invited Borah to take his place on the platform of Madison Square Garden, March 27 (1933), when our Congress first brought to the attention of the American people an understanding of the tragedy that lay before the world. Senator Borah replied, "I would like to do what you ask, but I think I can do more through dealing with the gentlemen whom you have seen in the outer office. They represent Hitler himself, and through their offices I may be able to bring about mitigation of anti-Jewish severity, and even a change of attitude on Hitler's part to the whole Jewish problem." The men in the outer chamber were just run-of-the-mill newspaper men, purporting to be endowed with authority by Hitler—actually there as espionage agents of the

new regime, and seeking to make Borah believe that if he
would refrain from protest, he might yet be influential
in affecting the Hitler government. After some years
Senator Borah regretted that he had been momentarily
beguiled by men without power, who purported to be
authentic representatives of a regime which Senator
Borah loathed, because he was a man of honor, to whom
principles of fair dealing and international justice were
sacred.

A last important contact with Senator Borah was in
relation to the succession to Justice Oliver Wendell
Holmes. I happened to be in Washington on the day the
latter resigned his office, and to be in the office of Senator
Borah, who at once said, "The only man in the country to
succeed Mr. Justice Holmes is Chief Justice Cardozo." It
rejoiced my heart to hear his word of profound appreciation of the greatness as jurist of my beloved friend.
Throughout the weeks of discussion Senator Borah again
and again urged President Hoover to name Justice Cardozo, whom the Bar and the Law Schools and the Federal
Judges of America were virtually unanimous in desiring.

There are conflicting versions of what I am about to
tell, and President Hoover's secretary made some manner
of denial of what is to follow. It is, however, no violation
of confidence to tell that Senator Borah, on the Sunday
night which preceded the Monday morning of Cardozo's
appointment, informed President Hoover in the course
of a friendly conversation that none of the men whom
President Hoover had in mind, including an honored
colleague of Senator Borah in the United States Senate,
would be ratified by the Senate. It would not be unintelligible that President Hoover might have urged that
Justice Brandeis, a Jew, was one of the Justices of the
Supreme Court. In any event, without telling more than

may be told, Senator Borah urged President Hoover, "This is the time to lay the ghost of anti-Semitism in America by appointing to the Supreme Court a man whom the country wants, whom the American people know to be the best qualified man in the nation for the office." That Sunday night I learned from Senator Borah over the telephone that on the following morning Chief Justice Cardozo would be named successor to Justice Holmes. And so it came to pass.

I do not at this time write more about Senator Borah, of whom there will be more to say in other connections. Suffice it to say at this moment that Senator Borah was a great American and a great Senator. Whether it was a regrettable self-limitation on his part never to have crossed the Atlantic, never to have looked upon the chaos of inextricably joined and disjoined European nations, history alone will decide. He did his duty as he saw it in opposing the great Wilson program of nations leagued together in common defence. Borah felt that America must stand alone in the pride of its unmatched strength, and have no part or traffic in the never-ending quarrels and wars of the European peoples.

Curiously and perhaps sadly enough, it was this isolationist point of view which kept America out of the League of Nations, and made the League of Nations the shadow of what it might and ought to have been. He sought the honor of his country and the peace of the nations. By his convictions he stood without faltering. America will never forget a man equal to himself, who served in the United States Senate with character, with dignity, with power. "He never sold the truth to serve the hour" nor sought less than to keep his country upon the highest level of equal law and unfailing justice.

— 1940

Vladimir Jabotinsky

THE death of Vladimir Jabotinsky means a great sorrow to the Jewish world, the more so since those who differed from him never ceased to hope that some day the barriers would fall and he would find his way home again. Jabotinsky was much more than a dynamic figure, which is a conventional term: he was Dunamis, electric in power, dazzling in brilliance. And his strength he devoted to one cause, the cause of regathering his scattered and homeless people and enabling them to live their own inevitably creative, possibly secure life in their own ancient and cherished Homeland.

He was not only one of the most eloquent men of his time—and that in many tongues—but he was one of the bravest of men in setting out to make real his ideal, in struggling for the attainment of that in which he believed, in defying them who are unjust to Israel. He was one of the few men who, like Herzl and Brandeis, become legendary whilst yet they live. His limitation was that he could not bear to be a Grand Vizier, second in command. Feeling born to lead, and indeed, possessed of an undeniable flair for leadership, he was ill at ease in enduring a mere Lieutenancy. He was ill favored, too, in his following, which was pitiably unequal to its Commander.

But this is no time to dwell upon the limitation and failures of Jabotinsky. Manfully he wrought, valiantly he fought for Zion, dearer to him than all else. The World War tested him. The current World War should have brought him to an unchallenging and unchallenged place beside the leadership of the Zionist movement. Alas, that it was not to be, that pride of will or contempt for caution or inhospitality and unforbearance of antagonists kept him outside the gates!

Born to command, he obeyed but one impulse—to set his people free. His was "wisdom in the scorn of consequences" in a world which insists that consequences must be weighed by him who essays the leadership of a people. He was a puissant figure, and as such he will be gratefully remembered. His life was gain, his death is loss to his people. No man merits loftier epitaph. He clad himself in the armor of his people's hope. He wore it worthily. The quarrels that he provoked, the conflicts that gathered around his name will be forgotten. But his name and heroic deeds will be remembered and will shine forever in the firmament of his imperishable people.

— 1940

Henrietta Szold

IT IS no exaggeration to say that world Jewry, as far as it is free, joined in celebrating the eightieth birthday of her whom the pulpit of the Free Synagogue described as "foremost among Jewish women." Henrietta Szold is as clearly and indubitably foremost among Jewish women as Justice Brandeis is foremost among Jewish men the world over. These have something of the same impressive and moving moral quality which is the surest passport to the temple of immortality.

Henrietta Szold, daughter of fine and scholarly Rabbi Benjamin Szold of Baltimore, gave a generation of her full life to Jewish learning, to teaching, in the early eighties, of the East European immigrants to our shores. She will be remembered as the guiding spirit, though such was not her title, of the Jewish Publication Society, perhaps her most important service in that office having been her admirable translation of Graetz's monumental history of the Jews, and the preparation of an invaluable index.

Always at the side of her father, a Zionist from the very beginnings of the Zionist Movement in America, with the coming of the world war she entered into more active and continuous relation to the Zionist Movement. Hadassah is her creation, though it must in fairness be added that in the founding of Hadassah she had the help of one identified throughout her life with Zionism, Mrs. Richard Gottheil, wife of the late Professor Gottheil, who might justly be described as co-founder of Hadassah.

Much that is finest in the work of Hadassah and in the quality of its membership derives from the impact and the influence of Henrietta Szold. She is truly a great woman, who exacts much from others and most from herself. Her contemporaries will never forget the zeal and consecration with which she set herself in 1916 to the task of organizing the first Hadassah Nurse war unit in Palestine. For two decades she has been an honored figure in Palestine, holding indeed an unique place among all the dwellers of the Yishub. Incredibly humble, literally untiring and always giving and asking the best, she stands today as perhaps the most notable contribution of American Jewry to the life of Palestine. OPINION adds the deepfelt congratulations of its Editorial Board and of tens of thousands of its readers to those wishes which go out to one whose eye is undimmed and whose strength is unabated. So to live, so to dream, so to toil, so to serve the highest in a people's life: "This is not broken age but ageless youth!"

— 1941

Brandeis — Our Very Own

BEFORE I FIRST MET Brandeis, nearly thirty years ago, someone said to me, "I find that every meeting with Brandeis is a spiritual experience." I quickly came to see the accuracy of that observation. One felt as one sat with him in his modest little study, unadorned save by the radiance of his personality, that one had drawn a little nearer to the sources of truth and justice. In his moving tribute to Mr. Brandeis, Justice Frankfurter quoted the lines of Malachi, "the law of truth was in his mouth and unrighteousness was not found upon his lips." Sometimes as I listened to him at his finest and truest, I felt as if I were at the side of one who, without being oracular or dogmatic, had gained for himself the treasure of truth and was sharing it with those who listened.

He was our very own as leader in the most critical years of American history, in the years of Israel's most urgent need, when the lofty quality of his ethical idealism meant much to the fortunes of Israel. It was a providential conjuncture that matched the man and the need, that made his the decisive contribution in the working out of Jewish destiny at a time when America had become supremely important in the leadership of world affairs. Whatever may be believed touching his return as an active participant in Jewish affairs, who can think of Louis Brandeis without rising to the hope that something of his own spiritual quality might pervade the leadership of American Israel.

Nor may we forget that Brandeis has been one of the commanding figures in the realm of democracy. As much as any man of his generation, he has been a leader of the forces of liberalism, not spasmodically nor melodramatically but consistently and selflessly. Throughout a genera-

tion he made the imperiled interests of the people his
own, so that it was not a matter of chance that President
Wilson named him, as he assured me again and again,
with the deepest personal satisfaction as "an inevitable
choice for the United States Supreme Court."

Brandeis was an American prophet, but the prophet
within his being was enriched and ennobled in the last
generation of his life by reason of his self-identification
with the Jewish people. If he did not enter into affiliation
with the Synagogue, he did that which established the im-
mediacy of his relationship to his people—gave himself
to the cause of Zionism—and I use the term gave himself
advisedly—gave his time, his strength, his intellectual
and moral counsel, gave with unknown and unbelievable
generosity to every great interest and cause of Palestine
rebuilding.

The term "prophet" should not be lightly used, least of
all by Jews. When it is used, it must be in relation to one
who is dowered with that insight into truth which inevitably translates itself into foresight with respect to the future, with that moral grandeur which compels men to
undertake and achieve the impossible.

Brandeis was a proud Jew. He wore his Jewish badge
not only with dignity but with joyous pride. Sometimes I
have felt as I sat with him that he exaggerated the virtue
of his people, that he over-estimated the capacity of his
people to rise to his own height, to share his dreams, to
give as he gave himself for the honor of his people, thru
the re-establishment of the Jewish National Home.

Since the day of Herzl, who passed in 1903, Brandeis
was indisputably and incomparably our greatest. I thank
God for the fullness of his years and the richness of his
days, for what he wrought and above all for what he was.
Speaking on the eightieth birthday of Justice Brandeis,

I said of him that "Brandeis belongs to America; Brandeis has become a world figure; but we Zionists have the ineffable satisfaction of knowing that he who is at one and the same time the greatest of living Jews and one of the greatest Americans, belongs peculiarly to us. What he has meant to the Zionist cause and to the leadership for nearly a generation will not be known until after the decades, when the annals shall have been laid bare and become known."

Brandeis made an unique contribution both to the Zionist cause and to the cause of democracy in Jewish life, through the American Jewish Congress. I think not of his gifts as an economist, not even of his genius as a statesman; least of all, of his boundless personal generosity. Rather do I think of a spirit that he has brought to our cause, that I can best describe by using the old Hebrew term "Kedushah"—holiness.

He did not give himself to the cause of rebuilding the Jewish people thru the resettlement of the Jewish land as to one of many causes which are entitled to help, but he dedicated to that cause the finest mind and the noblest heart in all the Jewish world. I, who, in common with a number of the older American Zionists, am—alas, was—privileged to be in close touch with him, thank God for that privilege—which I cherish as few things in life—of having worked year after year, and day after day with a man whose spirit has given me a fresh insight into the possibility of the Jew at his highest.

The Conscience of the Senate

IT is not seemly for a non-political journal to discuss matters that impinge upon the world of political affairs. But the defeat of Senator Norris at the last election is not an occasion for partisan regret over the almost inexplicable defeat of the least party-tied member of the United States Senate. It is cause for sorrow that the foremost of Senators, honored, beloved, revered, should have been denied re-election to the Senate by the State which he had notably served for more than forty years. It may be too late or too early for postmortem election analyses, but certain it is that a nation-wide plebiscite of his fellow Americans would have resulted in the virtually unanimous re-election of Senator Norris. Writing this editorial note in Boston, the Editor of OPINION recalls the great Senator of Massachusetts who bore the distinguishing title, "a Senator with a conscience." Senator Norris was not a senator with a conscience; he was pre-eminently the conscience of the Senate. Even when surrounded and supported by its finest members, Senator Norris stood out as the great apostle and servant of democracy. The people of his own State might for a time forsake him, but the common people of every State, and of estate high and low, know and love him for their own.

No American since the day of Lincoln was more truly of the people, by the people, and for the people. He recognized and acted upon the imperatives of social-economic as well as political democracy, and sought to move his country to live by them and in obedience to their commands. Herein he was yoked in fellowship with yet another younger leader of democracy who, like him, trusts the American people and serves them greatly. Each of the mighty battles Senator Norris fought will abide as an inspiring memory to his fellow Americans, and the last of the battles he fought reveals the stature of this American who was Jeffersonian in his political idealism, Lincolnian in his American simplicity, Rooseveltian in his illimitable dedication to the democratic hope of his country and of mankind at its highest.

— 1942

George Brandes' Centenary

IT IS INDEED TO THE honor of the Danish people that they did not permit the Centenary of George Brandes, famous literary critic and author, to pass, February 4, without fitting celebration thereof. It could not have been easy thus to defy the Nazi rulers, but it was done, much to the honor of the natives of brave, unmilitary little Denmark. Best of all, it was Denmark's student body, which at the University of Copenhagen persisted, to its peril, in arranging a celebration to commemorate Brandes' (Morris Cohen) "contribution to European Culture and the contribution of his people to world civilization." The Brandes' meeting was heavily guarded but it was held. So must the now flickering lights of civilization be vigilantly guarded by all peoples to whom life is unthinkable without light— the light of the human spirit groping toward the highest, which it will see only to love.

Brandes' position in Denmark during his life was unusual. He was one of the most eminent of the devotees of the Shakespeare cult, and held a unique position in the literary life and circles of his day. How tragic to think that the land which gave him birth and opportunity, which tendered him such honor as his unique position in the heart of Danish culture merited, should now be under the feet of that government for which culture has only

one meaning—avenue to power over others. Against Nazified Germany and its morally lawless rule the civilized
world feels nothing but scorn and loathing. Its victims
engage the sympathy of men who still understand that the
only values that abide are moral, and that every brave little people, from Denmark and Holland to Jugoslavia and
Greece, that still dares as it can to resist the oppressor,
stands higher in the role of human aspiration and achievement than hated, loathsome, doomed Nazi Germany.

— 1942

A Grand Old Man

UNDERSTANDING Americans will take heart at the thought
of an early visit to this country by one of the grand, old
men of current history. Marshal Smuts is become since the
death of President Masaryk one of the two surviving key
figures of the first World War and the peace that followed, his only surviving contemporary of the first magnitude being former Prime Minister Lloyd George. Field
Marshal Smuts is not only a great citizen and leader of his
own country and indeed of the British Commonwealth
of nations, but stands out as one of the foremost citizens
of the world of freemen. In his youth he fought England
on behalf of the Dutch. In the eighth decade of his life he
stands at the side of England for the second time, in order
to devote the immensity of his mind and the majesty of
his purposes to the winning of the war against the mighti-
est foes freedom has ever known.

Like many of the greatest of his contemporaries, Wilson and Lloyd George, Balfour and Masaryk, Field Marshal Smuts has spoken and acted on behalf of Zionism.
The prophet in him has uttered his soul with clarion
notes of understanding and heartening to the Jewish peo-

ple. His knowledge and love of the Old Testament have made him a Cromwell in our time. His message for the twenty-fourth anniversary of Balfour Day will be treasured as one of the classics of Zionist utterance by one who is himself a devout Christian a true mystic and a great servant of man's highest hopes. America will do well to bid the warmest welcome to Field Marshal Jan Christian Smuts, a friend of Zionism, helper of Weizmann and, over and above all, with life utterly dedicated upon the altar of human freedom.

— 1943

In Memoriam: Josiah Wedgwood

I DO not know the name of a living non-Jew which has meant as much to Jews the world over as that of Josiah Wedgwood. Years ago in the pages of OPINION I said of him that, "what'er the wrong done the Jews of a Polish or Roumanian village, these rested confident that their cause would have a hearing in the world's foremost Parliament because of the never-failing championship of the wronged by Josiah Wedgwood."

Wedgwood's relation to the Jewish people dates from his espousal of the Zionist cause. He became sharply intolerant of Jews who opposed Zionism—indeed, could not even understand them. Zionism meant these things to him, the resumption of Jewish self-respect, the restoration of the collective and creative life of the Jewish people, and, for him above all, a deed of historic reparation from the nations of Christendom to the Jew. That great wrong, as he saw it, could thus alone be righted, and the righting of it seemed doubly desirable because Zion might be set up as the Seventh Dominion within the British Empire. This possibility was calculated to make the Jew-

ish redemption of Zion still more precious to his British
soul.

I have seen Josiah Wedgwood in the House, a veritable
gadfly to the ignoble steeds of the Colonial Office, blazing
with righteous wrath and moving governmental anti-
Zionists not to noble anger but to bitter recrimination
against the universally respected, often exasperating, but
always loved Wedgwood. Members of the House, usually
his opponents, including even Jewish supporters of Zionism, often spoke of Wedgwood as indiscreet and impatient. If to call unfairness by its right name without equivocation was indiscreet, he rose at times to the summit
of indiscretion; if to be impatient with injustice, whether
to Chinese coolies or Indian untouchables or Jewish
dreamers of Zion, was unstatesmanlike, there was no
statesmanship in this Englishman, with an Englishman's
conscience and an Englishman's passion for freedom.

One remembers well his radio address of two years
ago to the American Palestine Committee's dinner at
Washington for Dr. Weizmann. He might have been
courteous in studied circumlocution, and particularly
discreet as an Englishman speaking to Americans. Instead of that, he was direct and blunt and unequivocal.
Some of his timid, particularly Jewish, hearers were
shocked. The British Broadcasting Company was forced
to offer explanations. He stood his ground, as all his life
he stood his ground, whether in South Africa or Gallipoli,
whether on the Hustings or in the House, whether as
Commander in the Navy or Colonel in the Army.

In other days I have seen him at work on his task of
many years, the History of the English Parliament. On
that testing ground he won a lasting fame, because men
recognize and honor integrity, even when it becomes irritating in its ceaseless insistence upon the right in scorn of

consequences. Other hands will complete the work Wedgwood carried on throughout a generation. In all the many tomes of that Chronicle, it will not be possible to find the story of a Commoner, only in his last years a Peer, who served his country with a nobler will and a more generous ardor for human freedom. When his country was right he sought to keep it right and true, but whenever his country was wrong and unequal to itself, he dared to set it right.

World Jewry has suffered a great loss in his passing, even as his life fortified the Jew everywhere. In all the non-Jewish world there is no Josiah Wedgwood left to die.

— 1943

V

Toward Peace and Justice

The Need for Jeremiah

JOY is turned into mourning! What promised to be epochal days in the story of man's abolition of war are become days of anguish and world-woe. The scene of human interest has been shifted from Geneva to Shanghai. A solemn farce may yet be enacted at Geneva in these days, while at Shanghai the gathering portents threaten tragedy.

If Shanghai is to supersede Geneva, is it not in part because Geneva has never been equal to itself, to men's best hope or deepest need? If it now be too late to avert the Sino-Japanese war which is already that in all but name, it is the most awful indictment of the futility of Geneva and the fatuity of its leadership.

Why should men place their trust in Geneva and its Disarmament Conference, seeing that the two most effective European figures in the field of internationalism are not to be there? Robert Cecil's place is taken by some British cabinet nonentity and Briand is virtually banished and a'fishing while the French jingoes prepare to take a leading part in the farce.

No less a figure than Jeremiah were needed to depict this sombre hour of disillusionment. For if Shanghai is to be the Serajevo of 1932, the human family will be plunged into unfathomable horror. And yet Shanghai is almost an alternative to Geneva. The world will either resolve at Geneva to move forward rationally through disarmament to warlessness, or Shanghai will prove to be the first scene in the tragedy of world dissolution. How long halt ye between two opinions? The Shanghai way is the sorrowful and bitter way of death. Geneva—if England, France, Germany, and our own country dare take the lead—may yet promise life and peace. — 1932

What Good Is Good-Will?

THERE are many current good-will movements. Some of
them are all but frankly political maneuvers: some are
little more than individual or collective conscience-
twinges amplified: yet other good-will movements grow
out of the recognition on the part of the "good-willers"
that ill-will does not pay, in any event, is not nice nor
seemly.

The most notable of the good-will phenomena is bound
up with Christian-Jewish relations in our land. For a
decade or more, the realists in the realm of inter-racial
and inter-religious conflicts have seen that Christians
could not afford to remain passive or neutral while war of
one kind or another was being waged against Jews by
various groups holding aloft—or trailing in the mire—
Christian banners. These good-will committees and
groups and associations got themselves organized with
the help of not a little genuine Christian good-will, stimu-
lated by markedly undiffident Jewish cooperation. This
Jewish stimulation has occasionally assumed such gro-
tesque forms as singling out some conspicuous and admirable Christian, lay or clerical, as the most aggressive
or effective of the year's "good-willers." The professional
advocates of good-will were resolved that good-will should
not ineffectually beat its wings in the intense inane—and
good-will goes marching on.

From time to time an unwelcome doubt obtrudes itself
upon the thinking of one Jewish "good-willer." What
good is good-will, unless in times of crisis and emergency
it energize itself into action, substituting the act of beneficence or well-doing for the mere past of benevolence or
"good-willing"?

Such was the good-will of a group which some years ago

was about to set forth and collate facts with regard to the extent of the "Christians only" anti-Jewish employment boycott. Then something happened and the quest halted or, what is likelier, was halted. Frustrate action need leave no scars of defeat if it has been undertaken with vigor and valiancy. But what could be psychologically more hurtful than organized good-will forever left unutilized, however urgent the appeal for it to dare enter the field of action!

Otherwise it may come to pass that good-will may be accepted as an attitude or pose, wherever, for any reason, it is bound to be inert and ineffectual, and rejected as an obligation wherever it may be translated into effectiveness. It has well been said that tolerance is only less intolerable than intolerance. Must it be that good-will is to become as unlovely as either tolerance or intolerance because many men of good-will have not learned the distinction between feebly wishing and firmly willing.

— 1931

True Christians and Jews

WITHIN THE MONTH two great utterances of outstanding Christian men, one Catholic and the other Protestant, have come to light. In a recently published volume under the title "I Was In Hell With Niemoeller," Dr. Leo Stein, who was a German Jew, fully quotes the more recent attitude of Niemoeller to Jews. It was for years deeply painful to know that Niemoeller would have been prepared to give his support to Nazism without any reservation save that which drove him to accept the torture of Sachsenhausen rather than do obeisance to Hitler in the place of Niemoeller's Divine Master. Niemoeller apparently took no exception to Hitler's treatment of Jews but now Dr. Stein reports Niemoeller as saying "I certainly

am not free from reproach because for a time certain
restrictions against the Jews seemed to me tolerable. I did
not realize that we would have to pay for these restrictions
with our own liberty. I did not fully take into account
that equality had been given to Jews during our epoch of
liberalism and that any restriction imposed on Jews
would mean the end of that epoch and possibly the end
of individual liberty including the right to worship. In
other words, to deprive the Jews of political equality
would mean turning back the wheels of history. That is
the truth I learned. It is not sufficiently realized by the
anti-Semites in our countries."

This expresses some manner of penitence but it will
not be deeply satisfying to those who feel that Niemoeller's repentance should have rested itself on higher
grounds than those of self-interest and that his wrath
should have been as a flaming sword against a regime
which dealt with Jews as Nazism did. It may be that these
are only the first fruits of penitence and that Niemoeller,
if he is to survive, will yet see the truth that the religious
man cannot assent to injustice to any man, whatever his
faith or race even though such injustice be not followed
by injustice to one's self.

A truer and nobler declaration on anti-Semitism has
come from the lips of the Cardinal of England, a declaration so significant that it deserves to rank with the immortal utterance of the late Pope who declared, "Spiritually
we are all Semites." The English Cardinal phrases it differently but he fully assents to the word of Pius XI. Cardinal Hinsley deals with the matter of anti-Semitism as
an Englishman and Christian. On both counts and from
both points of view he finds it reprehensible, incompati-
ble with the viewpoint of a civilized person and intolerable from the position of a Christian.

Would that such followers of Coughlin, as are still his dupes, would remember the word of Pope Pius or the word of England's Cardinal. It is these in the breadth of their understanding and the catholicity of their fraternal, and even paternal, regard for men which should be accepted by true sons and daughters of the Catholic communion rather than the savage outcries of intolerance and bigotry and hatred which are the staple of *Social Justice* soon perhaps to be no more. Even a Jew has the right to say that the Catholic Church is more truly represented by the Pope and England's Cardinal to say nothing of many, many Catholic leaders who might be quoted, than by the Priest of Detroit who, while erecting a shrine, has builded an instrument of betrayal to his country and dishonor to his Church.

— 1942

Il Duce's Threat

IT had been imagined that the cup of Jewish bitterness was full to overflowing. But it has been left for the personal organ of Mussolini to add the last embittering and empoisoning drop to the cup of Jewish misery. Hitler brought the question of race into the arena of discussion and judgment. Mussolini's organ has done something worse. It has laid down the law in terms that are shocking and yet not startling to them that understand, that the Jews must become enthusiastic devotees of the cause of Fascism in Italy and that Italian Jews must give their approval to the Nazi cause in Germany.

It is difficult at this moment to foresee to what compromises of action this fiat of Il Duce will lead. It must be taken for granted that Italian Jews will bear themselves with dignity and self-reverence in scorn of every conse-

quence. The real question is what will be the attitude of
the Jewish world. Will it be prepared to bend the knee or
will its answer be in a language that Italy will understand
—*non possumus!* This is the uttermost indignity to the
Jewish people, not only bidden to be lawful but to expose
its innermost soul and surrender all in order that it may
preserve the outer form of life. Israel has met mightier
masters than Il Duce. It has survived them. It will survive
him. Let him be warned betimes that the ultimate ideal
of Jews is not safety but honor, that Jews will not choose
outwardly to survive in order that they may inwardly
perish.

This is the time for the great Christian communions to
rise up and utter their word of most solemn protest
against an unutterable wrong. May it not be added that
Hitler's first assault was upon Jews. Today Catholic and
Protestant are become the objective of Nazism's enven-
omed attack. Whatever Christianity resolves to do for the
Jew and against a wrong will not only redound to the
honor of Christianity but ultimately to the saving of
pagan-threatened Christianity.

— 1937

China's Freedom Is Our Concern

THE Panay incident will remain closed unless Japan
chooses to reopen it. Congress will now devote itself to
discussion of the Ludlow amendment which may yet
prove to be democracy's supreme gift to the Fascist Powers. Ludlow and his supporters may not understand it, but
it is such parliamentary ineptitude as the proposed Ludlow amendment which accelerated the death of most
parliaments.

In a democracy such as our own, the government which

is the Administration, legislative and executive, chosen for a term by the people, prescribes the rules under which it is to proceed in any given circumstances. But it does not presume to regulate the daily conduct of its citizenship over the wide area of voluntary choices as long as these are not in conflict with law and statute. Thus our government has decided to accept the apology of the Japanese government. But it does not and could not prescribe what shall be the attitude of the American citizen toward Japan. The latter's unprecedentedly savage war is as yet undeclared, so that even neutrality in act may not be imposed upon us.

It will be recalled by some that after the advent of Hitler, it was easy to see that the Administration was wholly out of sympathy on every ground with that authoritarian absolutism which usurped the place of the Weimar Republic. But it did no more than send a democratic and libertarian ambassador to Berlin. Not even the jejune timidities of the B'nai B'rith nor yet the more articulate patrioteering of some members of the American Jewish Committee could move our government to stop the anti-Nazi boycott activities of the Congress, of the Untermyer-Silver and the Jewish Labor Committee groups, above all, of the American Federation of Labor. These say that while our government might not feel itself free to break off relations with a usurpatory Nazi regime, we as Americans remain free, severally and collectively, to have no relation of any type with the Nazi government and people and that the severance of such ties must include our refusal to have any relation to Nazidom which, through purchase of its wares or use of its services, might add an atom to the strength of the regime. Millions of Americans have done this and, if it be said ineffectually, for Hitlerism still stands, the obvious answer is that boycott values are moral rather than economic and that we who share in boycott measures are bent upon keeping our own souls undefiled by any contact which is assent to a monstrous wrong.

Again I revert to Japan. It has done that which is a stench in the nostrils of civilization. Shall we, who rose up against Nazi Germany, be unconcerned in the presence of deeds as foul as earth has known, because committed in a far-off continent in which there is a minimum of Jews? We have said that if Nazism had insulted German Jews by singling them out for favor, we would be no less the foes of Nazism than we are. Japan has committed a three-fold crime. It has on the flimsiest excuse waged war against a peaceable people. It has provoked the most terrible of wars in order to strengthen itself for the mighty war which it plans to wage against Soviet Communism. It purports, most dastardly of lies, to defend itself against the anti-Japanese sentiment of the Chinese Republic, which has within three months found tragic vindication at the hands of Nipponese madmen bettering Nazi instruction.

Not for us to prognosticate how this tragedy will end! We only know that we covet for our people the distinction of leadership in defense of a great and peaceable people, to whom war at its most cruel and terrible is overwhelming. We cannot be sure that the Chinese Republic can be saved or the Chinese people effectively defended. But we may be sure that here we must speak and act as we for the most part vainly expect other peoples to rally to our side, when wrong is perpetrated against us. Governments must hesitate lest war ensue. But we who are American Jews must make clear to ourselves and to all mankind that we are not insensitive, as is often alleged, to wrong when not committed against us.

Japan has chosen to place the world's crown of infamy upon its own head. One hesitates to indulge in the commonplace about American women holding the decision in their hands or on their feet. This effort must not be limited to women alone. Unlike Christian churches, we have not sought to religionize Japan. But we would not have Japan become a threat and most terrible of menaces to all the world, at least not without solemn protest on our part. The Jewish population of Japan is most limited; that of China little larger. Our own duty is nonetheless clear. This gravest of affronts to civilization, this unspeakable violation of every instinct of morality must be sternly dealt with. Who better fitted than we, oldest of the peoples of a moral code, to give of moral support by the side of all who care, to another great and ancient people threatened with subjugation if not extinction!

— 1938

"Through Gentile Eyes"

THE AUTHOR of "Through Gentile Eyes" calls it a plea for tolerance and good-will. It is all of that and it is definitely more. If I were asked in a few words to explain and interpret the volume, I should say it is a mighty challenge to two worlds: the Christian world and the Jewish world. To the Christian world, to be just; to the Jewish world, to be worthy of and equal to itself. I venture to predict that this volumn "Through Gentile Eyes" will yet take its place with the great Christian classics of irenic Christian-Jewish literature. I am thinking of such volumes and such pleas as those of Abbè Gregòire of the 18th century., Count Coudenhove, whose book on anti-Semitism is the fullest, finest statement of the defense against anti-Semitism ever written by a non-Jew. The second edition has just appeared from the pen of his son, the author having been forced to flee from Austria and find refuge in Czecho-

slovakia because he is anti-Nazi; and then of course there
is that third classic written and spoken by Lord Macauley
ninety years ago.

This volume of John Haynes Holmes takes its place
in that collection of immortal things immortally spoken.
I have used the term challenge. It is more than challenge
—this book is a cry of penitence of the Christian world.
The author speaks contritely for those whose contriteness
and penitence he does not require to share. If this were
Christianity, if Christianity lived by this book, there were
another story to tell. Christendom would not be dishon-
ored; Jewry would not be broken. The author is funda-
mentally a progressive, socially radical Christian, and
therefore a great-hearted humanitarian. He is one of the
enlightened and most enlightening of modern religion-
ists and he is shocked, startled and humiliated by what
he sees and knows of Christian-Jewish relations. The guilt
of Christendom respecting the Jew weighs upon his soul,
though less perhaps than any Christian living has he
shared in that guilt. As a humanitarian, he is shaken; as
a Christian he feels guilty; as a neighbor to the Jew he
urges the Jew to be himself, not to succumb either to
the Christian world, or to something equally imperiling,
namely, Jewish self-scorn or self-contempt. He urges the
Jew to be equal to the best, and by way of climax to all
else, worthily, honorably, greatly to rebuild the Jewish
National Home, Palestine. Best of all, this book is written not by one who was said to be pro-Jewish or to be a
friend of Jews, but by one whose passion for justice revealed throughout a great and prophetic ministry, one
of the three or four great and prophetic ministries of our
age, moves him to face what he calls man's supreme injustice, namely, Christendom's attitude to the Jew.

"My sin, the sin of Christendom do I acknowledge,"

writes the author. The writer's soul is deeply stirred as a great liberal soul is inevitably stirred by the emergence of the Jew from the helplessness of the past century, and the will of Jews once again to live creatively not against nations, but with the nations, in the midst of nations as prophets of Democracy, as haters of war and as battlers for peace, not asking for tolerance and good-will for the Jew alone. He challenges the Jew to take his place among the leaders of mankind struggling, striving, battling, sacrificing for the highest we know, for those political, social, ethical and spiritual ideals of which the Jew at his truest has always been the protagonist and because of his defense of which he is the scorn and the mockery of them that loathe him. For these know whether in Berlin or in Belgrade, in Wilna or in Riga, that the Jew cannot be trusted to be silent and uncomplaining in the presence of political injustice, of social inequity or moral wrong.

Not since the days of Theodor Herzl, Max Nordau, and Brandeis has any man, whether Jew or Christian, spoken and written of Zion and Zionism as writes and speaks the author of these pages. Joy fills his heart as he contemplates the great achievement of the Jewish people and he is not afraid for them though he loves them. He glories as a friend of justice in the rebirth of Palestine of which he says, "Palestine belongs to the Jew not by the conquest of the sword but by that nobler conquest of the heart, which quickens into life the soil, the land, the cause which it devotedly loves!"

Consider the story of the American Jewish Congress and the World Jewish Congress which we formed a few years ago. "I am reminded again," writes Dr. Holmes, "that I am a gentile. But even so, I am truly as any Jew a member of a minority group. I share something of the experience of the minorities. It is from this standpoint that, very humbly, in answer to the belief of some Jews that they cannot afford to hold a World Jewish Congress, because they are Jews, I beg to say that Jews cannot afford *not* to have a World Congress *because they are Jews!*" That is the spirit of a man who respects us, who wishes the Jew not to be safe through submission to material power but whose soul so respects us, that he challenges the Jew to stand in the vanguard of battling humanity, not fearful and slinking away from his fate, that he may be safe, but joyfully hazarding every risk and every hurt and thus fulfilling the destiny of the Jew.

This book will live even as its author will live. Place copies of the book in the hands of our friends, place them in the hands of those who do not understand the Jew, let them be read by those who are unjust to the Jew. "Through Gentile Eyes" is a message of brotherhood, of understanding, of love, which I commend to the minds and hearts of Jew and Christian alike.

— 1938

Our Democratic Faith — A Reply to D'Annunzio

A CLEAR though contradictory statement of the Italian race problem has appeared in the *New York Herald Tribune* over the signature of a son of D'Annunzio. Clear, insofar as it rather accurately portrays the part played by Jews throughout the centuries of Italian history, with special reference to the place of the Jew in recent days. Much that Jews have contributed to the arts and sciences, learning and letters, army and politics, is set forth with seeming fairness. Suddenly and with barely a word of transition, the writer bursts into the angry and awkwardly phrased query: "Why have the Jews outside of Italy

made themselves responsible for a reaction against their
brethren in Italy? That is a question that they themselves
must answer."

Thus sharply and frankly, the race mask is torn off and
the Fascist land reveals itself as prepared for deeds of
vengeance and reprisal against its own Jews, because, so
it is alleged, Jews generally are against Fascism, and,
"Jewish press and pulpit throughout the world daily
denounce Italian Fascism." Whither has the race question fled, seeing that D'Annunzio concludes his argument
with the threat, "the Jewish problem of Italy has now become a problem for Jews throughout the world to solve.
And upon their decision rests the fate of the Jews in
Italy." This is the Nazi theory of hostages, plus a delicate
touch of Blackhandism. What could be more unashamed-
ly brutal than to announce to world Jewry that in its
hands, upon its decision, rests the fate of the Jews in
Italy. Heinous though this declaration be, it offers a challenge which Jews cannot, indeed dare not, ignore. The
question of race is hardly involved, although the weirdly
ludicrous doctrine of race purity has suddenly been borrowed by Mussolini in behalf of that mixed race which
Hitler in "Mein Kampf" repeatedly describes as "Ne-
groid."

D'Annunzio quotes an authoritative Italian spokesman: "The Jews have in every country in the world, with
their men and their means, formed the general staff of
anti-Fascism. . . . Jewish anti-Fascism has struck and
Fascism struck back. And in this exchange of blows Fascism was not the loser." The issue is thus presented une-
quivocally. Will Jews likewise make answer, as they are
invited to do, without equivocation?

Needless to say that there is an absurd measure of overstatement in the charge of D'Annunzio that "Jews have

in every country of the world, with their men and their means, formed the general staff of anti-Fascism." In replying, however, to such rhetorical blast, there is one thing that we must not do. That is, we dare not fail to make clear, first, that the statement that Jewish men and women have in every country formed the general staff of anti-Fascism is ludicrously exaggerated; second, while there is no such thing as "Jewish anti-Fascism which has struck," Jews in every land, unless they are under the compulsion of obedience to Fascist Governments, are the native foes of governmental tyranny. Whether or not Signor D'Annunzio is prepared to exploit my statement, I claim, not admit, the Jew everywhere is potentially, and in many countries actually, anti-Fascist. His history, his tradition, his instinct, have made of him an invincible anti-Fascist. His history, beginning with Bible days, is the story of a never-ending quest of liberty under law. Out of that passion grew the Moses-led revolt against Pharaoh. The ages have not dulled the Jewish instinct for freedom: centuries of exile have not moved the Jew to renounce his conviction that life without liberty is death.

As a Jew, I sorrow over the circumstance that Italian Jews, who have been an enriching part of its life for more than twenty centuries, should be penalized because of that uncancelable instinct of freedom, which has brought Jews in Democratic lands into the vanguard of Fascist foes. The normal Jew outside of Fascist lands—and none other is free—hates every form and manner of human tyranny whether it be Hitler Nazism or Mussolini Fascism or Franco Insurgency or Mikado Imperialism. It may be, to revert to our brother Jews in Italy, that they will increasingly become the victims of the spirit that lusts for hostages.

But one thing we cannot do for Italian Jews. We will

not disavow our democratic faith in order to soften the rigor of the blows which may fall upon them. If we were to do that—and there are those who begin to urge "piping down" against Fascism—then and only then the charge of "Internationalism" might be brought against us. The price which D'Annunzio asks Jews to pay for the sake of ransoming Jewish hostages in Italy, Jews will never pay. To the Jew, Democracy and all that it means is not a passing type or process of Government. Democracy is the political faith of the Jew, and this were true even if it were not bound up with his fate. In an enslaved world, the Jew would choose not to live. Unhappy Jews, whose lines are cast in the unpleasant places of Fascist tyranny as in Italy or Germany! Il Duce and all of his American disciples may yet learn that the Jew has never made security his goal, but ever hungered for justice and freedom. Fascism will not be humanity's last word. The spirit of freedom by which and under which alone the Jew lives, cannot die.

— 1938

The Fall of France

To philosophize on the reasons for France's failure would be meaningless, only if France were not again to be. No analysis of the causes of France's fall may omit the chiefest factors, however little known, that led thereto. OPINION, which is familiar with the French press, states without reservation that the press of France did not tell the truth to the French people throughout the first Nazi years about what Nazism meant, what it wrought, how it affected the people under the Nazi regime, what oceanic evils within and without the Nazi Reich were bound up with it. It is as if a conspiracy, perhaps it were better to say an arrangement, had been entered into between the Nazi Reich and

the French press to withhold the truth from the people
of France.

Today, the Nazis have, alas, taken over the government
and virtually the territory of France. But long before the
Nazis conquered France, they had taken over the press,
not of course without certain exceptions. It was the
French press more than any other single factor which constituted the Nazi fifth column in France. Seeing that the
French people did not know the truth about what Hitlerism meant, naturally enough they were unprepared and
unready either to make the effort or the sacrifices which
were needed during the years that went before the war.
The French press was not utterly silent with regard to the
unmeasured iniquities of the Nazi regime, of which
France today is become the victim, but the French press,
if not silent, never told a tithe of the truth about Nazi
horror and Nazi shame. When the press of one country
becomes the fifth column of a neighboring enemy, there
can be no hope for them that are to be invaded.

But there were other reasons. Throughout the years
during which France failed to prepare itself for the war,
French partisanship raged at its maddest. No government
commanded the complete support of the French people.
France has been undermined for a decade by Communists on the one hand and Fascists on the other, and it is not
easy to apportion the exact measure of blame, save that
guilt obviously attaches to both within France. The tragedy thus became inevitable. Partisanship, divisiveness,
either a wretchedly ineffective information service or a
lack of understanding on the part of governments, which
preferred to remain uninformed, these are the things that
brought about a tragedy too deep for tears.

When Poland fell, the consensus of the world's opinion
was that Poland was weakened and undermined by its

own Endek or Fascist groups. This is no less true about France, though we knew it not before France was undone. Even England, if the truth is to be told, has been far too tolerant of its fifth columnists. If Mosley and his coadjutors have trafficked with the enemy, why should not the British Government deal with utter sternness with traitors whose infamy is the more infamous because place and title and power were their own?

As for our own country, let it bethink itself. Let it not fail to remember that descendants of the Mayflower, as was well said in a recent radio symposium, may dwell within the Nazi Trojan Horse as truly as newly arrived aliens. The time has come for those nations which up to this time have survived the onset of Fascist forces to bethink themselves lest they, too, be betrayed to the enemies. The race of Mosleys, Quislings, Kuhns and Coughlins has not yet utterly perished.

— 1940

How I Shall Vote

IT MUST BE cause for rejoicing to true liberals throughout the land that the record of President Roosevelt as well as a ringing utterance by Wendell Willkie alike promise to take the so-called religious issue completely out of the campaign. In his Fourth of July message to the Council Against Intolerance, read at the Temple of Religion Exercises, the President made clear again his abhorrence—it might be called his one intolerance—of anything savoring of ill-will between race and race, faith and faith. President Roosevelt might almost be said to have supplemented the Bill of Rights, which is law, by his prophetic pleas for true understanding among the peoples and faiths, whose oneness is America.

Good indeed that the first published reaction of Mr. Willkie to the same problem should be no less emphatic and equally courageous. To speak of anti-Semitism as "a possibly criminal movement" and to warn against the spread of anti-Jewish feeling as a "calamity" is to reveal a clear grasp of the deeper meaning of anti-Semitism in its anti-Democratic portent. OPINION has reason to believe that the candidate of the Republican party is deeply in earnest with respect to this problem, and that the Bund and other divisive and anti-democratic groups will find as scant comfort in the words of Wendell Willkie as in the luminous record of Roosevelt in all that makes for integral and indivisible Americanism!

It will be noted that this editorial comment was free from partisanship and was an expression of rejoicing on the part of OPINION—not its editor alone— that an utterance of the Republican candidate "promises to take the so-called religious issue completely out of the campaign." Throughout August and up to mid-September I continued to hope that the campaign would not be marred by the raising of any racial or religious issue. Since mid-September, however, something has come to pass with which I must deal frankly inasmuch as it is of deepest moment to American Jewry.

Within recent weeks the election has taken a turn which bodes ill to the entire nation. Knowing that some Jewish citizens—perhaps many Jewish citizens—would vote for the President on any one of the many grounds on which American voters will decide to vote for him, a group of Jews, not large in number nor in themselves of the slightest consequence, because for the most part utterly unknown to Jewish life, have conjured up the spectre of a *Jewish vote*. A handful of shysters and curb manipulators have cried out aloud concerning the necessity of doing something to prevent the hurt to Jews that would be done by the general recognition of the truth—that the so-called Jewish vote is for the President. In a word, in order to benefit the Republican candidate, a group of Jews, becoming vocal Jewishly only throughout the election period, have done Jewish life in America the immeasurable damage of pretending that there is a Jewish vote. As far as these gentlemen know anything, they know better. And if Jews throughout the country were to follow them in their false and dishonest warnings against the Roosevelt dictatorship, there would be no further mention of a Jewish vote; that is, provided it were to be cast for the Republican candidate.

As if it were not evil enough for the Republican National Committee and its state and city followers to raise the issue of a Jewish vote, their Jewish gangsters have gone further in seeking to coerce Jews to refrain from voting for the President lest such vote be counted against them: "lest danger ensue to the Jewish people" throughout the country if it be shown by the election that many of them cast their votes for the President rather than for the Republican candidate.

HERE and now it must be said that the most loathesome means and methods have been used in order to terrorize Jewish supporters of the President to forswear their allegiance to the Democratic party and its candidate; to desert him in whom they believe, and to cast their ballots for one for whom "Jews must vote if they are to be safe in America." I am not drawing upon my imagination. On every hand there come to me proofs of such disgusting coercion on the part of Jewish friends of the Republican candidate. Personally I prefer to believe that the latter

does not know and, if he knew, would be ashamed of the
base tactics of such Jews as are prepared by their methods
of Jewish terrorism to accept for the American Jew the
status of second-class citizenship. For, if any Jew whether
in the Bronx or in Seattle, is to vote on November 5th
with fear in his heart that a vote for the President will
bring hurt to the Jewish people, then the Jew has ceased
to be first-class citizen of the nation and to enjoy complete
equality with all his fellow-citizens.

If the time has come when the Jews of America may
through threat be moved to vote for one candidate or another on the ground that their Jewish interests are involved, then it will not be needful for Hitler to assume
the sovereignty in our land, for this country will by such
token have been reduced to a chattel of Hitlerism. Publicly and with utmost frankness and directness, I charge
these shameless Jewish terrorists with the betrayal of their
country and the betrayal of their faith and its ideals. In
order to secure partisan advantage for their candidate,
they are dragging the Jewish name and Jewish honor into
the dust, and purporting to have power to "swing" the
so-called Jewish vote from the Democratic to the Republican candidate.

This is a matter, it need hardly be urged, of the gravest
moment. Therefore it is that I write in condemnation of
Jews ready to sell the honor of their people for a mess of
partisan pottage. It is they who must be rebuked. Jewish
citizens of America, in the face of this cyclone of terrorism against them, need to be reminded that they are free
men, that they may vote as they choose; that they are not
under duress or coercion to vote for either candidate, and
that nothing shall be permitted to impugn such elementary right of American citizenship.

I do not charge Jews, who will vote for the Republican

candidate, with voting for him because they are Jews. The privilege of choice is their own and must in the American spirit be conceded to them. But if any of the underling Jewish gangsters of the Republican National Committee charges me, an American Jew—at least as much of an American as these partisan hucksters—with voting for President Roosevelt because I am a Jew, I tell them that they say or imply that which they know to be false—false in every sense.

I shall vote for Franklin D. Roosevelt because, in the exercise of my inalienable right, I have decided for my-self that the President has rendered high and memorable service to his country at home and abroad. I shall vote for the President's re-election because I refuse to believe that one, who is the very embodiment of the democratic spirit, is to be transformed into a dictator by reason of what is to be a vote of confidence in him as leader of the Democracy by a large plurality of the American people. I shall vote for the President's re-election because he came to the presidency amidst the very chaos of political and social bankruptcy, superinduced by the twelve years of adminis-tration that had gone before. He found a most imperiling national situation, and overcame it by facing with clear vision and democratic purpose the needs of the nation, and, above all, the needs of those who would have been doomed to physical extinction if the New Deal had not been initiated as a measure of inner nationwide defense. I shall vote for the President's re-election because he, more than any American or European, has urged a quarantine against the aggressor nations, and because meanwhile, despite the ceaseless opposition on the part of the Repub-lican Party, he has prepared the nation to defend itself against those autocracies that would destroy us as they have destroyed the democracies of Europe, and now threaten the destruction of England. I shall vote for the President's re-election because I have faith in my country and in Franklin D. Roosevelt, who has served it greatly. He has defended its moral and spiritual interests, and he stands out today as the greatest living exponent of the imperishable democratic way of life.

— 1940

The Tragedy of France

NOTHING could be harder for one who loves France and has twice been honored by its Government than to speak critically of France, long and rightfully said to have been the second fatherland of every civilized man. The tragedy of a year ago shocked and overwhelmed the world, for the greatest army of Europe, as the French army was believed to be, fell and surrendered virtually without a struggle.

Alas, that was only the beginning of the tragedy of France. After having read scores of so-called explanations of the tragedy, certain things are clear beyond peradventure of doubt. The fall of France was not military, save in its closing scene. The tragedy, which is swiftly moving forward to a most inglorious climax, did not derive from its army, but from its leadership, lay, parliamentary and ecclesiastical.

The tragedy of France betrayed has moved continuously forward until it is about to be revealed as France betraying. We are now at the eve or threshold of the third chapter of the tragedy of France. First scene of the drama was French life, in utter divisiveness and disunion, preparing for its debacle. The second scene was the planning for and the actual invocation of the defeat by the military agents of the Parliamentary traitors. The third scene was the surrender by France, not wholly under compulsion, at the time of much that was the truest glory of France, including the real religion of the French people rather than its Church, as expressed in Liberty, Equality, Fraternity. Now comes the fourth, but not last, scene in the drama, the so-called collaboration of a handful of rulers of France with their conquerors, the height or depth of the tragedy being the full and explicit assent of France to the faith and spirit of Nazism.

Verily the deepest horror of the tragedy lies not in France betrayed, but in France betraying, and that France is betraying Democracy today has long been known in the political circles of all the governments of men, through facilitation of war supplies to Germany, including the helping of Nazis by the French sending all military supplies through the North African colonies of the French Empire. Now comes the clearest and most terrible of all the signs of the surrender of France—Syria, the most flagrant and flagitious of the crimes of Nazified France, which has willed to betray as truly as it was betrayed.

Syria, like Palestine, is mandated territory under the League of Nations. Today France virtually hands over Syria to the Nazis, permitting them to use it under one disguise or another for military purposes, against Iraq, independent, and against the British mandated territory of Palestine, with the result that the Axis powers may be doubly armed against the British in the Near East generally and in Palestine particularly.

Even this is not the whole or the worst of the betrayal, but merely another sign or token of the tragedy steadily moving on to its climax. It seems as if Admiral Darlan, who is either the voice or the commander of Marshal Petain, was not intelligent enough to comprehend the

meaning of his own words, maintaining that Hitler had
said nothing to him with regard to the French fleet and
similar questions. Is is not, assuming the statement to be
true, because it is no longer necessary for Hitler to speak,
because Hitler knows that France is utterly, completely,
unreservedly in his hands?

In order to realize the measure of France's betrayal and
the gravity of France's betraying conduct, one need but
contrast France today with lesser lands, such as Norway
and Holland. Norway has its Quisling, but he is loathed
throughout his country and reviled by all its people. Holland has its Quisling, but he is not yet in the seat of power
and the Dutch people abhor him, and when and as they
can, utter their unlimited scorn of him.

But Petain, Darlan and Laval, the trinity of betrayers,
are in power and they threaten to lead France into the
greatest tragedy of all this immeasurable horror, namely,
the union of France, in war against England, with and by
the side of Germany.

THE writer's own special reasons for speaking about and
against this tragedy of tragedies are in truth not political
in character. For one thing, how long will our country
maintain the fiction of continuing friendly relations with
Hitler's France, greatest of his conquered provinces in
and for Nazidom? France, alas, is dead, the France of Vic-
tor Hugo and Emile Zola and Georges Clemenceau, but
even in death France is being surrendered by its leaders
to Hitler. On the other hand, there is a rebirth of France,
which, for the world bears the name of Free France.
France Forever it rightfully calls itself in our own country. Why should not our Government recognize and give
help to the only France that is, the France that survives,
the France that alone is worthy of the honored name, that

France that would remain free. It is become the surest duty of all Americans to help Free France, to support and strengthen France Forever, the American representation of General de Gaulle's Free France.

May not an American be forgiven if he offers a very special plea to all Frenchmen who have lived in America for a generation or even for generations—to give their help and aid to Free France, not to Nazi France, but to what remains of the democratic France that is to be revived. Is it necessary to appeal to French men and women who have come to our hospitable shores within recent years to prove their love for their own deathless country by giving not limited and stinted support, but help in unlimited measure to Free France.

Even at the risk of being misunderstood, if French Jews who have found refuge here in America would serve America and the highest Jewish interests, they would live in the simplest possible fashion in America today and give all for Free France. The France of Hitler has spewed them out; the France of de Gaulle, whatever the future may be, is their, our, only hope. Even though American Jews seem to be unable to comprehend the graveness of the crisis that is upon us, French Jews in America have had reason to know and understand what Nazism means for them and for all Jews whom it can victimize—insecurity, homelessness, degradation. OPINION dares to demand that every Jew in America, who lived in France yesterday and throughout the years, shall stand sturdily, helpfully, sacrificially by the side of General de Gaulle and under the banner of Free France.

— 1941

Symbol of Victory

THE GREAT and outstanding event of these months was
the Atlantic meeting of England's Prime Minister and
our President. Supremely significant as symbol of the new
unity of the two English-speaking commonwealths, it
might almost be described as the "Atlantic Battle Won."
All mankind, including perhaps the peoples unconquered
as well as conquered, must have felt the dawn of a new
freedom. Even as the Bill of Rights crowned the Constitution of the United States, so the Atlantic Declaration
completed the promise of the Four Freedoms for all mankind. Not, as the Isolationists impudently say, that we
are fighting to impose these upon a reluctant world; but
the world-wide war can result in nothing less than the
winning of these freedoms by a world, which the defeat of
the democracies would behold enslaved. If the stress lay
upon two rather than all four Freedoms, it was because
of the high insight of the two statesmen, who understand
that fear enslaves and prepares the way for utter subjec-
tion, and that want must be vanquished if peoples are
ever to live peaceably side by side.

The Atlantic meeting was in very truth a rendezvous
with destiny—not the destiny that lies in the gain of a few
and the hurt of many, but in the liberation of all mankind. For the leaders and the peoples know that democratic victory must ensure the liberation of man, not
merely some men and nations, even as the defeat of the
Democraccies would spell human subjugation. One
wishes that the Chinese Republic and the Soviet Union
might have been present by their representatives at the
Atlantic Meeting, but that omission will in a sense be
remedied. The Atlantic Rendezvous challenges destiny,
and to it offers the hostage of the plighted honor of Run-

nymede's Magna Charta and Philadelphia's Declaration
of Independence.

— 1941

The True France

OPINION IS HAPPY TO RECORD two events from out of the
continent of Europe, one spiritually and the other politically significant. The Federation of Protestant Churches
in France adopted as its own its President's message
of sympathy to the afflicted Jews, "Our church which
in the past has known all the horrors of persecution, feels
an intense sympathy for your communities, in which
freedom of worship has been put in jeopardy, and for
your followers who have so suddenly been plunged into
misfortune. Our church has already taken steps, and will
continue to do so, in negotiating for an essential revocation of the law."

In fact, these words are as honoring to those who spoke
them as to those for whom they were meant. Rightly was
it said of this message, "These brave words breathe the
only kind of devotion to religious liberty and social justice that has much value—one which is not satisfied with
security or liberty for one's own group but is fired with
a noble indignation when any religious group is oppressed."

But of even greater significance is a message which has
come to the President of the American Jewish Congress
in connection with the One Hundred and Fiftieth Anniversary of the emancipation of the Jews of France. General de Gaulle utters the historic words, "The celebrated
Decree on the Emancipation of the Jews of France, as
well as the Proclamation of Human Rights and of the
Rights of the Citizen are still in force and cannot be abrogated by the men of Vichy. We consider indeed as null

and void the changes in the Constitution and in French laws made by the so-called Vichy Government, whose origin and actions are anti-constitutional and illegal."

At one and the same time, General de Gaulle, leader of Free France, cancels the annulments by which the Vichy government has sullied the record of France, and reaffirms those basic principles which have been the glory of France for a century and a half. The French of tomorrow thus binds itself to recreate the free, proud France of 150 years ago. May that restoration of Free France to life, to honor and to freedom be achieved speedily. God give it!

— 1941

We Are At War

WE ARE AT WAR—our country as truly as Britain or the Axis Powers. That we were bombed into war by Japan was an infamy beyond credence, but that infamy resolved many doubts, chiefly the oft-iterated doubt "whether we would ever be forced to go to war." The war-mongers are now seen not to have been the Administration, whose leader made a noble appeal for peace to Japan's Emperor within twenty-four hours of Japan's crime. The war-mongers were the isolationists whose evil-doing was two-fold. For it led the Axis Powers to imagine that we were a divided people remote from every thought of self-defense, and in the meanwhile gave to the Axis time to prepare and to organize its synchronized attacks upon the democracies.

Our country was transformed within an hour. Now we have all become an America First Committee and people, resolved with confident strength to do all that a mighty nation can do in defense of its life and freedom.

But America first is not to mean that we are to relax our toil and our vigilance in support of the nations which have long ere this defended their anti-Fascist way of life. Each of these—America, China, Russia—offered such resistance to Fascist savagery as redounds to their immortal glory, whatever their immediate loss and hurt. The Axis Powers stand and war together for the wrong. We shall stand and war together for the right.

It is too early and too late to speak of the failure of the democracies, including our own, sooner to have recognized the inevitableness of this world conflict. The rise of Nazism should have been accepted and acted upon by the West and the Soviet as a summons to battle. We should not have given Hitler and his confederates in crime years and years wherein to thrice-arm. We shall pay the price; we have had no end of a lesson, and it may yet do us no end of good. From the rise of Hitler's evil day, peoples who were free faced three alternatives—surrender, negotiate, resist. The pitiable peoples surrendered. The blind or terrorized nations deemed negotiation possible, and have now learned what follows upon negotiation, which meant mounting shame and deepening dishonor. Britain resisted with a heroism the record of which becomes the glory and despair of history. Russia, after a lamentable but not wholly inexplicable lapse, has stood with finest fortitude against the mechanized devils of Hitler. There is no other way, and America faces today the need of unparalled resistance against the over-organized forces of destructiveness. We will resist to the end and beyond the end, for the American people, in the strength and by the side of its Allies, is determined that never again shall the right of men to be free be challenged, and the inalienable privilege of a national and personal self-determination be under attack.

OPINION has only one word of counsel to offer to
American Jews. It knows that these would give their all
to their country, to which no one owes more, which no
one loves more deeply and loyally than do American
Jews. But is not this the time for a coming together of all
American-Jewish groups in order that they may be doubly
effective in service, not in the fictitious togetherness of
the unvital General Jewish Council but in the togetherness of a common and resistless purpose to serve democratically as alone becomes every group, most particularly
our own, within the American Democracy.

— 1942

The United Nations

PERHAPS the greatest event of the year, it may even be of
many generations, will prove to have been what happened
in Washington on the first day of January, when, under
the leadership of the two statesmen of Democracy, Roosevelt and Churchill, the United Nations were organized.
It may be that the United Nations will prove to be what
the League of Nations never became nor could become.
If the United Nations are to supersede the League of Nations, it is because of what the world has learned to its
sorrow and because even our own country has come to
understand that isolation is a worn out superstition which
has no place in a world of planes and tanks.

Nothing is fraught with richer promise for the future
world order than that union of nations which the political genius and moral leadership of the President and the
British Prime Minister effected on the first day of the year
1942. In a sense, it is little more than a summoning of
other nations to the acceptance of the Atlantic Charter.
Many nations have responded, more will respond, and

it seems at this hour as if the civilized peoples of earth had finally become united against the Axis nations of lawlessness, violence and enslavement.

The war has assumed greater proportions not only because we are involved therein, not primarily because of what happened on the seventh day of December in Hawaii, but because of the acceptance by the people of the United States of the truth that civilized peoples will be destroyed one by one or they will be united to resist, to check and to disarm the Axis oppressors.

Whether the Jewish people should be included within the United Nations is a problem still to be faced. The Jewish Agency for Palestine in a very real sense is a Jewish government, and was recognized by the League of Nations that was. It has the right to ask admittance for the Jewish Palestine, to which the Peace Conference is bound to give the status of a Jewish commonwealth, either under British Mandate or under a condominium, or best of all under the mandate of the United Nations. Jews who think of themselves as disembodied spirits as far as everything that is Jewish is concerned may protest, but red-blooded Jews with understanding and memories and soul unashamed will avow themselves as prepared to defend the integrity of a Jewish commonwealth of Palestine within the United Nations, only those Jews being or to be citizens of the Jewish Commonwealth of Palestine who dwell within its boundaries.

— 1942

Post War Punishment

ONE READS with reluctance and assents with sorrow to all proposals by those who insist that punishment is to be meted out after the democratic victory, to those responsible for the excesses and crimes committed against the natives of the invaded and conquered territories. Those who are shocked by the mere thought of punishment however just of the arch criminals in the Nazi conspiracy against the sanities and sanctities of mankind would have done well to have appealed betimes to Himmler and his Gestapo gangsters to refrain from doing the deeds which civilization can hardly leave unwhipped of justice. The United Press correspondent in Stockholm reports that in Lithuania and Latvia Jews have either been executed or the survivors are slaving in labor battalions and that Himmler, the Gestapo chief, has ordered the shooting of all German Jews, except those over sixty or Jewish workers in armament factories and that in fulfillment of this command 100,000 Jews were slaughtered.

This is the time to plead for mercy. Why should not they who dream of a mild and soft peace for the sake of the German people now direct their warnings to the heads of the German government? While it cannot be hoped to equal the Nazis in ruthlessness and brutality of conduct, the Himmlers and Heydrichs, whose goings up and down throughout Europe are marked by trails of blood, many understand that not vengeance but decency will call for the expiation of their crimes and infamies throughout the years. One already hears the Bund-inspired organizations crying for mercy for those who never showed a trace of mercy in their dealings with tens of thousands of unoffending people. This is the time for mercy but it is denied. The time will come not for reprisal nor for vengeance, but for such stern punishment of them that are responsible for the infamies of these years that never again will men undertake to bathe a continent in a sea of blood.

This does not mean that we accept the Hitler program. For the Hitler program destroys the innocent. But we do accept a program of sternest, swiftest punishment within the processes of law of such as have ended for a time the civilization of Europe and inaugurated once again the horrors of the jungle. And the world is already assured that they who are cruelest and most bloody in their deeds will be most plaintive in their pleas for mercy.

— 1942

I Am An American

I AM AN AMERICAN. I was not ever thus. My Fathers were not Americans. They dwelt on the Continent of Europe for many centuries. But my parents chose, within a year after my birth, to become Americans. My father, on the day after Lincoln's death, announced to his friends at a German University: "Some day I mean to live in the land of Lincoln." When I told that story to President Theodore Roosevelt and added that he did not come to America until ten years later, President Roosevelt said: "Then your Father was a good American ten years before he arrived in America."

I am an American. I am doubly an American, because I am foreign-born. It may be that native-born Americans take America for granted. Foreign-born Americans like myself do not take America for granted. We look upon American citizenship as the most precious and sacred of boons. We understand what it is that we have left behind us—of denial of the freedoms of man, and we know what it is that has come to be our high destiny, to be a sharer in American freedom, to be a bearer of American responsibility, to be a devotee of the American Democracy, to use American freedom not for one's own advantage but for the service of the American Democracy, and in these days of war, for the preservation of its loftiest ideals and purposes.

I am an American. I thank God that my parents brought me to this country. I thank God that my children and children's children have been born in this country. They have entered into and become sharers in the most precious heritage which can fall to the lot of man, and I have faith that they will prove equal to and worthy of the high opportunities of life which American citizenship affords. They, like me, will give their deepest, truest loyalty to the America which is today, to the greater, freer, nobler America that is to be on the morrow.

I am an American, I say, not boastfully, but with deepest faith in my country's destiny. For more than one hundred and fifty years my country has held aloft the torch of human freedom that other peoples might watch and learn how men live under the law of freedom. Today that freedom is under attack by those powers of darkness whom the light of American freedom offends and moves to derision and to attempted destruction. My country is in the midst of war, a war which it has not willed to wage, which it has not chosen to engage in. But now that America is under attack by the enslaving despotisms, America and its people which hate war, are resolved to spare no effort and substance that world tyranny may be broken, that human enslavement may be halted, and that human freedom may be saved.

I am an American, an American Jew who, because he is a Jew, proudly recalls that on the Independence Bell, which, on the 4th day of July, 1776, proclaimed the glad-

dest tidings that human ears ever heard, there were in-
scribed the words of the Hebrew Bible, "And ye shall proclaim liberty throughout the land unto all the inhabitants
thereof." On this, "I Am An American" Day, I know, and
I thank God because I am permitted to know, that the
Bible verse "And ye shall proclaim liberty throughout the
land unto all the inhabitants thereof" has, since the 7th
day of December, 1941, yea since the 3rd of September,
1939, yea since the 4th day of March, 1933, translated itself into the larger term "And ye Americans shall proclaim liberty throughout the lands unto all the inhabitants thereof."

I am an American. Because I am an American, I am
free. Because I am an American, I shall live and labor to
the end that all men be set free and that the spirit of
American freedom rule over all the sons and daughters
of men.   — 1942

"Priorities to the Stars"

THIS singular and apparently unintelligible term is become the very glory of France. In occupied France, where
it is least safe, and in unoccupied France, where it is almost equally unsafe, the French people are constantly
repeating the phrase, "Priorities to the Stars." And the
stars are the Shield of David, the historic *Magen David*,
and the French people in their magnificent reaction to the
attitude of the regime in occupied and unoccupied France
alike does not content itself merely with uttering this
fine formula but lives by it from day to day, takes risks in
its name, insists upon sharing whatever can be shared
with the haunted and hunted Jews of France. Many won-
drous things in the field of humaneness and considera-

tion are being done throughout France, including for example, the refusal of policemen to surrender Jewish children, and the glorious stand of the Catholic Priesthood and the Catholic Sisters who dare to wear the Stars in token of their sympathy with their persecuted fellow-Frenchmen and women, the Jews.

"Priority to the Stars," which is only another way of saying we dare not for a moment forget the Jews; we must help them; we must save them, does much indeed to redeem the shame of France. A people that is equal in the face of penalties and peril to cry out, "Priority to the Stars," and by that gesture show that they are ashamed of their country's dealing with the Jews, will not and cannot remain enslaved. It will be liberated, it will together with the United Nations liberate itself. Frenchmen were not born to be slaves. They are freemen at heart and they shall be freemen again who are inwardly free, even when governmentally enslaved.

— 1943

Mexico — As I Saw It

I REALLY wonder what it was and is about Mexico that thrilled me most. The country is unbelievably beautiful. It has all the loveliness and charm of the Mediterranean plus that unique background which might be called either Indian or Mexican. One cannot help feeling as one gets a glimpse of Mexico and its people rather than peoples that, whatever may have been the former difficulties and problems of admixture of populations, there has been a wonderful adjustment of Europeans, the Spanish, to the American Indians, who, with their Hispanic foreground, constitute the heart of the Mexican people.

What I found almost as exciting as the matchlessly

beautiful days and nights of Mexico was the feeling that
became my own that at last, after a century and more, we
have been able to reach a *modus vivendi* with the Mexican people. A number of causes have been contributory
to such adjustment, the wise and far-visioning leadership
of President Roosevelt, the kindly and understanding
ministrations of the Mexican Ambassadors of yesterday
and the day before, Josephus Daniels and Dwight Morrow, and today George Messersmith, the pressure of a
Fascist world, which has moved Mexican leaders to see
that the Mexican Republic will lose every gain it has
achieved unless it stands inseparably at our side, the leadership of the present Administration and some of the pre-
ceding governments, with the Mexican people apparently placing their fullest trust in two men, their own President and the President of the United States, Manuel
Avila Camacho and Franklin Delano Roosevelt.

As Jew and as President of the American Jewish Congress and sharing the responsibility for the work of its
collateral bodies, the World Jewish Congress, the Institute of Jewish Affairs, the Inter-American Jewish Council
and the United Jewish War Effort, I came, to my heart's
delight, upon a Jewish community which is a credit to
itself and to the Jewish name, and which, above all, is of
high service to the whole of Mexico. What a joy to hear
a distinguished Mexican say at a meeting: "There are
Jews in Mexico but there is no Jewish problem. The
Mexican Jews are a part of the life of Mexico and we think
of them not as foreigners resident in Mexico but as our
fellow-Mexicans, as our neighbors and friends."

I found that this attitude obtains not only among a few
eminent leaders of Government, such as I met, but in
wider circles. What is more, I found the Jewish community meriting the good-will which the Mexican people feel

toward them and the part they play in the development
of Mexican life and commerce and letters, and the larger
part which the Jewish community is to play in the Mexico
of tomorrow. I do not dream of attempting to give an
estimate of Mexico's social and economic or even cultural
values. A more daring visitor might, after a week's residence in Mexico, undertake to do this; not I, who recognize the limitations imposed upon me by the brevity of
my stay, and above all, by reason of my concentration
upon the affairs and the program arranged for Dr. Goldmann and myself by the Jewish community.

The Mexican Jewish community is made up of a number of strata. As far as I could learn, there are no survivors
of the earliest Jewish settlers in Mexico in the sixteenth
century, unless these be the Indian Jews, who are un-
swervingly loyal in their Jewishness; whose one request
to me was to make it possible for them to receive an additional Sefer Torah, or several Sifre Torah. The Jewish
population, which is under twenty thousand in the whole
of Mexico, may be divided into these groups; the two
divisions of Sephardic Jewry, namely, the Asia-Minor or
Levantine Jews and the Postuguese-Spanish Jews; the
East East European Jews, who constitute the chief
strength and vitality of Mexican Jewry, and finally the
refugees from Germany, Czechoslovakia, Austria, and
other German-speaking lands, who are of recent arrival.
In all these Jewish circles, to my unmeasured satisfaction,
I found a blending of utter loyalty to Mexico, its people,
its future, its ideals, an unchanging loyalty to the Jewish
tradition, to Jewish hopes, to Jewish ideals and over and
above all else the ideal of reestablishing the Jewish National Home in Palestine.

To indicate how thoroughly and unreservedly Zion-
istic the Jewish population of Mexico City is, it is not

too much to say that of the twelve thousand Jews of that
city, one-half, or six thousand, sought to gain admittance
into the Palace of Fine Arts, in which the twenty-fifth
anniversary Balfour Day celebration was held, with truly
notable addresses by a number of important representatives of the Mexican people, a brilliant address in French
and Yiddish by Dr. Goldmann, and my own word in
English. Four thousand and more people were jammed
into that rarely beautiful auditorium, the occupancy of
which was made possible by the very special courtesy
of the Government.

Mexican Jews are clear-sighted enough to understand
that it is not enough, however generously, to support the
Zionist Movement and to further the reestablishment of
the Jewish National Home. The Inter-American Jewish
Council, established in Baltimore, November, 1941, has
touched the imagination of the Jewish community, which
seems to understand that it is the part of statesmanship to
unify Jewish organizations throughout the Western
world, North America, Central America, Latin America,
and to bring about such coordination of democratic interests and of Jewish sympathies as shall ensure the maintenance of the Inter-American Jewish Council, the aim of
which is and must remain the strengthening and ever-en-
riching integration of Jewish communities into the life of
the American peoples and Governments, and the deepening of that democratic ideal which is the touchstone of
the Americas.

It gladdened my soul to come upon the concordant
loyalties of Mexican Jews, the oneness of their loyalty
as Mexicans with their loyalty as Jews, no contradiction,
no conflict, but a perfect concordance, which the two
United States visitors recognized, honored and it may
even be strengthened. All the groups in Mexican Jewish

life are doing well; otherwise the very generous gift which, without any campaign, was placed in our hands for the work of the Inter-American Jewish Council and the World Jewish Congress, by four of the leaders of the community, Senores Arturo Wolfowitz, Elias Surasky, San Wishniak and Leon Alazraki, would have been not only miraculous but impossible. The Jewish community is in the best sense of the term Jewishly self-conscious, conscious of its Jewish obligations and responsibilities, in a word, eager to share in the shaping of the life of Mexico on the morrow and the world that is to be, a free world, a world wherein the four freedoms are unchallengably to obtain.

I have reserved for the last a moment with the Minister for Foreign Affairs in Mexico, to whom, as Chairman of the Inter-American Jewish Council, I submitted our tentative plan to hold the second Session of the Inter-American Jewish Council in Mexico in the Spring or Fall of 1943. His Excellency, Minister Padilla, assented without a moment's hesitation, and when the writer offered to submit a memorandum on the question, the Minister for Foreign Affairs was graciously hospitable and courteous enough to reply: "No memorandum will be necessary. We will be happy to welcome the Inter-American Jewish Council as the guests of the Mexican Government and people." This is the new Mexico, the Mexico that is come of age, the Mexico made up of them with whom for nearly a century we had reached no understanding; today a people of neighbors and good-neighbors, of inseparable allies in the cause of human freedom.

— 1942

We Shall Not Forget

RARELY indeed in the last ten years have more joyous tidings reached Jewish ears than the news that, in response to the fiendish resolve of the Nazis to deport all the Jews of Denmark to Poland—meaning enslavement and ultimately death—the Danish government, in the spirit of its King and people, had undertaken to help its valued and honored Jewish citizens to escape from Denmark into Sweden and other countries. The utter gravity of the situation was disclosed by the announcement that hangman Himmler had been sent to Denmark to facilitate the deportation, and to avert the threatened escape of the victims.

Two things happened that will have permanent record. The Danish government, including the police and many other officials, at once intervened—the public collectively and singly—to prevent the arrest of the Danish Jews and their deportation. To their lasting honor it should be told that some of the Danish police have exposed themselves to the risk of being deported to Poland in the place of those Jews in whose deportation they refused to cooperate. And the second item must be especially mentioned. The American representative of the Danish Government, Minister Henrik de Kauffmann, who has been compelled to act without instructions from the Danish government which is itself in exile, undertook to make an offer to support for the duration all Danish Jews who might escape to Sweden and other lands. And a very large sum of money, now under his trusteeship, was mentioned by the Danish minister.

The third and equally important fact that should be widely and lastingly known is that the Swedish government acted in response to the Danish government in the

finest spirit, and not only declared that it was ready to receive Danish refugees, but even refugees from other countries who had, for a time, made their home in Denmark.

All in all it was a nothing less than perfect exhibition
of what democratic and Christian countries could do and
should do in behalf of those threatened, as the Jews of
Denmark were threatened, by the hellish Hitler-Himmler
regime. At the moment of writing, it is stated that more
than six thousand Jews, most of them native Danes, have
been able to escape from Denmark into Sweden, Denmark serving as the place of exit, and Sweden doing everything possible as the place of entry. What could be finer
than the word broadcast by the Swedish radio at Stockholm: "Fleeing Jews who now reach our coasts may feel
that they have come to a Nordic brother, and take refuge
with us until it will be possible for them to return to a free
and independent Denmark." Except for its use by a handful of religious teachers, OPINION cannot recall any case in
ten years in which the term "brother" was used in relation to Jews by any national, racial, or religious group!

One thing more remains to be added. If the great
European nations had acted in the last three years as
Sweden and Denmark have acted in this moment of crisis,
three million Jews would not have perished in the mire
of Nazi guilt. Hundreds of thousands of Jews might have
been rescued, as these six thousand Danish and other refugees have been saved, for a time in any event, unless the
Nazi government now invades Sweden. If only the greater
democratic nations had acted with a tithe of the prompt-
ness and vigor and courage with which the Scandinavian
countries have acted! This is not merely a reminder of
what might have been. It should serve as a mandate to the
great democratic nations, including our own, to act at
once in order to rescue those who may yet be saved from

the jaws of that hell which is the Himmler-Hitler deportation program.

At a luncheon recently tendered by the heads of the Joint Emergency Committee for European Jewish Affairs in honor of the Danish minister, it was stated that Jews know how to forgive, but they do not know how to forget. Jews have acquired the habit of forgiving the most grievous wrongs which have been done against them. They remember every kindness, every act of friendliness and neighborliness. And Jews, with their unsleeping memory, will for many generations cherish the remembrance of those two Scandinavian lands and peoples, together with their Kings, which at a moment of fate, bore themselves in such a way as to help save Jews who would otherwise have been doomed to death and worse than death. We shall not forget.

— 1943